M000072616

THE GOD OF MIRACLES

THE GOD OF Miracles

An Exegetical Examination of
God's Action in the World

C. John Collins

CROSSWAY BOOKS • WHEATON, ILLINOIS
A DIVISION OF GOOD NEWS PUBLISHERS

The God of Miracles: An Exegetical Examination of God's Action in the World

Copyright © 2000 by C. John Collins

Published by Crossway Books
   a division of Good News Publishers
   1300 Crescent Street
   Wheaton, Illinois 60187

All rights reserved. No part of this publication may be reproduced, stored in a retrieval system, or transmitted in any form by any means, electronic, mechanical, photocopy, recording, or otherwise, without the prior permission of the publisher, except as provided by USA copyright law.

Scripture references marked NIV are from the *Holy Bible: New International Version.*® Copyright © 1973, 1978, 1984 by International Bible Society. Used by permission of Zondervan Publishing House. All rights reserved.

The "NIV" and "New International Version" trademarks are registered in the United States Patent and Trademark Office by International Bible Society. Use of either trademark requires the permission of International Bible Society.

Scripture references marked NASB are from the *New American Standard Bible*® © Copyright The Lockman Foundation 1960, 1962, 1963, 1968, 1971, 1972, 1973, 1975, 1977, 1995. Used by permission.

Scripture references marked RSV are from the *Revised Standard Version.* Copyright © 1946, 1953, 1971, 1973 by the Division of Christian Education of the National Council of the Churches of Christ in the U.S.A.

Scripture references marked NRSV are from the *New Revised Standard Version.* Copyright © 1989 by the Division of Christian Education of the National Council of the Churches of Christ in the U.S.A. Published by Thomas Nelson, Inc. Used by permission of the National Council of the Churches of Christ in the U.S.A.

The Graeca II and Transliterator Semitica fonts used to print this work are available from Linguist's Software, Inc., P.O. Box 580, Edmonds, WA 98020-0580, telephone (206) 775-1130.

Cover design: Cindy Kiple

First printing, 2000

Printed in the United States of America

Library of Congress Cataloging-in-Publication Data

Collins, C. John, 1954–
   The God of miracles: an exegetical examination of God's action in the world / C. John Collins.
      p.   cm.
   Includes bibliographical references and indexes.
   ISBN 1-58134-141-5 (trade pbk. : alk. paper)
   1. Providence and government of God—Biblical teaching. 2. Miracles—Biblical teaching. 3. Bible and science. 4. Apologetics. I. Title.
BS544 C65 2000
231'.5—dc21   99-053546
                                             CIP

15	14	13	12	11	10	09	08	07	06	05	04	03	02	01	00
15	14	13	12	11	10	9	8	7	6	5	4	3	2	1	

Outline of Contents

Acknowledgments

I owe a debt of gratitude to many people, for their encouragement and interaction.

Thanks to Discovery Institute's Center for the Renewal of Science and Culture for a research fellowship, 1998–99, especially to its director, Stephen Meyer, who made it possible for me to do this work.

The Templeton Foundation's Science and Religion Course Program, 1996–97, got me started thinking about these questions.

At Covenant Theological Seminary, Bryan Chapell, the president, and Dan Doriani, the dean of faculty, as well as my fellow faculty members, gave me much kind support and intellectual stimulus. Serving with these people is a privilege beyond my deserts.

Stephen Bilynskyj's fascinating Ph.D. dissertation and cheerful offering of ideas were invaluable.

Students, with their questions, observations, researches, and criticisms, have been the most rewarding part of my own teaching and research: I especially appreciate the Summer 1998 E-mail discussion group—Jonathan Barlow, Blane Conklin, Bryan Cross (and his brother Troy), and Mike Farley; but I also thank Wayne Larson and Per Almquist for papers they wrote for me.

Wade Bradshaw, of the Francis Schaeffer Institute of Covenant Theological Seminary, has pushed me beyond my comfort zone in asking me to speak about these matters in "unsafe" venues such as the Friday night talks at the bookstore. The participants in the 1998 Summer Program at the Schaeffer Institute heard much of this material hot off my keyboard, and helped me to think about making myself understood.

My wife, Diane, by her love, devotion, and support for me and our children, makes our home a place worth living in. Watching and helping my children, Joy and Joseph, learn about the world has taught me more about rationality than anything else has. These three are clear evidence that God's providential arrangements for me are not limited to my merit!

Part One

Setting the Stage

One

Introduction

We often hear that the "modern scientific outlook" provides difficulties for traditional Christian belief, at least in the doctrines of creation, of human nature and the image of God, and of the interaction between God and his creation (providence and miracles). The influential German New Testament scholar Rudolph Bultmann made the following claim about what is allowable in understanding God's relation to the world and his action in it:[1]

> It is impossible to use the electric light and the wireless and to avail ourselves of modern medical and surgical discoveries, and at the same time to believe in the New Testament world of spirits and miracles. We may think we can manage it in our own lives, but to expect others to do so is to make the Christian faith unintelligible and unacceptable to the modern world.

We can take several avenues of response to such a statement. We can accept it and follow Bultmann's advice or perhaps give up the New Testament altogether. A better idea would be to ask some questions: What is this "modern scientific outlook," and what authority should it have in what I believe? Is the scientific *outlook* something separable from the *practice* of science itself? Or else we could examine more carefully the biblical materials, to make sure we really understand what they say and to see if the Bible is as untenable in our era as Bultmann suggested.

Although I will comment briefly on the philosophical questions about science, the main purpose of this study is to provide an exegetically based foundation for discussing God's action in the world within the framework of biblically based (Christian) theology.[2] This in turn will affect the way we

---

[1] Rudolph Bultmann, "The New Testament and Mythology," *Kerygma and Myth* (New York: Harper and Row, 1961), 5.

[2] I put the qualifier "Christian" in parentheses because that is the perspective both of myself and of most of the sources available on the subject. There are, of course, key points of contact with "traditional Jewish theism," and I have not hesitated to use Israeli commentaries. As a matter of fact, as we will see below, these issues have come up in Jewish and Islamic theology as well.

would treat the questions that have been raised about the believability of biblical "miracle claims," since it will clarify what those claims are and what believers and nonbelievers are invited to believe about them. This foundation, as we shall see, will also help us to evaluate the theological propriety of the "intelligent design" program.

My interest in this study arose from a number of places. For example, I have used C. S. Lewis's book *Miracles* as one of several texts for my class "Christian Faith in an Age of Science." Lewis's defense of miracles depends on an understanding of nature and divine action that I call "supernaturalism." We can summarize supernaturalism, which has had many prominent advocates in church history, as:

> God in his ordinary providence maketh use of means, yet is free to work without, above, and against them, at his pleasure. (*Westminster Confession of Faith*, 5:3)

This affirms the existence of something we can call "nature" (the "means," or "second causes"), which is divine action in the sense that God upholds it in existence and confirms its interactions; God's "interventions" in nature are qualitatively different (and detectably different) expressions of divine power.

However, I discovered several negative reviews of Lewis's book, and these reviews come not from skeptics but from people committed to Christianity.[3] In the reviewers' estimation, Lewis was operating with a defective understanding of "nature" and of divine action. An extensive presentation of one of these other approaches to divine action, generally called "occasionalism," appears in G. C. Berkouwer's volume on *The Providence of God*. A summary of this position would be:

> Laws of nature are not alternatives to divine activity but only our codification of that activity in its normal manifestation, and a miracle means nothing more than that God at a given moment wills a certain thing to occur differently than it had up to that moment been willed by him to occur.

In this view "natural" and "miraculous" are not qualitatively different expressions of God's activity, and the perception of a "miracle" depends primarily on the subjective response of its witnesses; hence there is no such thing as an "intervention" that is demonstrable to a nonbeliever.

---

[3] E.g., Stuart Judge, "How Not to Think About Miracles," *Science and Christian Belief* 3:1 (1991), 97-102; and John C. Sharp, "Miracles and the 'Laws of Nature,'" *Scottish Bulletin of Evangelical Theology* 6:1 (Spring 1988), 1-19.

On the other hand, the recent book *In Defense of Miracles*, edited by R. D. Geivett and G. R. Habermas,[4] is philosophically closer to Lewis, but it lacks an *exegetical* and *theological* discussion to establish its basis. It also gears its apologetic entirely toward objections in the tradition of David Hume, and hence lacks treatments of the Spinoza-Schleiermacher approach and of postmodern objections to the knowability of supernatural events. And it has no discussion of answered prayer.

Further, the "intelligent design" movement, as typified by, for example, Michael Behe's *Darwin's Black Box*, and the collection *The Creation Hypothesis* (edited by J. P. Moreland),[5] presupposes for its validity a model of divine action that it does not articulate or defend. This project as it is typically argued assumes, 1) that the supernaturalist model of divine action is correct, 2) that at least some supernatural events are detectable, and 3) that some specific events in the natural history of our planet have a (detectable) supernatural factor (such as the origin of life and of humans). The criticisms of this paradigm, for example from evangelical scientists such as Howard Van Till, commonly object to its alleged liability to the "God-of-the-gaps" fallacy. Van Till himself has offered his doctrine of "functional integrity," which he believes calls for strict complementarity between the faith-based and the scientific descriptions of events, especially regarding the origin and development of life and of humans (i.e., such descriptions are statements about separate and non-overlapping components and hence cannot conflict). Van Till's argument also presupposes a model of divine action of the sort that I will call "providentialism"; and the respective opponents do not always seem aware that the issue between them is their theological model of God's relation to his world. (Another criticism, that the intelligent design paradigm has too high a view of natural theology, needs to be handled separately.)

There have been important discussions of the issue of divine action, but these are primarily from the perspective of philosophy and philosophical theology. Examples include Stephen Bilynskyj's 1982 Ph.D. dissertation, *God, Nature, and the Concept of Miracle*, and Paul Gwynne's 1996 *Special Divine Action: Key Issues in the Contemporary Debate*, both of which are from the supernaturalist side.[6] The exegetical articulations of occasionalism appear most commonly in works influenced by the "biblical theology" movement, and have not yet taken account of the critiques of this movement

[4] Douglas Geivett and Gary Habermas, eds., *In Defense of Miracles* (Downers Grove, Ill.: InterVarsity, 1997).

[5] Michael Behe, *Darwin's Black Box* (New York: Free Press, 1996); J. P. Moreland, ed., *The Creation Hypothesis* (Downers Grove, Ill.: InterVarsity, 1994).

[6] Stephen Bilynskyj, *God, Nature, and the Concept of Miracle* (Ph.D. dissertation, University of Notre Dame, 1982); Paul Gwynne, *Special Divine Action: Key Issues in the Contemporary Debate* (Rome: Gregorian University Press, 1996).

launched by James Barr.[7] Indeed, in my conversations with theologians of both supernaturalist and occasionalist persuasion I have found agreement that the decisive *exegetical* study on the issue does not yet exist. Paul Gwynne's work allows me to focus my attention. His study is a detailed examination of the discussion in philosophical theology, especially in the years 1965–1995. As for the biblical material, he suggests that[8]

> . . . a vague distinction between direct and indirect SDA [Special Divine Action] seems to exist in the Scriptures even though people of that epoch had only an inchoate sense of an autonomous natural order.

However, Gwynne does not think that the biblical material itself has been shown to be decisively in favor of one position over another.[9] Here then I find my key questions: Does the *biblical* material actually favor one of the models for God's relationship with the created realm over another (perhaps with refinements)? By what hermeneutics could we answer that question? Is this model defensible against the critiques that come from, say, David Hume and empiricism, Benedict Spinoza and his influential brand of rationalism, and postmodernism; and if so, how? Would such a model allow us to say under what conditions "special divine action"—if there be such a thing—might be detectable by humans?

My goal, therefore, is to provide a more thorough exegetical treatment of the issues than has yet been offered, and to relate my exegetical results to the associated theological, philosophical, scientific, and apologetic questions. My particular interest is in the area of exegetical method informed by discourse linguistics. I also draw on recent studies in biblical historiography, since many of the same questions occur there.

When I cite a biblical text in this work, the translation reflects my own conclusions about the meaning of the original. If any grammatical point is

---

[7] For example, in such books as *The Semantics of Biblical Language* (Oxford, England: Oxford University Press, 1961); and *Biblical Words for Time* (London: SCM, 1969).

[8] Paul Gwynne, *Special Divine Action*, 65. Gwynne uses "SDA" to denote "special divine action," which he defines as "God brings it about that some particular outcome is different from what it would have been had only natural, created factors been operative" (24). "Direct SDA" is his term for what has traditionally been called "miracle," while "indirect SDA" denotes what is commonly called "special providence" (58). "Special providence" here denotes an event that is subjectively special in that it meets a human need and makes God's government especially visible to the pious, but for which we do not have to invoke a supernatural cause (e.g., being in the right place at the right time).

[9] Likewise, Alfred Freddoso, "Medieval Aristotelianism and the Case Against Secondary Causation in Nature," in T. V. Morris, ed., *Divine and Human Action: Essays in the Metaphysics of Theism* (Ithaca, N.Y.: Cornell University Press, 1988), 74-118, says, "The scriptural and patristic testimony cited by the Christian Aristotelians [who were 'supernaturalists'] in favor of secondary causation in nature is scanty and, more to the point, counterbalanced by other texts that seem to support occasionalism" (103-104). He says that Malebranche, an occasionalist, has the longest and most illuminating discussion of the exegesis.

controversial, I generally keep critical discussion to the footnotes (unless it is crucial to the argument). In some cases I simply quote a standard version for convenience, as long as any translation quibbles I have do not affect the point under discussion.[10] I intend citations of secondary sources to be thorough and fair, but make no claim to be exhaustive. Indeed, to try to be exhaustive in describing the historical and philosophical landscape would simply be to reinvent the wheel, since competent surveys in these fields already exist.[11] I generally limit references to technical works in biblical studies to scholars who have addressed the questions I am asking, whether in agreement or in disagreement.

In order to begin to address these questions, we must note that several important preliminary matters arise. For example, the way I have phrased my questions seems to presuppose that it is possible to speak of *a* biblical model of divine action, and even that such a model is ascertainable by us in our age. It is also true that there are many in biblical studies who attend, not to the texts we have, but to the hypothetical antecedents to those texts, i.e., their putative sources and redaction histories. Further, some suppose that these sources reflect differing ideologies, and that different traditions of the Bible are also at odds with each other (e.g., wisdom as contrasted to prophecy, Paul as opposed to Jesus or to Moses).

I do not intend to gloss over such matters, to the extent that they are relevant to the topic at hand; and I have a few comments before I begin. First, for theological purposes the text as we have it is the only text that is canonical, and this diminishes my religious interest in any prehistory to these texts, unless we can show that the prehistory had a bearing on how the audience of the final text was to interpret it. Second, it is usually possible to give the existing texts a coherent reading, which diminishes literary and exegetical interest in the putative sources. Third, the text as we have it is something with objective existence, and is hence an empirically appropriate object of exegesis; the putative sources do not satisfy such an empirical criterion. Moreover, even if it could be the case that there are sources and theological streams that reflect differing ideologies, it does not necessarily follow that these ideologies differ on the topics under the present investigation. This last point also applies to the relationship between what we call the "Old Testament" and the "New Testament," and the differences between

---

10 When I give no notation, the translation is my own. I use the standard designations RSV (Revised Standard Version), NASB (*New American Standard Bible*), NIV (*New International Version*), and NRSV (*New Revised Standard Version*).
11 If this were a Ph.D. dissertation in philosophy, I would of course be obligated to comment critically on everything I have read. I have contented myself, however, with focusing on the exegetical side and providing a fairly full bibliography for those who want to pursue the philosophical investigation.

Christians and Jews: It does not follow that they must differ on this particular point.[12]

As for the hermeneutical question, I am persuaded that the methods of
literary-linguistic study, especially those of discourse analysis, give us some
reliable tools for ascertaining how the biblical texts served as acts of communication between their authors and their audiences. It is in fact the failure to employ these tools on the part of many theologians and exegetes that
leads to misinterpretation and misapplication of the biblical material, as I
aim to show.

---

[12] Cf. the apostle Paul, in Acts 23:6-9, who aligns himself with one of the parties of Judaism in regard to
the particular point.

$\mathcal{T}wo$

Summary of Positions: Models for "God" and "the Creation"

To begin discussing the relationship of God to his creation we must first define what we mean both by "God" and by "the creation"; the answers to these questions yield several families or types of models of divine action.[1] We may also refer to these models as *metaphysics*. When I use that term, I mean one's convictions about what the world is like, how its parts interact with one another, and what role God has in it all. Discussions of metaphysics will also involve us in considering whether we can know anything about the world and about God's role in the world; and if so, how we might know.

I. ATHEISM

A. ATHEISTIC NATURALISM (E.G., RICHARD DAWKINS):

There is no transcendent creator, and nature works autonomously, according to its own laws, at least some of which are in principle intelligible to humans.

B. ATHEISTIC IRRATIONALISM (E.G., MANY POSTMODERNS):

There is no transcendent creator, nor is "nature" either rational or intelligible to us.

---

[1] In this summary of models it is not my intention to evaluate under guise of description (hence I shall shun provocative labels). (Contrast the classification schemes of Colin Russell in *Cross-currents: Interactions Between Science and Faith* [London: Christian Impact, 1995], 92-97, which apparently follows Reijer Hooykas, *The Principle of Uniformity in Geology, Biology, and Theology* [Leiden: E.J. Brill, 1963] in caricaturing the supernaturalistic position of, e.g., Aquinas, and calling it "semi-deism.") I also want to place theologians in the models that they themselves would agree to. The terms *theistic naturalism*, *providentialism*, and *limited theism* are terms of my own coinage.

II. DEISTIC NATURALISM (E.G., STEPHEN HAWKING AND PROBABLY CHARLES DARWIN)

God is a transcendent creator but he does not take an active role in events in the world since the creation. Events in the world unfurl according to the laws with which nature was endowed at the creation.

III. "TRADITIONAL (CHRISTIAN) THEISM"

This position includes the doctrines of God as the sovereign Creator who is independent of his creation with respect to his own being and is the cause of the existence of the creation, who continues to involve himself with his creation, both in the sense of maintaining it in being and of ruling it according to his own ends (providence). He is omniscient, omnipresent (in time and space, and any other dimension there might be), and omnipotent; he is also holy, just, and loving. He enters into covenantal relationship with his human creatures. Christianity asserts that in this one God there are three persons, the Father, the Son, and the Holy Spirit.

Among traditional (Christian) theists there are various ways of viewing the relationship between God and his creation:

A. "NATURAL PROPERTIES" EXIST:

God has given to created things a definite nature according to which they behave.

1. Theistic naturalism (e.g., Rudolph Bultmann, Maurice Wiles, "liberal" theology):

God does not "interfere" with the nature of his creation, because such interference would be inconsistent with the modern scientific worldview. (This contention is at the heart of liberal theology.) I distinguish this from deism, partly because its adherents make such a distinction, and partly because they usually think that this view does not preclude some kind of relationship with God. They generally acknowledge that this is not the "biblical" view (they usually suppose that the biblical view is either supernaturalism or occasionalism), but they are trying to salvage something of religion in the face of modern science.[2]

---

[2] It is possible to argue that at least some of the proponents of this position actually belong to a subset of deism; and Paul Gwynne, *Special Divine Action: Key Issues in the Contemporary Debate* (Rome: Gregorian University Press, 1996), 298-302, discusses precisely that in regard to Maurice Wiles. On page 301 he observes, "Whether Wiles' position is properly described as 'deistic' or not is probably a debatable question, since the term 'deism' can be difficult to pin down with precision. . . . It is possible that Wiles and others who deny SDA [special divine action] may not be deistic in the fullest sense of the term, but they are definitely heading away towards the deistic end of the spectrum." Although this is probably true, I have left this category under "traditional Christian theism" because, as noted, its proponents would do so (even though it is a severe contraction of that theism). I do not think this position is really compatible with traditional Christian theism, but the relevant point for my task is that proponents of this position do not claim it represents the biblical view, a view they consider untenable today. Hence I will not discuss them further, except in the context of apologetics.

2. Providentialism (e.g., Howard Van Till, R. J. Berry):

This view is somewhat similar to "theistic naturalism," in the sense that it rejects "interference" in the natural world. It is different, though, in that it is usually put forward as biblically faithful. In this view, God does not "interfere" with his creation, but he has set up its natural processes so that they accomplish his purposes. What are traditionally called "miracles" are by this view rather "special providences" which are distinguished from ordinary providences not by any mechanism but by our recognition of God's purpose in the event.[3] Howard Van Till's doctrine of "functional integrity" is the expression of this view in the realm of the origin of life and of humans.[4]

3. Supernaturalism (e.g., Aquinas, Protestant scholastics, Old Princeton, C. S. Lewis):

This class of views affirms that there is such a thing as "nature" as a web of cause and effect, and that God's ordinary providence is the preservation of the things that he made and concurrence in their effects. (For a definition of "concurrence," see chapter 3, under the subhead "Supernaturalism.") It also affirms, as we have seen, that God is free to work "without, above, and against them, at his pleasure" (*Westminster Confession of Faith* 5:3).

B. "NATURAL PROPERTIES" DO NOT EXIST:

1. Occasionalism (e.g., Nicolas Malebranche, George Berkeley, "Amsterdam School" [Abraham Kuyper, Reijer Hooykas, G. C. Berkouwer], "biblical theology"):

This position says that other views accord autonomy to nature but that the Bible does not do so. As noted above, according to occasionalists laws of nature are not alternatives to divine activity but only our codification of that activity in its normal manifestation, and a miracle means nothing more than that God at a given moment wills a certain thing to occur differently than it had up to that moment been willed by him to occur.

IV. "LIMITED THEISM"

This class of views generally results from modifying traditional theism by removing God's transcendence over time and his absolute sovereignty.[5]

---

[3] This is why I am suggesting the term *providentialism* for this model: It attributes every event to the providential working of ordinary natural properties.

[4] A difficulty is that an author may be "providentialist" in one field of study (e.g., the origin of life), but more properly "supernaturalist" in others (e.g., the special events in redemptive history).

[5] E.g., John Polkinghorne, *Quarks, Chaos and Christianity* (New York: Crossroad, 1996), 41-48; Ian Barbour, *Religion in an Age of Science* (New York: HarperSanFrancisco, 1990), 243-270. For our purposes it is important to note that, although these writers are major players in the "science and religion" arena, nevertheless their reasons for advocating "limited theism" are not the products of *scientific* advances as such; they are, as they always have been, *philosophical*, generally having to do with the problem of evil and the definition of human freedom.

A. KENOTIC (SELF-LIMITATION) (E.G., JOHN POLKINGHORNE):

God respects the integrity of his creation and the freedom of his creatures by willingly limiting his rule over the world and his knowledge of the future. The favored model is the relationship between a parent and a growing child. As Polkinghorne put it, "The suffering and evil of the world are not due to weakness, oversight, or callousness on God's part, but, rather, they are the inescapable cost of a creation allowed to be other than God, released from tight divine control, and permitted to be itself."[6]

B. ONTOLOGICAL LIMITATION (E.G., IAN BARBOUR AND PROCESS THOUGHT IN GENERAL):

God finds his own completion in the creation. In some writers this takes the form of comparing God's relationship to the world with the mind-body relationship; in others we may find God described as "the leader of a cosmic community" (Barbour). This means that God *cannot* control absolutely; he is instead involved with the creation, and exerts influence but not domination.

---

[6] John Polkinghorne, *Quarks, Chaos, and Christianity*, 47.

Three

The Options Within "Traditional (Christian) Theism" Presented and Contrasted

The summary of models of chapter 2 indicates that the chief competitors for representing the (or a) "biblical" understanding of God's relationship to his creation are found within what I have labeled "traditional (Christian) theism": providentialism, supernaturalism, and occasionalism. Proponents of the other categories do not claim that their positions represent the biblical materials; instead at best they see themselves as providing a corrective to untenable positions found in those materials.[1] (An exception to this would be the form of limited theism associated with the book titled *The Openness of God*, which I shall discuss in an excursus at the end of this chapter.)

SUPERNATURALISM

Supernaturalism, as I have indicated, affirms the existence of "nature" as a web of cause and effect, and it describes God's ordinary providence as the preservation of the things that he made and concurrence in their effects. The existence of "nature" and "cause and effect" is usually expressed in terms of "second causes"; that is, God is the "First Cause," the source of being, and created things are second causes. "Scholasticism," whether in its Lutheran, Reformed, or Roman Catholic form, generally treats this topic under the rubric of "providence," treating "creation" separately.[2] For

---

[1] Cf. the quote from Bultmann that begins chapter 1 and the citations of Polkinghorne and Barbour in chapter 2 under "Limited Theism."

[2] See, for example, Heinrich Schmid, *Doctrinal Theology of the Evangelical Lutheran Church*, Charles Hay and Henry Jacobs, trans. (Minneapolis: Augsburg, 1961 [originally 1875]), 170-194; Heinrich Heppe, *Reformed Dogmatics*, G. T. Thomson, trans. (Grand Rapids, Mich.: Baker, 1978 [originally 1950]), 251-280; and Alfred Freddoso (Roman Catholic), "God's General Concurrence with Secondary Causes: Why Conservation Is Not Enough," *Philosophical Perspectives* 5 (1991), 553-585. Some theologians dispute whether concurrence should be included, but Freddoso's essay is, I believe, proof that it must be. Such a notable theologian as William G. T. Shedd, *Dogmatic Theology* (Nashville: Nelson, 1980 [originally 1888-1894]), i:527-530, speaks only of preservation and government, but from his exposition it is clear that his definition of preservation *includes* concurrence.

example, Heinrich Schmid's compendium of the Lutheran scholastics puts it this way:[3]

> The Providence of God specially manifests itself: I, in His preserving what has been created in the world [Latin *conservatio*]; II, in His coöperating with all that occurs [*concursus*]; and III, in His leading and directing everything in the world [*gubernatio*]. . . .
> I. *Preservation* is the act of Divine Providence whereby God sustains all things created by Him, so that they continue in being with the properties implanted in their nature and the powers received in creation. The world would fall back again into nothing if God did not continually uphold, not only the various species of creatures and the individuals in them, but also the existing order of arrangement and coöperation which He has assigned the whole; for created things have no power of subsistence in themselves. . . . Therefore *preservation* is also designated as *continued creation.*[4]
> II. *Concurrence.* The doctrine of Divine Providence implies far more than merely that God creates and upholds the world. . . . The Holy Scriptures teach us that He is an active participant in all that transpires in the world; that nothing that occurs could take place without Him and His active co-operation. . . . In this, God is not, indeed, as in creation and preservation, the sole cause of that which happens; for God has given to living creatures[5] a will that is to be employed in actions, and has imparted even to inanimate things a power which we are to regard as the efficient cause of changes. . . . Concurrence, or the co-operation of God, is the act of Divine Providence whereby God, by a general and immediate influence, proportioned to the need and capacity of every creature, graciously takes part with second causes in their actions and effects.[6]
> III. *Government* is the act of Divine Providence by which God most excellently orders, regulates, and directs the affairs and actions

---

[3] All three schemes mentioned above are in agreement here. I cite Schmid 1) because he has clearly laid it out and 2) one has to choose someone!

[4] The term *continued creation* can cause some confusion, since different writers may mean different things by it. The Reformed compendium of Heppe uses similar language about "continued creation," but adds a clarification: "*conservatio* is to be conceived as a *continuata creatio*, resting upon the same command of God as creation. . . . At the same time preservation must not be conceived as a continued creation, as though by preservation the essential identity of the once created world were abolished" (Heppe, 257-258). We shall see that occasionalists such as Jonathan Edwards also speak of "continued creation," but mean something that is incompatible with the scholastic consensus.

[5] So Schmid; does he mean "*rational* creatures"?

[6] The expression "graciously takes part" is somewhat vague; it refers to God's confirming the interactions of the created things' causal properties. Heppe, 258, cites the Swiss theologian J. H. Heidegger (ca. 1700) for a definition: "Concurrence or co-operation is the operation of God by which he co-operates directly with the second causes as depending upon him alike in their essence as in their operation, so as to urge or move them to action and to operate along with them in a manner suitable to a first cause and adjusted to the nature of the second causes."

of creatures according to His own wisdom, justice, and goodness, for the glory of His name and the welfare of men. . . .
The Providence of God ordinarily employs second causes, and thus accomplishes its designs; but God is by no means restricted to the use of those second causes, for He often exercises His Providence without regard to them, and operates thus contrary to what we call the course of nature, and hence arises the difference between *ordinary* and *extraordinary* providence. [*Providence* is *extraordinary* when God operates either without means, or beyond or above means, or contrary to means and their nature, or, what is the same, above and beyond the order instituted by Himself . . . (all miracles are effects of the extraordinary providence of God).[7]][8]

There is no doubt in this scheme that both "ordinary" and "extraordinary" providence are expressions of God's active power. However, the mode of that expression of power is different, and, at least in principle, some of those differences are detectable by human observers.[9] God's ordinary providence is not physically detectable, since it is not part of the order of the world we experience with our senses.[10]

As Christian theologians discussed these matters, it became popular to refer to two modes of divine power, namely *potentia absoluta* (Latin for "unqualified power") and *potentia ordinata* ("ordained power"). As the Presbyterian William Shedd put it,[11]

The omnipotence of God exerted in the act of creation is denominated potentia absoluta. In this instance, there is no use made of anything that is in existence. It is the operation of the First Cause alone. The Divine omnipotence exerted in providence is called potentia ordinata. In this instance there is use made of existing things.

Under this terminology "miracles" are expressions of God's *potentia absoluta* or creative power. Since, however, there are some historical and conceptual

---

[7] "The form of divine *gubernatio* in which God is active without second causes or uses them in a manner deviating from their orderly appointment and activity is God's performance of miracle" (Heppe, 263).

[8] The bracketed portion is from Schmid's quote of Johann Quenstedt, page 193.

[9] Cf. Stephen T. Davis, "God's Actions," in R. D. Geivett and G. R. Habermas, eds., *In Defense of Miracles* (Downers Grove, Ill.: InterVarsity, 1997), 163-177, at 166. I say "at least in principle" and "some of those differences" because it is conceivable that a given special divine action is not distinguishable to us from a "natural event." Some that are clearly distinguishable, under the supernaturalist scheme, are the initial creation *ex nihilo* event; the virgin conception of Jesus; the turning of water into wine; the resurrection of Jesus; and the conversion of sinners, even at the hands of incompetent messengers.

[10] Cf. Paul Helm, *The Providence of God* (Downers Grove, Ill.: InterVarsity, 1994), 82, who helpfully says, "The exact sense in which objects which are distinct from God are yet upheld by him is difficult to get clear"; and (89), "It should be stressed that this upholding, being metaphysical or ontological in character, is physically undetectable." Other writers have referred to the hiddenness of the "causal joint" (Austin Farrer's term) between God and the creation. Note also Helm (146), where he virtually defines "providence" as "that great matrix of causes and effects through which God governs the world."

[11] Shedd, *Dogmatic Theology*, i:361.

difficulties associated with these terms, I will not use them here.[12] The crucial thing for us to note is that supernaturalism, at its best, asserts the reality and causal powers of created things and a direct expression of divine power in everything that happens. Supernaturalism may or may not be sound biblically, but in no way is it responsible to call it "semi-deism" or "deism plus miracles," as some have done, since the notion of concurrence asserts God's direct participation in every event.

PROVIDENTIALISM

What I am calling "providentialism" is, at its best, similar to supernaturalism in the sense that it affirms not only the existence of nature but also the radical dependence of nature on God's providential working. Where it differs is in its understanding of "special providences." Writers in this category will not accept the idea that God needs somehow to "tinker" with his creation or compromise his fidelity to it; instead, in choosing to create he bound himself to work within the created properties and capacities. Hence all "special providences," including those traditionally called miracles, are in principle explicable "scientifically" (which means in terms of the causes and effects of created things). This means that what makes an event a "miracle" is not any property of the event itself, but its appropriateness to a given set of circumstances, where it displays God's concern and power.

The most that writers in this category will allow is special divine influence on human decision making.[13] Paul Gwynne notes that,

All in all, many seem to hold that because a significant proportion of the processes operative in the physical arena are explainable in terms of scientific theory, there is little scope for SDA [special divine action] there, and thus "nature" miracles are deemed implausible. In contrast, the inner structures of the mind and its enigmatic influence over the body are still somewhat unexplored territory; this creates space for possible SDA and renders stories of amazing healings of bodies via mind-power more believable.[14]

---

[12] According to William J. Courtenay, "The Dialectic of Omnipotence in the High and Late Middle Ages," in T. Rudavsky, ed., *Divine Omniscience and Omnipotence in Medieval Philosophy* (Dordrecht: D. Reidel, 1985), 243-269 (also reprinted as article iv in Courtenay, *Covenant and Causality in Medieval Thought* [London: Variorum Reprints, 1984]), the original context for these terms was the medieval discussion of things that God could have done by virtue of his absolute power, versus the things he has decided to do by virtue of his decree. Later medievals began to apply the terms differently, in the way Shedd used them as quoted here.

[13] This category is what Paul Gwynne calls the "indirect SDA only" school in his *Special Divine Action* (Rome: Gregorian University Press, 1996).

[14] A potential drawback of this rationale is its liability to the charge of committing the "God-of-the-gaps" blunder: that is, we only posit special divine activity because we don't have a "scientific" (naturalistic) explanation yet.

It is difficult to find thoroughgoing providentialists; instead one finds people with tendencies in this direction or preferences for this kind of explanation. An example of this kind of thinking, though, is R. J. Berry's comment in the midst of exploring the biology of the doctrine of the virgin conception of Jesus: "Probably all miracles are susceptible to an explanation other than the supernatural."[15]

An expression of providentialism is the attempts to propose such explanations for the biblical "miracles"; one of the most influential of such attempts was a series of articles by Greta Hort on the plagues in Egypt and the wilderness events recorded in Exodus and Numbers.[16] Hort gives a very detailed examination of the material in Exodus and correlates her exegesis with known phenomena from Egypt such as the behavior of the Nile, various microorganisms, bugs, and so on. She stumbles over the tenth plague, attributing her difficulties to the literary history of the Exodus account. Likewise she explains the death and disappearance of Korah and company, who had rebelled against Moses' leadership (Num. 16:26-35), by reference to a *kewir*[17] and thunderstorm (which Moses, who alone of Israel had desert experience, saw happening and therefore used to his advantage). Hort herself identifies the credibility of the narratives with the availability of a naturalistic explanation. Not everyone who finds her treatment of the first nine Egyptian plagues helpful is persuaded to abandon supernaturalism for the tenth plague and for the death of Korah;[18] but some are.[19]

---

[15] R. J. Berry wrote "The Virgin Birth of Christ" for *Science and Christian Belief* 8:2 (1996), 101-110; the quotation is from his comment in reply to P. Addinall's response to his article in *Science and Christian Belief* 9:1 [1997], 77. In the original article, at 108-109, Berry suggests that a natural mechanism would not decrease the miraculous nature of the event.

[16] G. Hort, "The Plagues of Egypt," *Zeitschrift für die Alttestamentliche Wissenschaft* (ZAW) 69 (1957), 84-103; "The Plagues of Egypt (part ii)," *ZAW* 70 (1958), 48-59; "The Death of Qorah," *Australian Biblical Review* 7 (1959), 2-26.

[17] A *kewir* is a kind of mudflat one might find in such a desert. Hort explains: "They owe their existence to the configuration of the ground with its undrained depressions, into which the wadi floods and occasional rain showers pour their water from time to time, to the sand and dust carried by the wind, perhaps to wandering dunes, and above all, to the high evaporation, all of which factors working together result in a lake which instead of water consists of clayey ooze and salt, and whose surface may be a salt crust or/and a mud and sand crust, thick or thin, or which may have no crust at all, and show itself for what it is, a quite specially pernicious kind of bog, but which, when it has a mud crust, will look bone-dry in the dry season with yawning desiccation cracks, and which then may or may not be crossed with impunity" (Hort, "Qorah," 20). She supposes that the crust suddenly opened because Korah's company had disturbed it by pitching tents on it (and perhaps the thunderstorm, which she takes as the cause of the "fire from the Lord" in v. 35, contributed).

[18] E.g., James Hoffmeier, "Egypt, Plagues In," in David Freedman et al., eds., *Anchor Bible Dictionary* (New York: Doubleday, 1992), ii:374a-378a; K. A. Kitchen, "Plagues of Egypt," in J. D. Douglas et al., eds., *The New Bible Dictionary* (Downers Grove, Ill.: InterVarsity, 1982), 943a-944b, both of whom give arguments for taking the tenth plague as "wholly supernatural."

[19] An example would be the evangelical OT scholar R. K. Harrison, who inclined toward providentialist accounts of miracles whenever he could make them plausible. For example, see his commentary on the death of Korah in *Numbers* (Grand Rapids, Mich.: Baker, 1992), 238, and his *Introduction to the Old Testament* (Grand Rapids, Mich.: Eerdmans, 1969), 578, on the plagues, accepting Hort's arguments. I will be able to use Harrison as a representative of providentialist-type accounts in several instances in this work.

Or consider the following from Colin Brown (note the added italics):[20]

> Many of the other miraculous events in the OT did not involve the suspension of natural causes. . . . The parting of the Red Sea was caused by a "strong east wind" blowing all night (Exod. 14:21). In such instances the event is *a providential ordering of natural causes for the benefit of the people of God.* Similarly, the fire falling on the sacrifice of Elijah on Mount Carmel (1 Kings 18:38) was probably a thunderbolt. In the cases of the healing of Naaman (2 Kings 5) and the restoration to life of children (1 Kings 17:17-24; 2 Kings 4:18-37) we have instances of paranormal healings beyond normal medical explanation. . . . The sun dial of Ahaz (Isa. 38; 2 Kings 20) was probably a series of steps. . . . The return of the shadow ten degrees may have been due to the Shekinah Glory which lighted up the steps. . . . In the case of 2 Kings 6:5ff., John Gray comments, "The factual basis of the 'miracle' of the floating axe-head may be that Elisha with a long pole or stick probed about the spot indicated (an important point in the text) until he succeeded either in inserting the stick into the socket, or, having located the hard object on the muddy bottom, moved it until the man was able to recover it." . . . It may be noted that the text itself does not call the event a miracle or even a sign.[21] *Nevertheless, the event was evidently remembered as indicative of Yahweh's providential help.*
>   . . . A sudden gust of flame or explosion killed the men who brought Shadrach, Meshach and Abednego down to where the kilns were (Dn. 3:22), but the latter survived their ordeal possibly protected by their clothing mentioned in the narrative.

A difficulty with providentialism is that one may prefer providentialist explanations in some kinds of areas, but not necessarily in others.[22] An example is Howard Van Till, a physicist who has offered a doctrine of what he calls the "functional integrity" of the creation:[23]

---

[20] C. Brown's section in W. Mundle, O. Hufius, C. Brown, "Miracle, Wonder, Sign," in C. Brown, ed , *New International Dictionary of New Testament Theology* (Exeter, England: Paternoster, 1976), ii:620-635, at 628.

[21] On the linguistic error involved in this line of reasoning, see the final section of chapter 4.

[22] For this reason, while it is often hard to identify an author as a "pure providentialist," we can still speak of him as a "relative providentialist," i.e., as insisting on such explanations in certain disciplines of study. Also, we will find authors who are what we may call "supernaturalist-but-almost-providentialist," i.e., they have a pronounced preference for providentialist explanations and will accept supernatural ones with great reluctance. R. K. Harrison probably fits into this category, as does Donald MacKay most likely. Colin Brown, in the article cited above, does not completely exclude supernatural acts, but he does apparently prefer to minimize their number.

[23] Howard Van Till, "Basil, Augustine, and the Doctrine of Creation's Functional Integrity," *Science and Christian Belief* 8 (1996), 21-38, at 21-22, 23. As far as I know, Van Till means this doctrine to apply to the "natural history" of the cosmos and of life on this planet, and not necessarily to redemptive-historical acts of deliverance.

Scientific cosmology, for instance, proceeds on the presumption that the expanding universe of galaxies that we now observe, including the particular forms of matter of which it is composed, is the outcome of a continuous succession of form-producing processes and events—all such dynamic physical processes and events being manifestations of the capacities for action possessed by matter and by other forms of energy. Similarly, most modern biological theorizing regarding the formative history of life on our planet presumes the possibility of some historical scenario that proceeds from molecules to mankind along a continuous pathway of natural phenomena.

By "continuous pathway" we here mean an unbroken succession of natural processes and events not interrupted or blocked by physical, chemical or biological gaps of the sort that would require occasional bridging by "miraculous divine interventions" or by any other "special" divine activity. . . .

I find a substantial basis for articulating a "doctrine of Creation's functional integrity" that envisions a world that was brought into being (and is continuously sustained in being) only by the effective will of God, a world radically dependent upon God for every one of its capacities for creaturely action, a world gifted by God from the outset with all of the form-producing capacities necessary for the actualization of the multitude of physical structures and life forms that have appeared in the course of Creation's formative history, and a world whose formational fecundity can be understood only as a manifestation of the Creator's continuous blessing for fruitfulness. In such a Creation there would be no need for God to perform acts of "special creation" in time because it has no gaps in its developmental economy that would necessitate bridging by extraordinary divine interventions of the sort most often postulated by Special Creationism.

Van Till considers scientific explanations to be necessarily in terms of natural processes only, and strictly complementary to theological ones. He is steadfastly opposed to young earth creationism, progressive creationism, and the intelligent design movement, because they do not accept his principle of functional integrity, and he considers them therefore to be not only unscientific but also theologically wrongheaded.

OCCASIONALISM

The doctrine known as "occasionalism" appeared in a number of medieval Islamic writers, whom the Jew Maimonides and the Christian Aquinas opposed.[24] The form of it that we will consider comes from Nicolas Malebranche and Bishop George Berkeley, and then appears in the "biblical theology" writers of this century as well as the "Amsterdam school" of theologians and philosophers.

The motivation for occasionalism is to give an account of events in the world in a way that maximizes divine sovereignty over everything. It is based on a critique of supernaturalism, which, it is held, allows "nature" too much autonomy. Hence in this view laws of nature are "not alternatives to divine activity but only our codification of that activity in its normal manifestation," and a miracle "means nothing more than that God at a given moment wills a certain thing to occur differently than it had up to that moment been willed by him to occur."[25] According to this view, "God is not only the primary or first cause of every natural phenomenon, he is its only true cause."[26] However, "No important occasionalist has ever in fact intended to deny that there is such a thing as creaturely free choice or that such free choice involves a genuine active causal power to produce effects. . . . God is the sole efficient cause of every state of affairs that is brought about in 'pure' nature, i.e., in that segment of the universe not subject to the causal influence of creatures who are acting freely."[27]

Since I intend to focus on the exegetical issues, I will take as conversation partners those who have actually tried to offer an exegetical defense of this position. There are two principal sources on the modern scene: first, writers with "biblical theology" emphases, and second, the Amsterdam theologian G. C. Berkouwer.

Nevertheless perhaps a brief mention of Malebranche would be in order here. Nicolas Malebranche (1638–1715) was a French priest who was influenced by the French philosopher René Descartes (1596–1650). Descartes is known for his brand of soul-body dualism, which raises questions about the

---

[24] There are many historical questions that I shall here pass by, such as whether the Muslim al-Ghazali and the Christian Nominalists properly belong in this category; cf. William Courtenay, "The Critique on Natural Causality in the Mutakallimun and Nominalism," *Harvard Theological Review* 66 (1973), 77-94 (reprinted as article v in Courtenay, *Covenant and Causality in Medieval Thought* [London: Variorum Reprints, 1984]).

[25] The first quote is from John Sharp, "Miracles and the 'Laws of Nature,'" *Scottish Bulletin of Evangelical Theology* 6:1 (Spring 1988), 1-19, at 17, drawing on Donald MacKay; the second comes from G. C. Berkouwer, *The Providence of God* (Grand Rapids, Mich.: Eerdmans, 1952), 196, drawing on Abraham Kuyper. It is interesting to note that MacKay is probably best classified as a supernaturalist-but-almost-providentialist; the fact that Sharp can cite him, however, anticipates some of the confusions that arise between providentialism and occasionalism.

[26] Thomas V. Morris, "Introduction," in Morris, ed., *Divine and Human Action: Essays in the Metaphysics of Theism* (Ithaca, N.Y.: Cornell University Press, 1988), 1-9, at 5-6.

[27] Alfred Freddoso, "Medieval Aristotelianism and the Case Against Secondary Causation in Nature," in Morris, ed., *Divine and Human Action*, 74-118, at 81-82, 83. We should note that Freddoso is here speaking of "important occasionalists" in the history of philosophical theology. As we shall see shortly, the Dutch occasionalist theologian Abraham Kuyper comes quite close to denying that there is such a thing as creaturely free choice.

interaction of the soul and the body. Malebranche articulated his position in his most important work, *The Search after Truth* (French *De la Recherche de la Vérité*; first edition 1674–75; final edition 1712).[28] In his preface to the book he said,[29]

> In this work I combat several errors and especially those most universally received or those that cause a greater disorder of the mind, and I show that these errors are almost all consequences of the mind's union with the body. In several places I try to make the mind realize its servitude and dependence relative to all sensible things so that it might be awakened from its somnolence and make an effort to free itself.

The senses, which others (e.g., Aquinas) thought to be an important means of gaining knowledge, are actually, according to Malebranche, the problem for fallen humans because they are dominated by lust. Hence, though we may think that there is some interaction between our minds and bodies that results, say, in our moving our arms, this is a mistake; instead, our willing it is the *occasion* upon which God produces the effect of our arm raising.[30] Malebranche denied that our vision of objects is actually *caused* by the objects—the objects are instead the *occasions* on which we have the ideas of them present to our minds. He also denied that one ball knocking into another is properly the *cause* of the second ball's moving; it is instead the *occasion* on which God causes the motion. In his own words,[31]

> They should conclude not that objects transmit species resembling them because the soul ordinarily perceives them only when they are present, but only that the object is ordinarily necessary for the idea to be present to the mind. Finally, because a ball does not have the power to move itself, they should not judge that a ball in motion is the true and principal cause of the movement of the ball it finds in its path. They can judge only that the collision of the two balls is the occasion for the Author of all motion in matter to carry out the decree of His will, which is the universal cause of all things. He does so by communicating to the second ball part of the motion of the first, i.e., to speak more clearly, by willing that the latter ball should acquire as much motion in the same direction as the former loses, for the motor force of bodies can only be the will of Him who preserves them.

---

[28] Available in English in Nicolas Malebranche, *The Search after Truth and Elucidations of the Search after Truth*, T. M. Lennon and P. J. Oscamp, trans. (Columbus: Ohio State University Press, 1980).

[29] Malebranche, xxv.

[30] Malebranche, 449-450.

[31] Malebranche, 225.

Malebranche produced his *Elucidations of the Search after Truth* to accompany the third edition of his *Search after Truth* (1677–78); in *Elucidations* he replied to various objections to his philosophy. The sixth and final edition appeared in 1712. This work contains what Alfred Freddoso calls "the longest and most illuminating discussion" of scriptural and theological counterarguments to his theories in its fifteenth elucidation, and we shall bring some of these arguments to bear as we proceed.[32] He sums up his position:[33]

> Thus the philosophy that teaches us that the efficacy of secondary causes is a fiction of the mind, that Aristotle's, and certain other philosophers', *nature* is a chimera, that only God is strong enough not only to act in our soul but also to give the least motion to matter, this philosophy, I say, agrees perfectly with religion, the end of which is to join us to God in the closest way. . . .
>
> According to this philosophy, the bodies surrounding us do not act on the one we animate, and *a fortiori*, do not act on our mind. It is not the sun that illumines us and gives us movement and life. It does not cover the earth with fruits and flowers and does not provide us with our food. This philosophy teaches us, as does Scripture, that it is *God who provides the rain and regulates the seasons, who gives to our bodies their food and fills our hearts with joy, that only He can do us good, and that he never ceases to witness thereby what He is, although in ages past He suffered all nations to walk in their own ways* [reference to Acts 14:15-16; italics in the original]. Following the language of this philosophy, we must not say that *nature* provides us with goods; we must not say that it is God and nature.[34] We must say that it is God alone and speak in this way without equivocation in order not to deceive the simple.

Occasionalism had a major theological proponent in Jonathan Edwards (1703–1758). In *The Great Christian Doctrine of Original Sin Defended* (1758), Edwards was replying to a certain John Taylor (1694–1761).[35] Edwards quotes from Taylor, with apparent agreement, the following statement: "that God, the original of all being, is the *only cause* of all natural effects." In context, Edwards is dealing with the problem of identity of existence over time: e.g., how can a great tree be the same as the sapling with

---

[32] Freddoso, "Medieval Aristotelianism," 104 n. 56. He is referring to Malebranche, 672-685, which is the reply to the seventh proposed proof of natural causation, in the fifteenth elucidation.

[33] Malebranche, 681-682.

[34] Notice that he does not mention "God *via* nature," which is closer to the actual supernaturalist position.

[35] Jonathan Edwards, *The Works of Jonathan Edwards*, Sereno Dwight, ed. (Edinburgh: Banner of Truth, 1974), i:143-233. Discussion here refers to part iv, chapter iii, second difficulty (pages 222-224).

which it shares so few characteristics and probably no atoms? He makes an astonishing assertion:

> It will certainly follow from these things, that God's *preserving* of created things in being, is perfectly equivalent to a *continued creation*, or to his creating those things out of nothing at *each moment* of their existence. . . . It will follow from what has been observed, that God's upholding of created substance, or causing of its existence in each successive moment, is altogether equivalent to an *immediate production out of nothing*, at each moment. (italics in the original)

Let's turn now to the theological advocates of occasionalism from our time.

The field of what is called "biblical theology" is difficult to define, but, speaking broadly, a number of features bind this class of studies together: 1) an opposition between philosophy and philosophical theology as "Greek-influenced," and the more "dynamic" and passionate "Hebrew" thought world; 2) a related suspicion of systematic theology; and 3) an interest in broad themes as they develop historically through the Bible. These features can make an author who subscribes to a naturalistic theory of the origin of the biblical materials sound very pietistic or evangelical, using traditional theological language in good faith (because the question of whether the language refers to any historical and miraculous events is dismissed as "Greek-influenced."[36]

An early representative of this way of thinking was A. B. Davidson, who wrote,

> Two beliefs characterize the Hebrew mind from the beginning: first, the strong belief in causation—every change on the face of nature, or in the life of men, or nations, must be due to a cause; and secondly, the only conceivable causality is a personal agent. . . . Everything is supernatural, that is, direct divine operation.[37]

Similarly, consider these statements from J. P. Ross:

[36] Cf. H. Graf Reventlow, "Theology (Biblical, History of)" in D. N. Freedman et al., eds., *Anchor Bible Dictionary* (New York: Doubleday, 1992), vi:483b-505a; James Barr, "Biblical Theology," in K. R. Crim et al., eds., *Interpreter's Dictionary of the Bible, Supplement* (Nashville: Abingdon, 1976), 104a-111b. Barr is especially critical of the "Biblical theology movement," which took these features and wedded them to certain other ideological and methodological commitments, some of which we will examine in due course.
[37] A. B. Davidson, "God (in O.T.)," in James Hastings, ed., *A Dictionary of the Bible* (Peabody, Mass.: Hendrickson, 1988 [originally 1898]), ii:196a-205b.

Israel, on the other hand, could not concern itself about scientific irregularities or breaches of natural law [i.e., the modern notion of "miracles"], because it had no interest in science and did not think in terms of Nature. . . . When he is asked *why*, the answer that leaps to the Israelite's mind is in terms of God; the language of physical causation does not occur to him. . . . Every human act can also properly be regarded as an act of God. . . . Israel did not believe in an autonomous Nature, and consequently did not have to ask how God intervened in it—the modern problem of miracles.[38]

A very important "biblical theology" author is Walther Eichrodt, who wrote:[39]

It was possible just as spontaneously and axiomatically to portray natural events, which elsewhere might have been given an anthropomorphic life of their own, as *a direct act of God*, who controls both Nature and history by the omnipotence with which he fills all things. Thus the bestowal of rain and fertility is the direct gift of Yahweh; . . . [he gives a list of events God directly causes, cf. passages discussed in chapter 7 below] . . . the pious soul, overleaping all intermediate causes, sees God forming the universe at every moment. This conception is strikingly expressed in the fact that the Hebrew language has no special word for the sustaining of the universe, but for both creation and preservation uses the verb *bārā'* [Hebrew, "to create"]. It is hardly going too far to describe this Old Testament view of the maintenance of the world as *creatio continua*.[40]

Nevertheless Eichrodt recognized that some parts of the Old Testament do in fact show an awareness of nature as an ordered system; he ascribes this to development, especially under the influence of the "priestly writer," who is responsible for Genesis 1:1–2:4a according to the standard source-critical scheme.[41]

---

[38] J. P. Ross, "Some Notes on Miracle in the Old Testament," in C. F. D. Moule, ed., *Miracles: Cambridge Studies in Their Philosophy and History* (London: Mowbray, 1965), 43-60.

[39] Walther Eichrodt, *Theology of the Old Testament*, J. A. Baker, trans. (English translation, London: SCM, 1967), ii:153-154.

[40] This last sentiment is, of course, founded on an error in linguistic method that Barr would have pounced on (namely, identification of the *word* [*bārā'*] and the *thing* [the idea of creation]). We will see this kind of error in operation, and discuss it, in other contexts as well.

[41] Another important "biblical theology" writer, H. Wheeler Robinson, *Inspiration and Revelation in the Old Testament* (Oxford, England: Oxford University Press, 1946), is quite similar: On page 1 he asserts that the Hebrews had no word for "nature," instead to them that would just be "God"; while on page 24 he acknowledges that "this continued maintenance of Nature is effected through established ordinances and inherent energies, as the reference to the seed-containing fruit of Genesis i implies." This toleration of rival and incompatible explanations (on these authors' terms) can be handled either by positing historical development as reflected in the strata of the OT, or by assuming that the Hebrew mind was not "philosophical" and thus would not perceive the problem.

The sophisticated and influential theologian G. C. Berkouwer is very much in the occasionalist camp. In his work on divine providence, in the chapter titled "A Third Aspect?" he addresses and rejects the doctrine of concurrence.[42] He sees the doctrine of concurrence as a reaction to deism and a product of Protestant scholasticism, "first developed when the florescence of the Reformation had begun to decline."[43] He suggests that it originated from an effort to explain the relation between God and human sin, but he feels that it fails to do so. Berkouwer's hero is the Dutch polymath Abraham Kuyper (1837–1920), who said "that God not only provides the ability so that through it the sinner can work, 'but that He Himself is the "Worker" in everything.' . . . There is a Divine energy in all things: 'the energy, by which sin is committed, is a power of God.'" Berkouwer, of course, does not want to make God a partner in sin, and explains the difficulty by saying that is as far as human understanding can take us. Berkouwer's interest is to maximize the role of divine sovereignty.

Later in the chapter Berkouwer rejects the formulation of first cause and second causes. In his view, "The use of the terms first and second causes implies that God is only the most important cause among equal causes." He connects this with the "staticizing of the God-concept" which he considers an inevitable consequence of Roman Catholic arguments for the existence of God. He thinks the Scriptures leave no room for such a distinction: "We are unmistakably taught the absolute dependence of all creatures on the work of God. There is no terrain in which man can escape being defined by the activity of God."

Berkouwer continues this tack in his chapter on "Providence and Miracles."[44] He follows Kuyper, who "refused to accept miracles as an incidental intervention into an otherwise hermetically sealed nature" (i.e., opposing his caricature of supernaturalism). Berkouwer takes his definition of *miracle* from Kuyper: "nothing more than that God at a given moment wills a certain thing to occur differently than it had up to that moment been willed by Him to occur. . . . They are new, extraordinary ways of God's rule over all things." We cannot speak of miracles as *contra naturam* ("against nature"), since there is no such thing as "nature," only the constant activity of God.

I shall revisit and evaluate these arguments in chapter 8.

---

[42] G. C. Berkouwer, *The Providence of God* (Grand Rapids, Mich.: Eerdmans, 1952), 125-160.
[43] Berkouwer is in error here unless he means only in the Protestant world; Malebranche opposed the idea and treated it as entrenched in *Search after Truth*, 676-678.
[44] Berkouwer, *Providence*, 188-231.

HOW THESE OPTIONS COMPARE IN THEIR VIEWS
OF SECOND CAUSES, MIRACLES, AND THE
RELATION OF SCIENCE AND FAITH

Here we may summarize our description so far. Supernaturalism is the view that God maintains his created things in existence with their causal properties. The interaction of these properties gives us the regularity of nature. Supernatural events may occur when God transcends these natural properties to achieve some purpose. Providentialism is similar, but leaves out supernatural causation. Occasionalism denies that created things have any natural causal properties; instead, every event is entirely "supernatural."

In this section we will see that the metaphysical position one takes will have far-reaching consequences for how one views the scientific enterprise, the knowability of the natural world, the relation of science and faith (and their potential conflict or harmonization), and the apologetic value of miracles.

The *supernaturalist* position is the more conventional one, although the notion of concurrence is often not prominent in popular presentations of it (and hence there is some justice in the complaint that supernaturalists sound like deists who allow the occasional miracle). As we have seen, supernaturalism endorses the idea of a regular order of nature, not independent of God at any point but endowed by him with cause-and-effect relations which God supports at every moment. Ordinary science is the study of these cause-and-effect relations, and this metaphysic allows for *critical realism* in science, namely the conviction that what we study is objectively there and that, at least in principle, we can get genuine knowledge of it (hence *realism*), although our finitude and fallenness can and do interfere (hence the *critical* part). God can, according to his will, also act qualitatively differently, e.g., by not confirming a causal connection, by adding some new energy or object, by imposing organization, or by enabling some created object to do what its natural powers would never have equipped it to do. These are not problems for science, since no "laws" or causal powers are abrogated; supernaturalists will differ among themselves as to the degree to which unbelievers should be able to acknowledge the presence of a supernatural effect.

Providentialism is similar to supernaturalism in its view of science and of critical realism. Since the providentialists' dominant image of the created world is a well-made machine, they feel it would be an insult to God's workmanship to say that he had in any way "interfered" with its working. Hence in their view, miracles are detectable by believers because they answer in a timely way to their needs. The mechanism for these timely operations is then some combination of God's pre-planning the properties and conditions of events so that they accomplish his will, with his influence on human minds—both in their deciding what to do and in their perceiving his presence. This means that mention of God is *never* appropriate in *any* scientific description of events, except as the originator, preserver, and goal of nature.

Occasionalism in its most consistent form will promote what Alfred Freddoso calls "explanatory antirealism" in science:

> That is, they [occasionalists] hold that the purpose of natural science is not to discover the real causes of natural phenomena or the natures of those causes, but to discover and systematize regularities and correlations among the Real Cause's observable effects in nature, and on this basis to make accurate predictions.[45]

Occasionalists have argued that our sense of observing *causal* relations in natural events is not endorsed by Scripture and cannot be proved from experience (in this last point having an important connection to David Hume, as we shall see). In this scheme, miracles are not detectable as qualitatively different expressions of divine power, since there is no such thing as nature. Hence, like the providentialist, the occasionalist will locate the detectability of a miracle in the believing observer.[46]

This virtual identity between the occasionalist and the providentialist practical definition of miracles is remarkable when one considers how different these metaphysical models are. The similarity stems from both positions' common rejection of the detectability of special divine action against a backdrop of "nature" (or ordinary providence): Occasionalism rejects the distinction between natural and supernatural by excluding the natural; providentialism rejects the distinction by excluding the supernatural and subsuming everything under "nature."

An interesting confusion results from this close similarity: Namely, one finds authors mixing arguments from providentialists and occasionalists to oppose supernaturalism, apparently unaware of the contradictions. One example will suffice. In his article on "Miracles" in *The New Bible Dictionary* (a reference work I regard highly), M. H. Cressey wrote the following:[47] "Scripture does not sharply distinguish between God's constant sovereign providence and his particular acts. . . . Thus when biblical writers refer to the mighty acts of God they cannot be supposed to distinguish them from

---

[45] Freddoso, "Medieval Aristotelianism," 112, followed by proof texts from Malebranche and Berkeley.
[46] Gwynne, *Special Divine Action*, 110, notices this as well, although not in these terms.
[47] M. H. Cressey, "Miracles," in J. D. Douglas et al., eds., *The New Bible Dictionary* (Downers Grove, Ill.: InterVarsity, 1982), 782a-784a. Quotations are all from 782, section on "Miracles and the Natural Order."

'the course of nature' by their peculiar causation, since they think of all events as caused by God's sovereign power." This sounds occasionalist. But then in the next paragraph he said, "The discovery of, say, causal connections between the different plagues of Egypt, a repetition of the blocking of the Jordan, or increased knowledge of psychosomatic medicine could not of themselves contradict the biblical assertion that the deliverance from Egypt, the entry to Canaan and the healing works of Christ were mighty acts of God." This line of thought is most properly providentialist.

I suggest that these two incompatible lines of argument are merged here because of the very similar understandings of the detectability of "miracles" from both camps. Cressey went on to say, "Miracles are events which dramatically reveal this living, personal nature of God, active in history not as mere Destiny but as a Redeemer who saves and guides his people. . . . It is clear that Scripture speaks of many events which are extraordinary or even unique so far as our general experience of nature goes." This statement would suit both the occasionalist and the providentialist, but does not clarify the yawning gulf that separates their metaphysics.

We will do well to avoid such confusion at the metaphysical level by careful attention to an author's actual position.

I find that many authors in the British journal *Science and Christian Belief* and the American *Perspectives on Science and Christian Faith* write from the assumption that either providentialism or occasionalism are scientifically, theologically, and philosophically respectable but that supernaturalism cannot be. If I were to speculate about what makes these views attractive to their proponents, I would suspect that providentialism has the benefit of eliminating most opportunities for "conflict" between science statements and faith statements, since they are complementary. Providentialists are able to say that atheistic science writers such as Richard Dawkins or Carl Sagan have made unwarranted and improper extrapolations from their scientific theories into metaphysics. They can say in good conscience, "We know from our faith *that* God did certain things; and our science simply tells us *how* he did it" (that is, the two realms of description are complementary). Indeed, some of the "natural" explanations for some biblical events sound pretty plausible.

The attractiveness of occasionalism, at least today, is more complex. I think the influence of Abraham Kuyper may help to explain it. To begin with, its scientific anti-realism humbles human knowledge, since it tells people they don't know as much as they think they know. It is also compatible with Kuyper's view that there are really two different kinds of science, that done by Christian believers and that done by everyone else. And no one can doubt that a non-theist is unlikely to give a pure occasionalist description of the world! The philosophically aware advocates of this group are also struck by the problem of whether we can prove the existence of causal relations between objects just by observing those objects; they find the problem as David Hume (a Scottish philosopher, 1711–1776, a skeptic and not an occasionalist!) posed it in his *Enquiry Concerning Human Understanding* (iv. 2) to be compelling. (We will come back to Hume later.)

The supernaturalist will conclude, however, that both providentialism and occasionalism seriously undermine the Christian critique of the naturalistic worldview that dominates the public face of the sciences. To the supernaturalist, providentialism has the feel of a too-easy accommodation to naturalism, while occasionalism seems to abandon all notion of a kernel of knowledge of the world shared by believer and nonbeliever, for which the believer claims to have the better explanation. It becomes hard for the supernaturalist to see how, in either of these alternatives, faith can have any relevance, let alone intellectual vigor, in the rough-and-tumble of the marketplace.

HISTORICAL NOTE: WERE AUGUSTINE AND CALVIN OCCASIONALISTS, SUPERNATURALISTS, OR PROVIDENTIALISTS?

Although this study is focused on the biblical writers themselves, it is worth a small aside to consider two authors to whom scholars frequently appeal as exemplary holders of "biblical" views. Unfortunately, such references to them are not in terms of evaluating their positions but often for the purpose of enlisting their support for the writer's own position. This leads to their being claimed for the providentialists, occasionalists, and supernaturalists!

Augustine (354–430) is held in high regard by Catholics and Protestants alike. His definition of "miracle" as something which is "not contrary to nature, but contrary to what is known as nature," his view that any event that reveals the goodness of the Creator could be a miracle, and his view that ordinary natural processes are often more wondrous than the extraordinary miracles narrated in the Bible, all seem to distance him from the supernaturalist camp.[48] We may make Augustine out to be a providentialist if we suppose his doctrine of seminal reasons implanted in the creation at the beginning of time excludes the possibility of anything "new" in the world. We may make

---

[48] This discussion draws on Paul Gwynne, *Special Divine Action*, 65-68; R. M Grant, *Miracle and Natural Law in Graeco-Roman and Early Christian Thought* (Amsterdam: North-Holland Publishing, 1952), 217-219, 244-245; John Hardon, "The Concept of Miracle from St. Augustine to Modern Apologetics," *Theological Studies* 15 (1954), 229-257; and Chris Gousmett, "Creation Order and Miracle According to Augustine," *Evangelical Quarterly* (*EvQ*) 60 (1988), 217-240.

him out as an occasionalist if we attend to his skepticism concerning science and human knowledge in general, and his emphasis on God's will as the sole cause of events.

However, several factors should keep us from assigning Augustine to one of these categories. First, as Gwynne points out, Augustine was using a much broader definition of "nature" in his definition of miracle; for him "'nature' embraces not only the known regularities of the material cosmos, but the entire divine plan." Further, he did not think that we would ever be able fully to understand the processes of nature.[49] On the other hand, Augustine's position was "based on the fact that natural science was moribund."[50] Indeed, John Hardon points out that,

> To accuse Augustine of denying the supernaturality of miracles because he calls these seminal elements "natural" is to confuse two entirely different concepts: "natural" as applied to "the ordinary course of nature," and "natural" as applied to "something in nature which only a direct intervention of God can actuate."

It is possible that these interpretive difficulties are evidence that the question is anachronistic for Augustine. In any case we do not have a decisive voice from this theologian for one view over the others.

John Calvin (1509–1564) was a premier Protestant theologian who is often contrasted with the "Protestant scholastics" who followed him in the seventeenth century. Calvin sounds almost occasionalist if we read his *Institutes*, book i, chapter 16, on divine providence.[51] For example, in section 2 he says, "With regard to inanimate objects, again, we must hold that though each is possessed of its peculiar properties, yet all of them exert their force only in so far as directed by the immediate hand of God. . . . Every single year, month, and day, is regulated by a new and special providence of God." On the other hand, the Calvinist tradition has typically read him as a supernaturalist, as evidenced in the fact that Heppe (a supernaturalist) can cite this passage of Calvin's in the context of second causes and concurrence and say, "Calvin means exactly the same thing . . ."![52]

---

49 Gwynne, 67-68.
50 Grant, 219. According to Grant, Augustine was the heir of "ancient Academic [i.e., the philosophical school descended from Plato] scepticism."
51 Gary B. Deason, "Reformation Theology and the Mechanistic Conception of Nature," in David Lindberg and Ronald Numbers, *God and Nature: Historical Essays on the Encounter Between Christianity and Science* (Berkeley, Calif.: University of California Press, 1986), 167-191, makes Luther and Calvin out to be basically occasionalist. His thesis is that their theology helped to undermine the medieval Aristotelian synthesis, and thus to promote the mechanical worldview of modernity. On his page 178 he contrasts Calvin with the Protestant scholastics compiled in Heppe.
52 Heppe, *Reformed Dogmatics*, 261 (chapter 12, §11).

Benjamin Warfield tried to portray Calvin as essentially a providential-ist, at least with respect to the origin and development of life and even of human bodies.[53] Warfield argued that, "Calvin's doctrine of creation is, if we have understood it aright, for all except the souls of men, an evolutionary one. . . . All that has come into being since [the original *ex nihilo* fiat]— except the souls of men alone—has arisen as a modification of this original world-stuff by means of the interactions of its intrinsic forces."[54] However, the theologian John Murray (1898–1975), who was in so many ways an heir to Warfield and his theological tradition, showed that Warfield had misun-derstood the relevant material in Calvin.[55] He concluded, "Calvin conceived of creative factors as entering into the process by which the heavens and the earth were perfected so that we are not able to characterize the process, as he conceived of it, as 'a very pure evolutionary scheme.'"[56]

Murray showed himself a supernaturalist when he continued, "While it is true that God is present and active in every event, which is just saying that God's providence embraces all that occurs, yet it is all-important to distin-guish the differing modes of the divine agency." It is most likely that this in fact represents Calvin's own view pretty accurately, since Calvin said (*Institutes*, I.14.20),

> From this history [i.e., Genesis 1] we learn that God by the power of his word and his Spirit created the heavens and the earth out of nothing; that thereafter he produced things inanimate and animate of every kind, arranging an innumerable variety of objects in admirable order, giving each kind its *proper nature*, office, place, and station; at the same time, as all things were liable to corruption, providing for the perpetuation of each single species, cherishing some by secret methods, and, as it were, from time to time instill-ing new vigour into them, and bestowing on others *a power of con-tinuing their race*. (italics added)

If we connect this with the mention in I.16.2 of "peculiar properties," we can see that the Reformed tradition that took Calvin as a supernaturalist with a very strong doctrine of divine governance is probably the most accurate.[57]

---

[53] Benjamin B. Warfield, "Calvin's Doctrine of the Creation," in Warfield, *Calvin and Calvinism* (New York: Oxford University Press, 1931), 287-349 (originally published in *Princeton Theological Review* 13 [1915], 190-255).

[54] Warfield, *Calvin and Calvinism*, 304.

[55] John Murray, "Calvin's Doctrine of Creation," *Westminster Theological Journal* 17 (1954), 21-43.

[56] Murray, "Calvin's Doctrine of Creation," 42, quoting from Warfield, *Calvin and Calvinism*, 305.

[57] Even so, Deason, "Reformation Theology," collects enough passages from Calvin to show that the pic-ture is not straightforward. It is possible that Calvin was not entirely consistent, since he was not a philoso-pher of nature; it is also possible that Deason has not always paid attention to the contexts and rhetorical purposes of Calvin's individual remarks.

EXCURSUS: REGARDING "THE OPENNESS OF GOD" THEISM

An interesting book made its appearance in 1994, titled *The Openness of God*.[58] What makes the book interesting for our purposes is that it argues for a form of what I have called "limited theism," all the time claiming that this better represents the biblical picture than does traditional Christian theism (a claim that sets it apart from other kinds of "limited theism"). In the book Richard Rice makes the exegetical case, John Sanders tries to account for the historical factors that led to traditional theism being the default view, Clark Pinnock offers a systematic theology treatment, William Hasker gives a philosophical perspective, and David Basinger explores the practical implications of this view of God. Because of the focus of this work, I intend to evaluate primarily whether this view has a fair claim to being a biblically based view, which means I shall be particularly concerned with Rice's article.[59] Although I cannot here give a full review of the book,[60] I can say that it merits our attention because it leads to serious limitations on God's range of possibilities for action in his world. That is, while these authors would most likely affirm the existence of nature and natural properties, their view would restrict the possible modes of God's interaction with (and especially, his overriding of) natural objects and their capacities.

According to this approach to God, Rice contends that (15-16),

> Love is the most important quality we attribute to God, and love is more than care and commitment; it involves being sensitive and responsive as well. These convictions lead the contributors to this book to think of God's relation to the world in dynamic rather than static terms. This conclusion has important consequences. For one thing, it means that God interacts with his creatures. Not only does he influence them, but they also exert an influence on him. . . . Thus history is the combined result of what God and his creatures decide to do. . . .
>
> As an aspect of his experience, God's knowledge of the world is also dynamic rather than static. Instead of perceiving the entire course of human existence in one timeless moment, God comes to know events as they take place. He learns something from what transpires.

---

[58] Clark Pinnock, Richard Rice, John Sanders, William Hasker, and David Basinger, *The Openness of God* (Downers Grove, Ill.: InterVarsity, 1994).

[59] Richard Rice, "Biblical Support for a New Perspective," in Pinnock et al., *Openness*, 11-58.

[60] Cf. the reviews of Michael Williams in *Journal of the Evangelical Theological Society* 40:3 (1997), 498-502; Alfred J. Freddoso, in *Christian Scholar's Review* 28:1 (Fall 1998), 124-133.

Based on this statement, it is probably right to take "the openness of God" theism as a member of the "divine self-limitation" category of "limited theism." Although these authors take pains to distance themselves from the ontological limitations on God found in process theology, it is not always clear that they reject *all* ontological limitations on God (but this may be due to their not having considered things in these terms).

At its heart, "the openness of God" theism stems from a strong view of human freedom, namely that God does not exercise total control over human decisions. Unlike the Arminianism with which it has important connections, this view denies that God knows the future, because, 1) God is *in* time and not *transcendent over* it; and 2) the future is the product of the free choices we and God make. Interestingly, there is no in-depth exegetical examination of either of these points, nor of the eschatological certainties expressed by biblical writers (e.g., 1 Cor. 15:23-25; Phil. 1:6), nor is there significant acknowledgment that these matters have a history of treatment in the church.

Rice cites 1 John 4:8, "God is love," and insists that "a doctrine of God that is faithful to the Bible must show that all of God's characteristics derive from love" (21). He defends the open view from the Old Testament by referring to passages that depict God's feelings (e.g., his distress at the unfaithfulness of Israel in Hosea), his intentions ("God's plans . . . are not ironclad decrees," 26), and his actions (he acts in time and reacts to his creatures). From the New Testament he refers to Jesus' life and ministry ("an obvious feature [of the ministry of Jesus] is the fact that his life was characterized by *service to* and *suffering with* rather than *power over* human beings," 40); Jesus' death ("the idea of a suffering God is the antithesis of traditional divine attributes such as immutability and impassibility," 46); and finally he addresses three groups of "problem passages," namely those dealing with divine changelessness, predictive prophecy (he particularly looks at conditional prophecy), and foreknowledge and predestination. He says (55-56):

> The traditional view of foreknowledge and predestination draws broader conclusions than the evidence warrants in three important ways. [1] The fact that God foreknows or predestines something does not guarantee that it will happen, [2] the fact that God determines part of history does not mean that he determines all of history, and [3] the fact that God extends a specific call to certain people does not mean that he similarly calls all people.

In general I would say that this argument fails for at least three reasons. First, Rice does not do justice to the full range of biblical material or of theological grappling with that material. For example, he leaves out of consideration such texts as Ephesians 1:11 (God is "the one who works out all things according to the counsel of his will") and Isaiah 14:26-27 ("This is the purpose that is purposed upon all the earth, and this is the hand that is stretched out over all the nations. For the Lord of Hosts has purposed, and who will frustrate [his purpose]; and his hand is stretched out, and who will turn it back?"), which are fairly plain about the determinative role of God's will.

Further, the claim that "a doctrine of God that is faithful to the Bible must show that all of God's characteristics derive from love," based on 1 John 4:8b, really needs a substantial amount of contextual exegesis of the statement in 1 John and extensive biblical and systematic support. It gets neither. In the context of 1 John the text is used to support the necessity of practical love being a part of the life of a professing Christian, since such a person is claiming to have been touched by God's love. Since John also insists that believers must display practical holiness (2:1-6) and adherence to God's truth revealed through the apostles (4:1-6), it hardly seems that 4:8b is set forth as an exhaustive statement of God's being. Besides, a controlling confession of the Old Testament is Exodus 34:6-7, which reads:[61]

> (6) And the Lord [Yahweh] passed before him [Moses] and called out, "Yahweh, Yahweh, a God compassionate and favorably disposed, slow of anger and full of grace and truth; (7) keeping grace to thousands, forgiving iniquity and transgression and sin. And he will certainly not acquit [whom? most likely the impenitent]; he visits the iniquity of fathers upon sons, and upon sons' sons, upon the third and upon the fourth [generations]."

Verses 6-7a describe God's benevolence, while verse 7b describes his justice, which will punish those who will not receive his benevolence. That is, a balanced view of God recognizes that a single attribute is not adequate to describe him.

Additionally, Rice's treatment of fulfilled prophecy is seriously inadequate. Patrick Fairbairn (a traditional theist) wrote a valuable manual on interpreting prophecy, and he deals with conditional prophecy quite fully.[62] He showed that there are three categories of prophetic predictions: 1) those disclosing God's purpose of grace for his people, and these are not conditioned on human response (e.g., Gen. 3:15; Isa. 9:6-7); 2) those referring to

---

[61] For detailed exegesis see my forthcoming study, "Exodus 34:6-7: Filling in the Blanks."
[62] Patrick Fairbairn, *The Interpretation of Prophecy* (Edinburgh: Banner of Truth, 1993 [originally 1865]). See especially his chapter iv, pages 58-82.

God's plans to judge foreign nations who oppress his own people, but which are addressed to his people for their comfort, and these are also unconditional (since the Gentiles are given no chance to repent); and then 3) all other prophecies, which are conditional (precisely because their chief aim is the moral response of the audience). Rice seems unaware of these issues. Further, the second major part of Isaiah's book uses fulfilled prophecy for apologetic purposes (e.g., 41:26; 42:9; 44:7-8, 26; 45:21; 46:10; 48:5-6). The interest of these passages is not simply that God *knows* the future (in itself this is damaging to Rice's case); it is rather that he *controls* it for his purposes (cf. 46:10-11). It is hard to see how these passages can make any sense at all under the openness view.

In dealing with the suffering of the earthly Jesus, Rice has no comments on its place in redemptive history, nor on the present status of the exalted Christ. Indeed, his theology of the incarnation seems to emphasize seeing it as a fuller revelation of God's character, which is not the primary focus of the apostolic message. For example, according to Scripture Christ suffered, died, and rose from the dead as his people's representative, to suffer for them what they deserve. Now that he has done so, he claims that "all authority in heaven and earth has been given to me" (Matt. 28:18; cf. Phil. 2:9-11; 1 Cor. 15:24-25; Eph. 1:20-23). None of this requires us to think that God must have changed during the process; instead the traditional explanation, namely that the assumption of a human nature was necessary in order to have a representative who could undergo all these events, fits the biblical evidence quite well.[63]

Second, it seems to me that Rice does not adequately deal with the requirements placed upon us by the fact that God is greater than we are and that we must therefore use analogical language to speak about him.[64] Rice often writes of traditional theists who dismiss biblical statements as anthropomorphisms or anthropopathisms, "which have no application to his real life" (49). This is a caricature of traditional theism, which does not treat anthropomorphisms as irrelevant or meaningless statements. They are meaningful, they describe something real, and they have limitations.[65]

---

[63] Classically, it is understood that the union of two natures gives us a situation in which each nature contributes what is proper to it. For example, the *Westminster Confession of Faith*, 8:7, declares, "Christ, in the work of mediation, acts according to both natures, by each nature doing that which is proper to itself; yet, by reason of the unity of the person, that which is proper to one nature is sometimes in Scripture attributed to the person denominated by the other nature." This declaration is in harmony with classical Christology as expressed in the Chalcedonian Definition (see translation with notes in P. Schaff, *History of the Christian Church* [New York: Scribner's, 1910], iii:744-746), and the Athanasian Creed (see translation in T. G. Tappert, *The Book of Concord* [Philadelphia: Fortress, 1959], 19-21).

[64] It seems to be a presupposition of the authors that our experience of God, which is of necessity temporal and changing, is adequate to describe the way God is in himself. They ought to have articulated this presupposition and defended it.

[65] Aquinas is clear about this, cf. *Summa Theologiae*, I, 13; and C. S. Lewis has a delightful way of putting it in *Prayer: Letters to Malcolm* (London: Collins, 1966), letter x.

Third, Rice falls foul of the *abusus usum non tollit* ("abuse does not take away proper use") fallacy. That is, whereas it is *possible* to articulate a traditional theism that is impersonal, it is not *necessary* to do so. When Rice wants to score traditional theism as presenting a God who is indifferent to our pains, he does so by drawing a caricature and without specific citations, e.g., (25):

> It is not uncommon for people to dismiss these emotional descriptions of God, numerous though they are, as poetic flights essentially unrelated to the central qualities that the Old Testament attributes to God. As they see it, the real God of the Bible is made of sterner stuff. He is powerful, authoritarian, and inflexible, so the tender feelings we read of in the prophets are merely examples of poetic license.

At the strongest, the texts adduced by Rice serve as a warning not to frame a doctrine of God that excludes the relational side of God. But this is not a problem that traditional theism *necessarily* suffers from.[66]

At the end of the day, the difficulty is that the Bible has a number of emphases that are in potential tension with each other, and we have to decide just how we are going to relate them. We may take the approach of some and declare that the Bible is self-contradictory, and that hence it is our task to choose those emphases we can support from other sources. Or we can try to find a pattern of harmony that respects the communicative intent of the various texts. Rice's essay does not have detailed exegesis of the texts with this latter end in view.

I do not think that traditional theism is as hard up for biblical support as these authors imply. Consider for example Isaiah 45. Several assertions about God underlie this passage:

1. God is *unique*, namely he alone is God. For example, in verse 5 the Lord says, "Besides me there is no God."[67] This one God is Yahweh; to use this name is to recall that he is the one who revealed his character to Moses (e.g., in Ex. 34:6-7).

2. God is *self-sufficient*, that is, he is the Creator, the source of everyone else's being. Therefore we exist at his pleasure, while he does not depend on

---

[66] Indeed, consider this statement from Adrio König that Rice cites with apparent approval: "Anyone who describes God's being in terms of disengagement, remoteness, or self-sufficiency, the ground or origin of all that is, has listened wrongly to the biblical message in general and the preaching of Jesus in particular" (50). This is a combination of caricature ("disengagement, remoteness") and the highly debatable ("self-sufficiency, the ground or origin of all that is," see below).

[67] Cf. vv. 5-6, 20-21; 44:6-8.

anyone else. This is why verse 18 speaks of the Lord who created the heavens and formed the earth.[68] He has neither beginning nor end (44:6; Rev. 1:8); he has no limits (Ps. 145:3); he is spiritual (i.e., since he caused the origin of matter, he is not himself material). This means that he transcends his creation, which includes matter, space, and time.[69] It also involves the power to bring about his purposes which he announced through his prophets (v. 21), even using unwitting Gentiles (vv. 1-4).

3. God is *personal*, that is, he has likes and dislikes, and acts accordingly. For example, verses 23-24 speak of his righteousness, which is his preference for what is right. Contrast this with the likes and dislikes of his rebellious people (46:12), and the impersonality of false gods (45:20). God's "name" is the revelation of his personal character, and its fundamental explanation is found in Exodus 34:6-7. His personal character includes wisdom, power, justice, goodness, and faithfulness.

4. God is *knowable;* he enters into relationships with people on the basis of his covenant (i.e., on his own terms). Thus, verse 6 speaks of all manner of people coming to know him as the one true God, while verse 19 speaks of his revealing himself to Jacob (a reference to his covenant, historically manifested).[70] To know God, to be rightly related to him through accepting his covenant, is life; not to know him this way is death and despair.

These assertions about God support traditional theism and are not compatible with limited theism.

---

[68] Cf. also vv. 7, 9-12, 18-21; 40:25-28; 44:24-28; 46:5-13.

[69] It is a legitimate task for systematic and philosophical theology to inquire as to just what is the best way to describe this transcendence.

[70] Cf. also vv. 18-20, 22, 25; 44:21-23; Ps. 147:19-20.

Part Two

———

PRESENTATION
OF EXEGETICAL
MATERIAL

———

Four

Some Hermeneutical Ground Rules

PHILOSOPHY, "COMMON SENSE," AND DISCOURSE ANALYSIS

When it comes to asking a question such as, "Which model of God's relation to the world he made does the Bible support?" we face a number of difficulties. The first is, should we believe that the Bible "supports" *any* of these models (providentialism, occasionalism, or supernaturalism)? Second, we may consider the question invalid from the start. After all, the Bible authors did not communicate their messages in philosophical form; nor are these messages intended primarily for philosophically oriented audiences (with the exception of Paul's speech in Acts 17:22-31). When one compares the biblical vividness with, say, the cool precision (and some would say hairsplitting) in traditional theological manuals such as Aquinas's *Summa Theologiae*, Heppe's *Reformed Dogmatics*, or Schmid's *Doctrinal Theology of the Evangelical Lutheran Church*, one can easily feel a yawning gulf between the Bible and the philosophical theologians; maybe the "biblical theology" authors have a point!

Nevertheless this need not imply that the scholastic effort is invalid, though it may of course be abused. With G. K. Chesterton we ought to recognize that, "Men have always one of two things: either a complete and conscious philosophy or the unconscious acceptance of the broken bits of some incomplete and often discredited philosophy. . . . Philosophy is merely thought that has been thought out. It is often a great bore. But man has no alternative, except between being influenced by thought that has been thought out and being influenced by thought that has not been thought out." In reference to a man who would respond to miracle claims with, "But my dear fellow, this is the twentieth century!" Chesterton observed, "In the mysterious depths of his being even that enormous ass does actually mean something. The point is that he cannot really explain what he means; and *that* is the argument for a better education in philosophy."[1]

Historically, it is fair to say that the Old Testament, and most of the New Testament, are not written in the mode that we associate with philosophy or philosophical theology (or even with the scholastic tradition of systematic theology). Some may interpret this to imply that such questions are at least unimportant and perhaps impertinent; and they may appeal to texts such as Colossians 2:8, "Watch carefully lest there be anyone who takes you captive through philosophy and empty deceit," or 1 Corinthians 1:18-31, which decries the Greeks' "wisdom of the world" as a barrier to belief in Christ. A simpler conclusion would be to note that 1) philosophers are not commonly in the original audiences of the biblical writers, nor are their questions generally in the range of topics addressed by them; and 2) while it is true that some forms of "philosophy" did provide barriers to belief, not all did. In fact, the earliest Jewish attempts to commend biblical faith to the Gentile world (and to Jews tempted to abandon their faith because of the pull of that world) include the apocryphal book called the Wisdom of Solomon, which makes judicious use of the philosophical concepts of its day.[2] Paul's own apologetic in Acts 14:15-17 and 17:22-31 and his theological background in Romans 1-2 reflect this tradition.[3] Further, it is simply false to suppose that being non-philosophical is the same as having no metaphysical implications. Indeed, it may be that careful exegesis can explicate the metaphysics implicit in a Bible text. So it does not seem to me that Paul would differ from Chesterton on this point.

C. S. Lewis, in *Letters to Malcolm*, Letter x, made the following helpful remarks about the respective roles of precise theological language and the vividness of the Bible:[4]

> We are constantly represented as exciting the Divine wrath or pity—even as "grieving" God. I know this language is analogical.

[1] G. K. Chesterton, "The Revival of Philosophy—Why?" in *The Common Man* (1950), cited from Chesterton, *As I Was Saying: A Chesterton Reader*, Robert Knille, ed. (Grand Rapids, Mich.: Eerdmans, 1985), 82-83.

[2] I hope no reader will suppose that I think that Greek philosophy is the benchmark of profundity; there is plenty of that in the Bible. Nevertheless, it does pose a set of questions, and presuppose ways of answering, that from a biblical perspective are not automatically invalid.

[3] To argue this at length would take us too far afield. See, for example, John J. Collins, "Natural Theology and Biblical Tradition: The Case of Hellenistic Judaism," *Catholic Biblical Quarterly* 60:1 (1998), 1-15; F. F. Bruce, *Acts* (New International Commentary on the New Testament; Grand Rapids, Mich.: Eerdmans, 1988), on the relevant passages; Michael Green, *Evangelism in the Early Church* (Grand Rapids, Mich.: Eerdmans, 1970); David DaSilva, "Paul and the Stoa: A Comparison," *Journal of the Evangelical Theological Society* 38:4 (1995), 549-564; N. Clayton Croy, "Hellenistic Philosophies and the Preaching of the Resurrection (Acts 17:18, 32)," *Novum Testamentum* 39:1 (1997), 21-39; and the discussion of creational revelation with extensive exegesis in my forthcoming *Christian Faith in an Age of Science*.

[4] C. S. Lewis, *Prayer: Letters to Malcolm* (London: Collins, 1966).

But when we say that, we must not smuggle in the idea that we can throw the analogy away and, as it were, get in behind it to a purely literal truth. All we can really substitute for the analogical expression is some theological abstraction. And the abstraction's value is almost entirely negative. It warns us against drawing absurd consequences from the analogical expression by prosaic extrapolations. . . .

   I suggest two rules for exegetics. (1) Never take the images literally. (2) When the *purport* of the images—what they say to our fear and hope and will and affections—seems to conflict with the theological abstractions, trust the purport of the images every time. For our abstract thinking is itself a tissue of analogies: a continual modeling of spiritual reality in legal or chemical or mechanical terms. Are these likely to be more adequate than the sensuous, organic, and personal images of scripture—light and darkness, river and well, seed and harvest, master and servant, hen and chickens, father and child? The footprints of the Divine are more visible in that rich soil than across rocks or slag-heaps. Hence what they now call "de-mythologising" Christianity can easily be "re-mythologising" it—and substituting a poorer mythology for a richer.

If we are going to ask philosophical questions of the Bible responsibly, we must make the effort to ascertain the "with-respect-to-whatness" of the biblical statements (that is, what questions were they actually trying to answer, and in what realm are they making truth-claims?), and to relate those statements to other biblical statements (being cautious of their communicative intents) and to the ways in which humans reason. Hence it is quite reasonable, say, to approach a biblical text about "the arm of the Lord," and to ask, "Does this imply that God has a body?" and "How shall we correlate this text with the texts that imply that God does not have a body?"[5] Hence good philosophy, like good theology, depends in the first place on careful attention to how words express meaning and how texts work to communicate.

   This leads us on to questions about the place of things such as "common sense" in theology and biblical philosophy. First, we shall have to define clearly what we mean by that term. I shall use the term *common sense* to denote the alleged fundamental apparatus by which humans function in the world: Namely, we have certain pre-reflective notions about the reality of our own existence and of our choices; about the existence and meaningful choices of other selves (perhaps also of God); and about the existence of the

---

[5] C. S. Lewis's chapter entitled "Horrid Red Things" in *Miracles* (New York: Macmillan, 1960) is an excellent discussion of some of these issues.

world and our ability to be successful agents in the world due to our (at least partial) knowing of (at least some of) the components of the world, and the cause-and-effect relations between those components. Does the Bible give any warrant for the validity of appeals to such "common sense"? Of course the answer is, it all depends on what those appeals are trying to establish.

Let us make a linguistic excursus to consider the role common sense plays in the act of communication. In their fine manual *Linguistics and Biblical Interpretation*,[6] Peter Cotterell and Max Turner describe what some discourse analysts call the "presupposition pool." This presupposition pool is the set of shared knowledge, beliefs, values, premises, worldview, etc., between an author and a receiver; an act of communication consists in the author "operating on" that pool—e.g., by adding to it or subtracting from it, by drawing attention to some part of it for the receiver to act upon, by revising it (even radically reorienting it), by aesthetic evocation of it. If the validity of a speaker's point depends on the affirmation of this common property, then we may say that such an affirmation, even when it is not explicit, is part of a good-faith act of communication.

For example, I have in my car a note in my wife's handwriting which says (in all capitals) "DON'T FORGET JOY." With only minimal information about my circumstances, someone might suppose that this is a general admonition to remember the character trait of "joy" (cf. Gal. 5:22), and conclude that I needed the reminder. Someone who knows I have a daughter named Joy might suppose that the note refers to her—perhaps to pray for her in a crisis or to get a gift for her birthday. Only the one who knows that I have agreed to pick my daughter up on my way home from work on a particular day will have enough of the shared "presupposition pool" between my wife and myself to understand the text. Indeed, the existence of the note indicates my wife's world-picture that I have the possibility of forgetting; and my placing the note prominently in my car indicates that I accept her world-picture—i.e., this is common ground between us, too.

Consider some examples from biblical interpretation. In Luke 20:27-40, the Sadducees question Jesus in an effort to show the absurdity of the resurrection. They posit a case based on Deuteronomy 25:5, which they say "Moses wrote for us. . . ." Jesus contests an important element of their premises, namely that life here and hereafter is identical; but he affirms as common property between them the notion that Moses wrote the passage in question. This comes out, not simply in his not disagreeing with that part of their case, but in his refutation of their conclusions using Exodus 3:6, which he also ascribes

---

[6] Peter Cotterell and Max Turner, *Linguistics and Biblical Interpretation* (Downers Grove, Ill.: InterVarsity, 1989), 90-97, 257-292.

to Moses. And this affirmation is essential to the discussion: Both sides agree that the passages are canonical Scripture, and that it is from Moses' authorship that they get their canonical status, because of his unique prophetic role.

Similarly, in Matthew 19:1-12, where Pharisees test Jesus with a question about divorce, Jesus' reply depends on a number of shared assumptions (i.e., a presupposition pool), e.g., that Moses wrote the law under discussion (Deut. 24:1-4), and that, nevertheless, the creation of humans narrated in Genesis 1:27; 2:24 was something earlier and represents a more pristine state of human existence. Christian ethical discussions of the text in Matthew also bring in the debates between the various Rabbinic schools on the matter, and when treating the propriety of remarriage they include discussion of the early Jewish divorce bills that have been discovered, considering these to be essential background to understanding the speech acts involved. In each case there are unstated shared assumptions, which figure crucially in Jesus' replies; if Jesus did not share these assumptions, then we would not be able to consider his arguments as *good-faith* acts of communication.

There are, however, instances in which a good-faith communication does *not* involve the speaker in endorsing whatever he might refer to by way of allusion. For example, if I refer to something that Sam and Frodo did, I am not necessarily claiming historicity for *The Lord of the Rings*. I would not be breaking faith with anyone unless I led them to believe the account was historical when I knew it was not. As a matter of fact, most people have the wherewithal to discern the generic clues (at least my children, before they were five, could tell the difference between the Chronicles of Narnia and the book of Acts).

In the Bible, there seem to be a number of references to assorted ancient Near Eastern myths; ought we assume that the author believed those myths to be true? In an important article, J. N. Oswalt showed that such an assumption is unwarranted; instead, the authors are using the ideas in a different setting from their original or making use of the emotional overtones of the mythic names.[7]

Take another example: In 1 Timothy 4:7, Paul tells Timothy to avoid "profane and old wives' myths" (Greek τοὺς βεβήλους καὶ γραώδεις μύθους, cf. NIV "godless myths and old wives' tales"). When he uses the adjective γραώδεις, "typical of old women," he is using a set phrase, found in other Greek writers, referring to stories not worth the attention of serious people.[8] Now it may (or may not) have been the case that these Greek

---

[7] J. N. Oswalt, "The Myth of the Dragon and Old Testament Faith," *EvQ* 49:3 (1977), 163-172. Oswalt also shows that some alleged mythic allusions are not allusions at all.

[8] For example Plato (428–347 B.C.) in his Theaetetus, 176B, dismisses a false motivation for virtue as "what is called old wives' chatter" (ὁ λεγόμενος γραῶν ὕθλος). The historian Strabo (ca. 64 B.C.—A.D. 19) in his Geography, 1.2.3, decries a man who makes Homer's poetical art out to be "old wives' mythology" (γραώδη μυθολογίαν).

authors had a low view of women's intellectual abilities, or that they thought older women had no capacity for serious discourse anyhow. But in no way does Paul's use of the expression commit him to such a view (especially since we can tell that he did not hold such a view, cf. 5:9-10; 2 Tim. 1:5; Titus 2:3),[9] nor does his point depend in any way on whether as a matter of statistics old wives actually tell such tales. Perhaps if we pressed Paul, he would say that these tales appeal to a certain kind of woman who is not sweetened by divine grace, and that comparable older men have their own kind of silliness; but this is no matter: We can identify the kind of tale he had in mind well enough.[10]

This indicates that we cannot simply assume either that the background ideas are or that they are not being endorsed, just because an author uses them. We shall have to concentrate on those cases in which the background ideas are bound up with the communicative intent.

If we assume that the biblical texts are first and foremost acts of communication, and that the original acts of communication between the authors and their first audiences hold primacy (or at least some kind of importance or interest), we can use this notion to get an idea of what we would expect the biblical texts to look like if, on the one hand, they were affirming (at least parts of) what I have designated "common sense," and what they might look like if their goal was to overthrow it.

There seems to be little room for dispute with Stephen Bilynskyj's observation that occasionalism "is contrary to common sense concerning our experience of causality in the physical world." He goes on to comment:[11]

> If the no-nature view is correct, then it is strictly false to say that "fire burns" or that "water cools" and the like. "Fire burns" is true only in a secondary sense. Burning is something that fire does only in the sense that fire is regularly connected with God's production of the effect of burning. "To do" something or other means, for every natu-

---

[9] The NASB rendering, "worldly fables fit only for old women," makes Paul sound like he did subscribe to such a view.

[10] Nicholas Wolterstorff, *Divine Discourse: Philosophical Reflections on the Claim That God Speaks* (Cambridge, England: Cambridge University Press, 1995), 209-216, addresses cases in which the presuppositions of a sentence may actually be false but the communication act still is successful. A biblical example would be the supposed geocentric cosmology in passages such as Ps. 93:1. In the first place, this is incorrect exegesis of the biblical texts, as I show in my forthcoming *Christian Faith in an Age of Science*. Second, such cases do not apply in this study, since I am trying to ascertain what the biblical authors *did* believe and try to inculcate.

[11] Stephen S. Bilynskyj, *God, Nature, and the Concept of Miracle* (Ph.D. dissertation, University of Notre Dame, 1982), 86. The Christian philosopher Paul Helm has little time for occasionalism, calling it "a classic case of a cure being worse than a disease," and the ideas of Jonathan Edwards quoted in chapter 3, "a preposterous view, for all sorts of reasons. But the chief reason, for our purposes, that it must be emphatically rejected is that there is no place in it for horizontal causation" (*The Providence of God* [Downers Grove, Ill.: InterVarsity, 1994], 84, 86). Unfortunately, Helm never explains *why* Christians ought to maintain a place for horizontal causation; apparently he thinks it is too obvious for discussion.

ral "agent," to be the occasion for God's "doing" something in the fullest and proper sense of asserting causal power. Our ordinary inclination to regard things as genuine causes is supposedly misguided.

That the occasionalist position does in fact require the overthrowing of our ordinary perceptions can be seen from Berkeley's reply to a similar objection:[12]

> It will upon this be demanded whether it does not seem absurd to take away Natural Causes and ascribe everything to the immediate operation of Spirits? We must no longer say upon these principles that fire heats, or water cools, but that a Spirit heats, and so forth. Would not a man be deservedly laughed at, who should talk after this manner? I answer, he would so; in such things we ought to "think with the learned, and speak with the vulgar." They who to demonstration are convinced of the truth of the Copernican system do nevertheless say "the sun rises," "the sun sets," or "comes to the meridian"; and if they affected a contrary style in common talk it would without doubt appear very ridiculous. A little reflection on what is here said will make it manifest that the common use of language would receive no manner of alteration or disturbance from the admission of our tenets.
>
> In the ordinary affairs of life, any phrases may be retained, so long as they incite in us proper sentiments, or dispositions to act in such a manner as is necessary for our well-being, how false soever they may be if taken in a strict and speculative sense.

I think the good bishop was mistaken: There is a great distance between what we think we are saying when we say "fire burns" and what occasionalists would have us mean. And his example of the Copernican system does not assuage the discomfort. One's theory of the solar system is an *inference* from a number of factors, and *not* a part of what I have called our common sense apparatus. Inferences are, after all, built on data, premises, meanings of terms, and chains of logic; "common sense" is one of our premises. To shift from a geocentric cosmology to a heliocentric one leaves this basic apparatus unaffected. Berkeley also raises questions about what constitutes a good-faith communication, when he allows ordinary speech primarily the function of arousing good sentiments. Some of us like to arouse good sentiments on the basis of what we think is true! It is just possible that some of the biblical authors may in fact have intended the same.[13]

---

[12] George Berkeley, *The Principles of Human Knowledge with Other Writings*, G. J. Warnock, ed. (Glasgow: Collins, 1969), 90 (§§51-52). Berkeley's *Principles* was first published in 1710.

[13] I will admit that Chesterton's influence on me makes me less confident than Berkeley that the learned rather than the vulgar will be right on such topics.

Unlike Berkeley, Malebranche, as we saw in chapter 3, would have us "say that it is God alone [who causes all effects] and speak in this way without equivocation in order not to deceive the simple." What would this mean? Malebranche did not give any examples, but we can imagine a few. Instead of saying in ordinary language to my daughter, "Be careful with that knife! It is sharp and you might cut yourself!" I ought to say, "Be careful with that knife! You don't want to give God the occasion to produce the effect of your being cut on your skin, because that could give him the occasion of producing other effects you won't like!"

Now from a philosophical perspective Bilynskyj has made the case that the burden of proof would lie on those who deny the existence of something we could legitimately call "nature," namely the occasionalists;[14] the linguistic observations made here suggest that *exegetically* the "no-nature" advocate also bears the burden of proof. This is because we must suppose that "common sense" is part of the shared presupposition pool. That is, for something like occasionalism to be true to the Bible we would need to find a group of texts whose communicative intent is clearly to overthrow commonsense perception of the world; on the other hand, to support either providentialism or supernaturalism, we would not need such explicit statements. Instead we would look to find texts whose arguments depend for their force or validity on there being such a thing as "nature," or that describe some created object as being the cause of some event. If we should find texts that assert the existence of "nature," "natural properties," or "causation" (terms defined below), that would be a bonus. If instead we find nothing decisive either way, we shall declare the Bible noncommittal and perhaps look to general philosophy for the decision.

These arguments may be compared with the hermeneutical principles advocated by Malebranche, who in his *Elucidations of the Search after Truth* offered the following guideline for exegesis:[15]

---

[14] It is this that is the basis of this famous incident in 1763, recorded in Boswell's *Life of Dr Johnson*: "After we came out of the church, we stood talking for some time together of Bishop Berkeley's ingenious sophistry to prove the non-existence of matter, and that everything in the universe is merely ideal. I observed, that though we are satisfied this doctrine is not true, it is impossible to refute it. I shall never forget the alacrity with which Johnson answered, striking his foot with mighty force against a large stone, 'I refute it thus.'" An editor has added a note from one Dr. Kearney: "Dr. Johnson seems to have been imperfectly acquainted with Berkeley's doctrine: as his experiment only proves that we have the sensation of solidity, which Berkeley did not deny. He admitted that we had sensations or ideas that are usually called sensible qualities, one of which is solidity: he only denied the existence of *matter*, i.e., an inert senseless substance, in which they are supposed to subsist. Johnson's exemplification concurs with the vulgar notion, that solidity is matter" (Everyman edition, i:292). But even though the experiment does not *disprove* the theory, the question must of course be, where lies the burden of proof?

[15] Nicolas Malebranche, *The Search after Truth and Elucidations of the Search after Truth*, T. M. Lennon and P. J. Oscamp, trans. (Columbus: Ohio State University Press, 1980), 672; discussed in Bilynskyj, *God, Nature, and the Concept of Miracle*, 69-70.

When an author seems to contradict himself [i.e., by affirming and not affirming "common sense"], and natural equity or some stronger reason obliges us to make him agree with himself, it seems to me that we have an infallible rule to discover his real view. For we have only to observe when this author speaks according to his lights, and when he speaks according to common opinion. When a man speaks as do others, that does not always signify that he is of their opinion. But when he positively says the opposite of what is customarily said, though he might say it only once, we have reason to judge that it is his view—provided that we know that he is speaking seriously, and after having given careful thought.

Now, we might decry this hermeneutic as elitist; but more importantly it is contrary to the cooperation that we assume between an author and his audience as described above. Indeed, what is to keep us from interpreting the "odd" statements of an author in the light of his more ordinary ones? Good exegesis will make no a priori commitments of Malebranche's sort; instead it will attend to the contextual factors such as genre, language conventions, knowledge of the referential world, and so on, to ascertain whether a statement is meant "literally" (and "literally" with-respect-to-what?).

If we decide that the Bible favors the existence of "nature," then, in order to decide between providentialism and supernaturalism we shall have to see, not only if there are passages that cannot be explained in terms of the ordinary functioning of the natural properties of created things, but also if there are texts that assert special supernatural agency.

SOME DEFINITIONS: "NATURE," "NATURAL PROPERTIES," AND "CAUSATION"

In a very insightful 1977 article,[16] John Rogerson addressed the Old Testament view of "nature" in an evaluation of several "biblical theology" writers who denied that the Hebrew writers *had* a concept of nature. For example, consider the opening sentences of H. Wheeler Robinson's *Inspiration and Revelation in the Old Testament*:[17]

> The Hebrew vocabulary includes no word equivalent to our term "Nature". This is not surprising, if by "Nature" we mean "The creative and regulative physical power which is conceived of as operating in the physical world and as the immediate cause of all its

[16] J. W. Rogerson, "The Old Testament View of Nature: Some Preliminary Questions," in H. A. Brongers et al., eds., *Instruction and Interpretation* (Oudtestamentische Studiën 20; Leiden: E. J. Brill, 1977), 67-84.
[17] H. Wheeler Robinson, *Inspiration and Revelation in the Old Testament* (Oxford, England: Oxford University Press, 1946), 1.

phenomena".[18] The only way to render this idea into Hebrew would be to say simply "God".

We need to note several things about this statement. First, although it is easy to find those who say that, because one language has no word equivalent to some word in another language, therefore the first language lacks the *concept*,[19] lexicographers will not countenance such an identification of lexical stock with conceptual stock.[20] Second, as Rogerson notes, Robinson has chosen one of several definitions of nature found in the *Shorter Oxford English Dictionary*. Had he instead chosen the entry "the material world, or its collective objects and phenomena, especially those with which man is most directly in contact," or some other, his conclusion that the only way to speak of nature in Hebrew is by saying "God" would not be nearly so clear.

In the interest therefore of clarity and precision, I shall draw on the work of a master of both, C. S. Lewis.[21] When in ordinary speech I speak of the "nature" of something, I mean the properties it has by virtue of being the kind of thing it is. I do not mean anything technical or microscopic by this: Rather, it is part of the nature of flint to be hard and sharpenable if you chip it right; it is part of the nature of red delicious apples to taste good (and to "keep the doctor away"?) and to produce seeds that have the nature to grow into apple trees; it is in the nature of cats to be predators; it is not in the nature of snakes to drink milk. Thus an equivalent expression for the nature of something is its "natural properties."[22]

In ordinary language, we speak of a "cause" as "that which produces an effect; that which gives rise to any action, phenomenon, or condition. *Cause* and *effect* are correlative terms."[23] Hence we can say that Mark McGwire's

---

[18] Robinson cites the *Shorter Oxford English Dictionary* for this definition.

[19] For example, besides Robinson, cf. R. H. Fuller, *Interpreting the Miracles* (Philadelphia: Westminster, 1963), 8; G. Harder, "Nature," in C. Brown, ed., *New International Dictionary of New Testament Theology* (Exeter, England: Paternoster, 1976), 2:656-662, at 658; John C. Sharp, "Miracles and the 'Laws of Nature,'" *Scottish Bulletin of Evangelical Theology* 6:1 (Spring 1988), 1-19, at 9 n.25.

[20] E.g., B. Siertsema, "Language and World View (Semantics for Theologians)," *The Bible Translator* 20 (1969), 3-21, at 12-13.

[21] Specifically, his chapter "Nature," in *Studies in Words* (Cambridge, England: Cambridge University Press, 1967), 24-74; and chapter 2 of *Miracles: A Preliminary Study* (New York: Macmillan, 1960).

[22] This is based on Lewis's analysis of the opposition between the "natural" and the "interfered with," *Studies in Words*, 44-47. A potential point of confusion is that we can speak of humans' "sinful nature" using the same opposition, but we recognize the difference between "we by nature prefer pleasure over pain" and "we by nature resist God's will." The first sentence refers to something we are by creation; the second, to something foreign to our created nature that has become a part of us, which must be removed by God's (special) action.

[23] From the *Oxford English Dictionary* (1971), s.v. "cause," sense I.1. This is along the lines of a philosopher's definition of cause in Alfred Freddoso, "Medieval Aristotelianism and the Case Against Secondary Causation in Nature," in T. V. Morris, ed., *Divine and Human Action: Essays in the Metaphysics of Theism* (Ithaca, N.Y.: Cornell University Press, 1988), 74-118, at 79-83. For fuller discussion see Stephen C. Meyer, *Of Clues and Causes: A Methodological Interpretation of Origin of Life Studies* (Ph.D. dissertation, University of Cambridge, 1990), especially chapters 2-3.

swing of the bat is the *cause* of the ball leaving the ballpark; the cat's hunger is the *cause* of its hunting, and the action of its claws and teeth is the *cause* of the mouse's death and disappearance. We may wish to refine the definition to "that which *contributes to producing* an effect," if we like, since we recognize that causes usually come in aggregates. Thus we can say more precisely that McGwire's swing is *one of the causes* of the ball's flight, since the wind speed and direction probably also have a role, not to mention the kind of pitch and even the properties of the ball (just imagine if it were a tomato!). The degree of specificity is relative to the kind of speech act we are performing: That is, in most cases of ordinary speech we are trying to isolate what we think to be the most interesting cause, and speaking of it as if it were the only one. To do so is not to deny the place of other contributing causes—such a denial needs to be made explicitly. (In other words, the key is to figure out just what question the speaker is trying to answer.)

Grammatically, to say that something is a cause is to say that it can be the subject of transitive action verbs (e.g., "the cat *killed* the mouse" implies that the cat *caused the death* of the mouse), or the object of a means-phrase ("McGwire hit the ball *by means of* the bat" implies that the bat's hardness and flight pattern *caused the trajectory* of the baseball), or part of an explanatory phrase ("the house fell *because* the structure was not strong enough for the wind" implies that the wind *caused the fall* of the house).

It follows from this that to speak of the nature of something is to speak of its causal contribution to the world: That is, at least part of the cause for there being a birch tree in my backyard is the fact that someone planted seeds from a birch tree, which have the property of growing into birch trees. Similarly, to speak of "causal power" is to refer to the capacity something has to be a cause in this ordinary sense. For example, a gas flame has the causal power to burn my skin, because of both its properties and the properties of my skin.

We can further speak of "nature," not as Robinson did, but as the great interlocking pattern of cause and effect that is the background for our lives and choices.

These definitions are based on what I take to be ordinary English usage. But we should notice that they also reflect what I have called the "commonsense" perception of ourselves and the world. I have the pre-theoretical sense that something has a nature because it exists; and I discover that it exists because I experience the effect of its nature on me and my surroundings. I also sense that the nature of something is independent both of my perception of it and of my wishes. Such intuitions are in fact the basis for many of what we take to be our most rational activities. For example, when we choose steel over cotton to make a knife blade, we think we are doing so because of the properties of steel and cotton. If I want a pet that is warm and cuddly, I'll choose a small mammal such as a dog rather than a cobra (and I'll keep the dog away from my anaconda, which has the nature of making small mammals disappear!). When we infer from seeing Stonehenge that it is the product of intelligent agents and not of natural forces, we do so because we do not believe its component stones (or any stones, for that matter) have the natural properties to form themselves into such a design.[24] Indeed, we feel intuitively that any philosophy that called into question the rationality of such activities would itself deserve rejection by any sensible person.

At a more sophisticated level, these intuitions are the basis of the famous warnings about the *post hoc ergo propter hoc* ("*after* this therefore *because of* this") fallacy in logic, which then becomes the ground for the statisticians' distinctions between correlation and causation, as Darrell Huff has so helpfully discussed in *How to Lie with Statistics*.[25]

We can make a few comments before moving on. First, nothing in these definitions *requires* any kind of "autonomy" from God for either natural properties or for nature; if any of the theories we are examining asserts autonomy for nature, that assertion does not arise by necessity from the word itself.[26] In view of the discussion of concurrence in chapter 3, Christians who are supernaturalists would probably do well to avoid the use of the word *autonomy*.

Second, the question between supernaturalists and providentialists on the one hand, and occasionalists on the other, is whether the biblical authors support the existence of "nature" and "causation" in the way defined here. The occasionalist must say that the commonsense view is an illusion. Interestingly enough, another kind of philosophy will also reject the commonsense view: one advocated by those impressed with the fact that we cannot prove the validity of common sense by our experience, so that arguments based on it are held to be circular; this group includes the skeptic David Hume and some postmoderns as well. We shall come back to them when we discuss apologetics.

---

[24] Interestingly enough, we know this to be rational even though we do not know who made Stonehenge or why they did it!

[25] Darrell Huff, *How to Lie with Statistics* (New York: Norton, 1954), 87-99 (chapter 8).

[26] Linguistically, this is equivalent to saying that to use a word in one sense does not imply all the other senses of the word. After all, I can be "proud" of my daughter's courage in facing a painful injection, without committing the sin of "pride," because these depend on different senses of the words involved (cf. C. S. Lewis, *Mere Christianity* [London: Geoffrey Bles, 1952], book iii, chapter 8 on "The Great Sin" for further discussion).

BIBLICAL VOCABULARY FOR "NATURE" AND "MIRACLES": ARE THERE TECHNICAL TERMS?

We have already noticed that the argument that "there is no word in biblical Hebrew for *nature* and therefore the Hebrews lacked the concept" has such severe flaws that it is not worth anything. But since many of the studies of this subject have focused on the vocabulary in the Old and New Testaments, it might help to see just what that vocabulary will and will not do for us.

Let's begin with the assertion, "There is no word for *nature* in biblical Hebrew," and see just what that means. First, we have to put the facts in more careful form. It is a philological fact that the word *ṭeba'*, which we translate "nature," is not attested in the biblical material and does not appear in a literary source until the Mishnaic period (the first few centuries of our era). This does not mean the word did not exist before the Mishnaic period—that would be quite difficult to prove;[27] all this means is that this particular word was not used to write about the idea in the Bible. The ordinary Hebrew way to say "I have something" is by the periphrasis "there is something to me," but we could not legitimately conclude from this philological fact that the Hebrew language lacks the capacity to speak of possession; and it would be just as illegitimate to infer that the lack of the word *ṭeba'* implies the lack of the concept *nature*.

As a matter of fact, there are some Hebrew words that can designate "natural process" in a sense related to what we mean in ordinary English. In a technical study I have argued that the noun *miqreh* can have the nuance "natural event," and the verbs in the semantic realm of "meet" (e.g., from the roots *q-r-h*, *ʾ-n-h*, *p-g-ʿ*, all roughly "to meet") can have the reference "to meet (in the ordinary natural course of things)."[28] Nevertheless, for reasons I shall explain shortly, these are not going to be the main focus of this research.

When it comes to New Testament vocabulary, the matter is pretty straightforward. That is, the Greek word φύσις, "nature," is used with a range of meanings that includes some relevant to us. Consider for example Romans 11:21, which speaks of "the *natural* branches" (οἱ κατὰ φύσιν κλάδοι) of a plant to denote those that it grows without interference. Then in verse 24 Paul refers to branches from "a tree which by *nature* is a wild olive tree" (ἡ κατὰ φύσιν ἀγριέλαιος), which "contrary to *nature*" (παρὰ φύσιν) have been grafted into a cultivated plant. Paul is trading on the obvious

---

[27] The verbal root to which this word is related, *ṭ-b-ʿ*, does appear in the OT, and the word formation for the noun is straightforward.
[28] Cf. C. John Collins, "*Miqreh* in 1 Samuel 6:9: 'Chance' or 'Event'?" forthcoming in *The Bible Translator* 51:1 (January 2000).

notion that some branches are the products of the "nature" or "natural properties" (φύσις) of a tree, while grafting involves interference with those natural properties and is hence "contrary" to them. The validity of this common sense notion underlies the illustration.

In James 3:7 we read of "every *natural kind* of beasts and birds" (πᾶσα φύσις θηρίων καὶ πετεινῶν) having been made tame to "the human *natural kind*" (ἡ φύσις ἡ ἀνθρωπίνη). This sense of the word depends on the members of the "kind" having similar "natures."

We even find the sense of "nature" in opposition to divine grace: Romans 2:14 speaks of Gentiles who do not have (God's) law doing *by nature* (φύσει) the mandates of God's law. Though some interpret this as "by instinct," this cannot be right: After all, surely Paul includes in this reference those Gentiles subjected to Aristotelian moral education (which goes beyond instinct). Therefore the sense is "by nature, i.e., in a condition outside the sphere of God's covenantal revelation and the impulse of the Holy Spirit"; the contrast is between "the natural" and "the interfered with."[29] The same usage appears in Ephesians 2:3, where believers were "by nature" (φύσει) children of wrath who have now received grace from God.

When it comes to vocabulary for "miracle," we have further difficulties. The English word *miracle* derives from a Latin word *miraculum*, which is related to a verb *miror*, "I am amazed." Thus, at least in etymology, the Latin word includes as part of its meaning the response of the onlookers to the event, namely wonder or amazement.[30] This is reflected in many of the discussions and definitions of the word in the history of the church.[31] For example, Aquinas gives the classical definition of miracle (*Summa Theologiae*, I, 105, 7): "The word *miracle* [Lat. *miraculum*] is derived from *admiration* [Lat. *admiratio*], which arises when an effect is manifest whereas its cause is hidden." The word *miraculum* is rare in the Latin Bible, but its cognate and synonym *mirabilis* appears often as the translation of some important words (influenced perhaps by the Greek equivalent θαυμάσια). It is not clear that dependence on etymology is actually implied in the *uses* we find, since that meaning component might not be prominent, i.e., we may

---

[29] Cf. the discussion of this passage in my forthcoming *Christian Faith in an Age of Science*, under "Natural Revelation."

[30] There is, however, evidence that the etymology of the Latin word did not entirely govern its usage: It could simply mean something like "prodigy, portentous event" (for examples from Livy [59 B.C.—A.D. 17] see H. Remus, "Does Terminology Distinguish Early Christian from Pagan Miracles?" *Journal of Biblical Literature* 101:4 [1982], 531-551, at 536 n.42).

[31] E.g., W. Mundle, O. Hufius, C. Brown, "Miracle, Wonder, Sign," in C. Brown, ed., *New International Dictionary of New Testament Theology* (Exeter, England: Paternoster, 1976), ii:620-635, at 621: "Etymologically the words miracle and wonder refer to the astonishment and amazement, created by an unusual or inexplicable event."

have a derived usage here.[32] Aquinas, however, followed Augustine and relied on the etymology (neither knew Hebrew).

The main Hebrew words usually discussed are *niplāʾôt / peleʾ*, "wonder" (but "extraordinary or incomprehensible thing, unattainable thing" is better, e.g., Ps. 139:6);[33] *ʾôt*, "sign"; *mōpēt*, "portent, symbol"; *gĕbûrâ*, "(act of) power." The main Greek ones are δύναμις, "(act of) power"; τέρας, "portent"; σημεῖον, "sign."[34]

None of these words can be shown to mean exclusively "miracle" in the sense of "supernatural event"; but that does not stop them from *designating* one in a given context. In such a case one would need to infer from the context and the nature of the thing talked about whether a "supernatural event" is in view. Some people might suppose that because the concepts are not distinguished at the lexical level, therefore to make the conceptual distinction is also invalid. To see that this is not so, consider an example: In 1 Samuel 6:7 the author calls the cows' young literally "their sons" (Hebrew *bĕnêhem*). But if anyone were to suggest that since the Hebrew does not distinguish between human and bovine young at the lexical level, therefore Hebrew speakers did not make such a conceptual distinction, would we take him seriously? The right way to do theological word study is not to suppose that words always mean the same thing, or that they have a one-to-one relationship with concepts; rather, we want to see what the use of a particular word (its "sense") contributes to our understanding of the thing being talked about (the "referent").

In many contexts the New Testament translator may be inclined to render the above Greek words *miracle* in the "supernatural" sense (e.g., Mark 6:5; Acts 2:22; Heb. 2:4). However, the English word *miracle* has been used for so many things that it may no longer be useful for clear communication (e.g., we can speak of a "medical miracle" when we are referring to an achievement of technological medicine that amazes us), so I recommend using the simple translation glosses given above : "(act of) power," "portent," and "sign."

The *Oxford English Dictionary* defines a miracle as "a marvellous event occurring within human experience, which cannot have been brought about by human power or by the operation of any natural agency, and must there-

---

[32] The *Oxford Latin Dictionary* says *mirabilis* may mean "extraordinary" (similarly Gk. θαυμάσιος, θαυμαστός, see Liddell-Scott's Greek lexicon); and *miraculum* can designate a supernatural occurrence. It is therefore quite possible that these are the factors that led to their choice as translations.

[33] See F. Brown, S. R. Driver, and C. A. Briggs, *A Hebrew and English Lexicon of the Old Testament* (Oxford, England: Oxford University Press, 1951), 810-811.

[34] Compare Yair Zakovitch, "Miracle (Old Testament)," in D. N. Freedman et al., eds., *Anchor Bible Dictionary* (New York: Doubleday, 1992), iv:845-856, especially 845b-846b; and H. E. Remus, "Miracle (New Testament)," in ibid., iv:856b-869b, at 856a-857b.

fore be ascribed to the special intervention of the Deity or of some super-natural being; chiefly, an act (e.g., of healing) exhibiting control over the laws of nature, and serving as evidence that the agent is either divine or is spe-cially favoured by God." This definition is quite full and technical, and seems more suited to a philosophical work employing tactical definitions than to a lexicon; but in any case, its restriction "within human experience" is sim-ilar to what one finds in authors who restrict the term *miracle* to events in *redemptive* history (and thus would exclude everything before the sixth "day" of Gen. 1). Indeed, such treatments then become dominated by con-cerns over the attestational quality of the miracles, perhaps even over whether they still happen today—important matters, but not my focus here. Under the *OED* definition, then, it is possible that the set of all *miracles* is a (proper) subset of the set of all *supernatural events*. The Hebrew and Greek vocabulary mentioned above does not help us to resolve the definitional question, since these words do not distinguish on this basis. However, the works of *both* creation *and* redemption are referred to as *niplā'ôt* ("wonders" or "extraordinary deeds") in Psalm 136:4ff., and perhaps we are not war-ranted in driving a firm wedge between them in respect to God's action.

For these reasons my own research is not particularly driven by the pres-ence or absence of "miracle terms," since that has little bearing on the kinds of things authors may be talking about. I shall instead focus on passages that seem to give us some idea of the mechanics behind the events they describe, and from there see if there is any specialized vocabulary. (But if there is none, that will matter little.)

Five

Passages Dealing with "Nature" and "Cause"

Now that we have set the stage for our investigation, it is time to look carefully at specific passages from the Bible and from other Jewish and Christian literature that will enable us to see the "presupposition pool" of the scriptural writers; this will extend over chapters 5–9 (the balance of Part 2 and all of Part 3). We will first consider texts that seem to *assert*, and not simply to *imply*, that there are such things as natural properties and causal powers involved in events. Related to this category is that class of texts which seem to presuppose the existence of causal powers in created objects, and which are worded in a way that is highly unsuited to occasionalism. If this apparent assertion and presupposition stands up under scrutiny, that will go a long way toward rejecting occasionalism as a biblically warranted model for God's action in the world.

Next, in chapter 6 we will consider groups of passages that appear to describe qualitatively special divine action in various realms. In these passages we are looking for both an affirmation of natural properties and an explicit identification of special divine action over and above those properties to produce the results. If these texts really do speak this way, this will make occasionalism still less attractive as a candidate for the biblical model; and it will also support supernaturalism over providentialism.

Finally, in chapter 7 we will consider the passages adduced by advocates of both occasionalism and providentialism in support of their views and in opposition to supernaturalism. We will pay attention to the communicative purposes of these verses, to see if they really do the work that is being asked of them.

Moving on to Part 3, "Theological Evaluation," chapter 8 will assess the different families of views (supernaturalism, occasionalism, and providentialism) against the biblical data. However, to choose a family is not the same as saying exactly how we should state the doctrine; thus in chapter 9 I intend to articulate what I take to be the metaphysic underlying the biblical material regarding God's action in the world.

PASSAGES THAT APPEAR TO ASSERT NATURAL AND CAUSAL POWERS

We begin by considering a passage from the book of Wisdom, which is in the apocryphal or deutero-canonical literature.[1] This book is one of the earliest attested efforts to commend the biblical religion to those steeped in the philosophical theology of the Greek philosophers, especially of the Middle Platonists and Middle Stoics.[2] As Derek Kidner puts it,[3]

> This book [Wisdom] is an essay in apologetics, presenting the faith of Israel to the rulers of the Gentile world, and indirectly to its own adherents who were living in that alien culture. The culture is Greek, therefore the thought-forms are Greek as far as possible; yet the teaching is, in its main intention, Israelite and biblical.

Wisdom 16:23 speaks of fire that "forgot its own power" (τῆς ἰδίας ἐπιλέλησται δυνάμεως). This assumes both that the fire has a native causal power, and that under God's control that power can be prevented from acting. This renders it beyond cavil that at least some Jews had the existence of nature, with definite natural properties in its components, as part of their world-picture.

Hebrews 11:34 expresses what appears to be precisely the same notion, when in reference to the episode of Daniel 3:23-28 (Shadrach, Meshach, and Abednego cast into the furnace but not burned because an angel protected them), it says "[Who by faith] quenched the power of fire" (ἔσβεσαν δύναμιν πυρός). Note that Hebrews, like Wisdom, refers to fire having a "power" (δύναμις). Franz Delitzsch comments on this expression,[4]

---

[1] Though this book is not in the Hebrew or Protestant canon, that does not mean Hebrews or Protestants should ignore it! (We would not ignore *Pilgrim's Progress!*) I begin with Wisdom because it has a clear statement that elucidates the presuppositions that underlie canonical texts, as we shall see. The author thought of himself as mainstream with respect to the biblical faith. (Similar comments apply to the citation of Ben Sira below.) Also, Wisdom is interesting to us because it represents an attempt to relate covenant faith to questions raised by philosophers. The apologetic approach of this book has important points of contact with that of the apostle Paul in Acts 17:22-31 and Rom. 1–2; but that goes outside the scope of this present study.

[2] Cf. John J. Collins, "Natural Theology and Biblical Tradition: The Case of Hellenistic Judaism," *Catholic Biblical Quarterly* 60:1 (1998), 1-15; Derek Kidner, *The Wisdom of Proverbs, Job, and Ecclesiastes* (Downers Grove, Ill.: InterVarsity, 1985), 149-157.

[3] Kidner, *The Wisdom of Proverbs, Job, and Ecclesiastes*, 152.

[4] Franz Delitzsch, *Commentary on the Epistle to the Hebrews* (English translation, Edinburgh: T and T Clark, 1868), ii:279.

He therefore says intentionally, as Theophylact observes, not φλόγα ["flame"] but δύναμιν πυρός ["power of fire"].[5] It was not only the flame, but the very nature of the fire, which in the power of faith they quenched and overcame.

This same view finds expression in Ben Sira 38:1-15, which speaks about the utility of physicians even for those who are truly pious.[6] The Lord "allocated"[7] physicians as part of his creation scheme and gave to these humans skill to heal. Both the patient and the physician should pray for the success of the diagnosis and medical treatment. In the course of this advice, Ben Sira tells us that God "causes medicinal herbs to come out from the ground,"[8] by means of which the physician heals. To make it clear that the herbs are seen as a cause (an instrument by which God carries out his purposes), the author in verse 5 says, "Was it not by a tree that water was made sweet, in order that its [or his?] strength might be made known?" (referring to Ex. 15:25). Does he specifically refer to the healing strength (ἰσχύς) of the wood, as the translation suggests, or does he instead speak of God's strength? Both the Hebrew (kōhô) and the Greek (τὴν ἰσχὺν αὐτοῦ) are potentially ambiguous: They could mean "his [God's] strength" or "its [the tree's] strength." Nevertheless the following factors support the NRSV interpretation "its": 1) the nearest referent for the pronoun in both language versions is "tree"; 2) the thrust of the context is that vegetable products have medicinal properties, which God has given physicians the skill to ascertain and employ (cf. vv. 4, 6-7); and 3) the Hebrew manuscript B has the marginal correction kôhām, "their strength," presumably using the plural as a reference to the medicines of verse 4 (at any rate it cannot be a reference to God). As the commentator W. O. E. Oesterley says on this passage,[9]

---

[5] Theophylact was an eleventh-century Greek commentator. The text can be found in J. P. Migne's *Patrologia Graeca*, vol. 125: Οὐκ εἶπε δὲ, Ἔσβεσαν πῦρ, ἀλλὰ δύναμιν πυρὸς ὃ καὶ μεῖζον· ἐξαπτόμενον γὰρ ὅλως δύναμιν τοῦ καίειν οὐκ εἶχε κατ' αὐτῶν ("He did not say, 'they quenched fire', but 'the power of fire', which is greater: for being kindled it did not at all have power to burn against them").

[6] On this book, also known as Ecclesiasticus, see Kidner, *The Wisdom of Proverbs, Job, and Ecclesiastes*, 142-148. Its author, Yeshua ben Sira, a wisdom teacher in Jerusalem, wrote the book in Hebrew, ca. 190–180 B.C. Unfortunately, not all of his Hebrew survives, nor can we always decide between some of the competing readings of the Hebrew manuscripts. Ben Sira's grandson, living in Egypt, translated the book into Greek in about 132 B.C. (at times being very interpretive). The vexing but fascinating problems of the Hebrew original, and the relation of the Greek to it, do not concern us here.

[7] The Hebrew verb is ḥlq, "allocated," while the Greek has ἔκτισεν, "created," which is interpretive; cf. Collins, *Homonymous Verbs in Biblical Hebrew: An Investigation of the Role of Comparative Philology* (Ph.D. dissertation, University of Liverpool, 1988), 170-175 for discussion of the use of this Hebrew verb translated with this Greek verb in Ben Sira.

[8] The Hebrew has môṣîᵊ, "causes to come out," while Greek has ἔκτισεν, "created," a past tense, interpreting reasonably as a reference to the creation account, Gen. 1:11-12.

[9] W. O. E. Oesterley, *The Wisdom of Jesus Son of Sirach* (Cambridge Bible for Schools and Colleges; Cambridge, England: Cambridge University Press, 1912), 245.

This reference to Exod. xv.23-25 is given in order to show the existence of healing powers in things which God has caused to grow out of the earth. It reads almost as though Ben-Sira did not regard the healing of the waters, referred to in the O.T. passage, as something miraculous, but as due to natural causes.

It appears from Oesterley's remarks that he thinks the Mosaic account is of something miraculous; we will discuss that passage in chapter 9 below. Be that as it may, the point is still that Ben Sira, who was clearly of the view that all things, including the effectiveness of divinely appointed instrumentalities, are at God's disposal, and that therefore we must pray when using those instrumentalities, found no discomfort in speaking of those instrumentalities as having causal powers.

Ben Sira's outlook is the same as that expressed in Deuteronomy. For example, Deuteronomy 8:17 warns the Israelites, once they have taken the land and have seen some measure of prosperity, against saying, "My own strength and the might of my hand [*kōḥî wĕʿōṣem yādî*] have made/caused [*ʿāśâ*] for me this wealth"; verse 18 requires them to remember that Yahweh is "the one who gives to you the strength to make/cause wealth [*kōaḥ laʿăśôt ḥāyil*]." The question Moses addresses is not whether people have causal power—he says they do—but where that power and its effectiveness come from.

These examples from Wisdom, Hebrews, Ben Sira, and Deuteronomy use words in the semantic field of "power, strength, ability" to refer to causal power—in Hebrew *kōaḥ* (Deut. 8:17-18; Sir. 38:5), in Greek δύναμις (Wisd. 16:23; Heb. 11:34) and ἰσχύς (Sir. 38:5; Deut. 8:17-18, LXX). These are not technical terms, of course, but they do indicate both the lexical ability and the interest on the part of biblical writers to discuss our topic.

Also in this semantic range is the expression found in Genesis 31:29, where Laban tells Jacob, "I have the power [Hebrew *yeš lĕʾēl yādî*, "it belongs to the strength of my hand"] to harm you"; the reason he has not exercised that power is because God warned him not to.

Further along these lines, we find passages that describe food as imparting "strength" (Hebrew *kōaḥ*). In 1 Samuel 28:20, for example, Saul fell headlong at the words of the ghost of Samuel, "moreover there was no *strength* in him because he had not eaten bread all the day and all the night" (note the causal explanation, "because"). In 1 Kings 19:8 Elijah has just had a specially provided meal: "And he went on the *strength* of that food for forty days and forty nights." Whether or not we are to suppose that the food itself is special, we nevertheless have a clear analogy with the ordinary causal effect of eating. And Psalm 104:15c refers to "bread which sustains [Hebrew *sāʿad*] "the heart of man," i.e., it causes the working man's strength to return.[10] At the headwaters of the Bible (Gen. 1:11), God expresses a wish:

> "Let the land vegetate with vegetation: herbs seeding seed each by its kind, fruit trees making fruit each by its kind, whose seed is in it."

Most commentators, even those of the "biblical theology" variety, acknowledge that this verse asserts that God made the different kinds of plants to be the kinds of things that reproduce after their own kinds (other things being equal; this says nothing about the "fixity of species"): Wheat plants produce wheat grains, which in turn grow into wheat plants, because that is the kind of things they are.[11] This text takes something that every human being knows full well—and agrarians like the early Israelites would stake their lives on it—and explains *why* the world works this way and why it is so reliable. It is this way because God made it this way, and at least part of his purpose was for the benefit of humans. (That this benefit includes dependence on the God who is not only the Creator but also the Ruler of everything becomes especially clear in the book of Deuteronomy.)

Derek Kidner observes that the communicative purpose of Genesis 1:11-12 is,[12]

> ... to show that God has bound together all creatures in a common dependence on their native elements, while giving each the distinctive character of its kind. Each has an origin which is from one angle natural and from another supernatural; and the natural process is made self-perpetuating and, under God, autonomous.

At this point I can imagine an occasionalist (or a "radical theist," as one author calls them)[13] objecting to the use of the word *autonomy;* and if Kidner meant what the "radical theist" takes the word to mean (i.e., having existence in some way independent of God), the Bible authors would likewise

---

[10] Cf. Gen. 18:5; Judg. 19:5, 8; 1 Kings 13:7, using this verb in this sense. Other texts that imply that humans are such that they need food and water to live (i.e., there is a causal connection between their presence and human longevity) include 1 Kings 17:6, 12; 18:13; 2 Kings 7:4; 8:1; 25:3 (these last three deal with the effects of famine); Deut. 23:24-25 (it is merciful to allow others to eat from one's own field).

[11] Cf. Walther Eichrodt, *Theology of the Old Testament* (English translation, London: SCM, 1967), ii:151: "The earth ... is endowed in its own sphere with the power of bringing forth plants and even animals as a permanent capability" (with a footnote giving Gen. 1:11, 20, 24 as examples). H. Wheeler Robinson, *Inspiration and Revelation in the Old Testament* (Oxford, England: Oxford University Press, 1946), 24: "This continued maintenance of Nature is effected through established ordinances and inherent energies, as the reference to the seed-containing fruit of Genesis i implies."

[12] Derek Kidner, *Genesis* (Tyndale Old Testament Commentary; Downers Grove, Ill.: InterVarsity, 1967), 48.

[13] Colin Russell, *Cross-currents: Interactions Between Science and Faith* (London: Christian Impact, 1995), 96-97.

object. But it is clear from the context that Kidner simply refers to these natural items being other than God and endowed with real causal powers that work, not independently of God, but under his government.[14]

The occasionalist might further object to Kidner's intent, however, by saying that we might just as easily imagine that the fact that wheat grains come from wheat plants (and so on) is a direct act of God that is not causally conditioned on anything like the "nature" of wheat plants but is simply the expression of God's faithfulness to his creatures.[15] This objection is more serious, and seems to get some headway from the fact that when Jeremiah 13:23 asks its question, it is not, "*Can* the Ethiopian change his skin or the leopard his spots?" (NASB) but more accurately "*Does* the Ethiopian change his skin or the leopard his spots?"[16] However, this objection founders when we look further. For example, James 3:11 asks, "A spring does not gush out from the same opening sweet water and bitter, does it?" and the occasionalist is unaffected; but verse 12 goes on to ask, "A fig tree, my brothers, *can* [Greek δύναται] not make olives, or a vine make figs, can it?" The context is about how our speech is an expression of the kind of people we are, and of how unfitting it is for professing believers, whose wisdom is from above (vv. 17-18), to act as if they are instead characterized by the wisdom from below (vv. 14-16). It is hard to avoid the interpretation of Peter Davids: "Springs like plants produce according to their natures (cf. Gen. 1:11)."[17] A similar pattern (including the use of δύναμαι, "can," in the later part of the question) appears in Matthew 7:16-18. Thus the ability denoted by δύναμαι (related to δύναμις, see above) is the "natural power" of the item in question.

---

[14] Cf. the comments about the word *autonomy* in chapter 4, in the section defining "nature," "natural properties," and "causation."

[15] This seems to me to be a weightier objection than what Malebranche himself actually said (*The Search after Truth and Elucidations of the Search after Truth*, T. M. Lennon and P. J. Oscamp, trans. [Columbus: Ohio State University Press, 1980], 674-675). He says "This way of explaining creation is accommodated to our way of speaking about the production of things. Thus it is not necessary to take it literally." He also contends that though the Vulgate reads, "Germinet terra herbam" [Gen. 1:11, "Let the earth sprout herbiage"] and other "expressions that might lead one to believe that the earth and the waters have received some true power to produce animals and plants," the original in Gen. 1:11 is better rendered, "Let the earth be verdant with verdure," etc. Unfortunately for his argument, though he might get away with his version of the volitional verb in v. 11, that is nothing to the point. The interesting thing is that these plants give seed each by their own kind, which is the property under discussion. We shall see in chapter 11 that Genesis in no way suggests that the earth has the property on its own to produce plants or animals. By the way, Malebranche's point about the meaning of Gen. 1:11 is defeated as well by noticing that v. 12, which describes the fulfillment of the wish of v. 11, says, "And the earth *produced* [a different verb] vegetation," etc.

[16] That is, the Hebrew verb is a simple future asking a question, which the NASB has interpreted as a question about possibilities. Whether this interpretation is valid or not depends on which model for God's action one accepts, so this verse cannot be used to prove one model.

[17] Peter Davids, *James* (New International Greek Testament Commentary; Grand Rapids, Mich.: Eerdmans, 1982), 148. Note that Davids draws the connection with Gen. 1:11.

Other passages seem to assert causal powers without specific vocabulary. For example, in Deuteronomy 11:13-17 (NIV) Moses declares,[18]

> So if you faithfully obey the commands I am giving you today—to love the LORD your God and to serve him with all your heart and with all your soul—then I will send rain on your land in its season, both autumn and spring rains, so that you may gather in your grain, new wine and oil. I will provide grass in the fields for your cattle, and you will eat and be satisfied.
>
> Be careful, or you will be enticed to turn away and worship other gods and bow down to them. Then the LORD 's anger will burn against you, and he will shut the heavens so that it will not rain and the ground will yield no produce, and you will soon perish from the good land the LORD is giving you.

It is hard to avoid the simple reading of this passage, namely that the rain is viewed as a "cause" of the land's fertility, and the lack of rain as the cause of its barrenness (cf. the definition of "cause" above).[19] Like Ben Sira, Moses affirms both the causal powers of created things and the radical dependency of the created order on the Lord's will.

PASSAGES THAT SEEM TO PRESUPPOSE THE REALITY OF NATURAL AND CAUSAL POWERS

Consideration of Deuteronomy 11:13-17 moves us to a group of passages that seem to speak of natural properties and causal contributions, but do so indirectly; that is, the notion seems to lie under the explicit statements. This is important, because even if the notion is not itself explicitly stated, it still might be a condition for the biblical statements to be good-faith acts of communication.

Let me begin at the beginning, namely the creation account of Genesis 1:1–2:3. Genesis 1:31 has God looking at what he had done and finding it

---

[18] To be accurate, we should note that the NIV has interpreted the Hebrew form in v. 14 "and you will gather" as "*so that you may gather*"; i.e., they have taken a simple consecutive future as a result. This is certainly within the bounds of the pragmatics of this form (cf. P. Joüon and T. Muraoka, *A Grammar of Biblical Hebrew* [Rome: Editrice Pontificio Istituto Biblico, 1993], §119e), and in view of v. 17 seems unavoidable. The result clause in v. 17, "so that it will not rain" renders a Hebrew form that is properly taken as a negative purpose clause (Joüon-Muraoka, §168b).

[19] Peter Craigie, *Deuteronomy* (New International Commentary on the Old Testament; Grand Rapids, Mich.: Eerdmans, 1976), 210, gives what seems to me to be the plain interpretation: "God promised to provide rain, in its season, which was necessary for the sustenance of men and beasts, provided that his people lived in accord with his requirements of them." Other texts on this topic are 1 Kings 17:1, where a drought meant dearth (cf. vv. 12, 14, and see James 5:17-18, which reflects on this event); 1 Kings 17:7 (the causal explanation for why a wadi was dry is that it had not rained); 18:45 (rain comes from the clouds; i.e., it is not a direct effect).

"very good." Interestingly, the supernaturalist Thomas Aquinas said (*Summa Theologiae*, I, 47, 1, *Respondeo*),

> for he [God] brought things into being in order that his goodness might be communicated to creatures, and be represented by them; and because his goodness could not be adequately represented by one creature alone, he produced many and diverse creatures, that what was wanting to one in the representation of the divine goodness might be supplied by another. For goodness, which in God is simple and uniform, in creatures is manifold and divided; and hence the whole universe together participates the divine goodness and represents it better than any single creature whatever.

That is, "very good" means sharing in God's own goodness! Earlier Aquinas attributed the imparting of the "dignity of causality to creatures" as due to the abundance of God's goodness rather than to any defect in God's own power (I, 22, 3, *Respondeo*). This puts the ascription of causal properties to created things in the light of the goodness of creation, i.e., its adequacy for the purposes for which God made it. Properly articulated, this view has no intention of crowding God out of his world. Indeed, if such properties exist, they are no "limitation" on God (other than that of his self-consistency), since they are after all "very good," which means they conform to his will.

Many of the following passages come from biblical wisdom material, especially the book of Proverbs and various biblical parables. It is well known that such material includes many instances of using observations of natural regularities as analogies for regularities in the moral and spiritual realm. Proverbs in particular is known for its emphasis on the consequences of our choices; as Derek Kidner put it so memorably, "Proverbs gets us to compare the 'now' of an act with its 'afterwards'"[20] (cf., e.g., Prov. 16:25; 19:20; 23:31-32; 25:16).

We may be inclined to infer from these considerations that a straightforward notion of natural cause and effect is therefore taken for granted in Proverbs. But the occasionalist will say, "Not so fast!" Indeed, Nicolas Malebranche himself was aware of the assertion that such efforts as plowing, planting, and watering, which the biblical authors (and especially Proverbs) certainly commend, would be pointless if these things were not causally related to their intended effects.[21] A possible occasionalist reply is that such

---

[20] Kidner, *The Wisdom of Proverbs, Job, and Ecclesiastes*, 29; cf. his whole discussion, 27-31.
[21] Malebranche, *The Search after Truth and Elucidations of the Search after Truth*, 663 (fifteenth elucidation, reply to third proof). Malebranche was replying to the assertion found in the work of the Spanish Jesuit Francisco Suarez (1548–1617), who defended the efficacy of second causes. I draw on the discussion in Stephen Bilynskyj, *God, Nature, and the Concept of Miracle*, 67. Again, though, I think that I have framed a better occasionalist reply than Malebranche himself actually did. Malebranche's own reply is in terms of the movement of water in plants, and since God alone causes motion, well, then, God alone acts. But Malebranche does not actually say why *we* should do anything.

efforts are not pointless, since even though God is able to produce, for example, a good crop without any particular prior arrangement of soil, seed, and water, he does not choose to do so. He chooses instead to dispose everything by general, consistent patterns. Thus the efforts, though they do not causally contribute, are still done in obedience to God's will.

There are probably few in contemporary Old Testament studies who would treat Proverbs this way,[22] but we cannot settle the matter simply by an appeal to "authority." Instead, we should look for passages that have the "common sense" notion so clearly bound up in them, or that speak so clearly incompatibly with the "no-nature" view that we can say that the "common sense" notion really is taken for granted.

We can start our survey by recognizing the obvious, namely that Proverbs and other wisdom-type material does not come in a vacuum; instead it comes to a group of people for whom the more explicit notions (of God's action in the world) that we found in the previous section are present. But let's see what the texts themselves say.

Proverbs 26:20-21 says the following:[23]

(20) Without wood a fire goes out;
   without a backbiter a quarrel goes silent.

(21) Charcoal (is) for embers and wood for fire,
   and a quarrelsome man (is) for kindling strife.

In verse 20 it seems clear that the wood is viewed as a causal condition for the presence of the fire (in the sense defined in chapter 4); but perhaps the occasionalist will deny that this conclusion is necessary. However, Franz Delitzsch remarks on verse 21,[24]

Black coal ["charcoal" in my version] is suited to glowing coal ["embers"], to nourish it; and wood to the fire, to sustain it; and a contentious man is suited for and serves this purpose, to kindle up strife. . . . The three—coal, wood, and the contentious man—are alike, in that they are a means to an end.

That is, the analogy does not work unless the author believes that the causal relation holds in all three parts of the analogy. (Remember, occasionalists do

[22] Cf., for example, R. N. Whybray, *Proverbs* (New Century Bible Commentary; Grand Rapids, Mich.: Eerdmans, 1994), or Franz Delitzsch, *Proverbs* (Keil-Delitzsch; English translation, Grand Rapids, Mich.: Eerdmans, 1980 [German original 1872]), on Prov. 27:23-27; 12:11/28:19; and 6:6-11/24:30-34 (passages that commend diligent work).
[23] English versions typically render v. 21 as a simile; but I have given a closer rendering of the Hebrew.
[24] Delitzsch, *Proverbs*, 2:192.

not necessarily deny that human agents can cause states of affairs in other humans.)

Similarly, Proverbs 30:33 declares:[25]

> For squeezing milk brings out butter,
>   and squeezing the nose brings out blood,
>   and squeezing anger brings out strife.

The verb rendered "brings out" or "produces" (*tôṣî'*) is a form which we could translate "causes to come out." The actual wording, therefore, does not invite the paraphrase "is the occasion on which God brings out" these things, which is what an occasionalist would say.

Consider Proverbs 25:16, 27 (NIV):

> (16) If you find honey, eat just enough—
>   too much of it, and you will vomit.

> (27) It is not good to eat too much honey,
>   nor is it honorable to seek one's own honor.[26]

Delitzsch is probably right in saying of verse 16, "that it is not to be understood in a purely dietetic sense (although thus interpreted it is a rule not to be despised!), is self-evident";[27] verse 16 extends by analogy to a whole range of areas in which there can be too much of a pleasant thing (the application in v. 27 is evidence of this). The usefulness of the proverb depends on our experience of having eaten too much of something sweet; we are accustomed to saying, "I feel sick *because* I ate too much honey." We make our future agency decisions on the basis of what we take to be experience of the properties of things in the world (e.g., we know what honey is "like" and will remember that next time).

Consider also 14:4 (NIV):

> Where there are no oxen, the manger is empty
>   [Hebrew *bār*, lit. "clean"],
> but from the strength [Hebrew *kōaḥ*] of an ox
>   comes an abundant harvest.

---

[25] Surprisingly, English versions do not render the threefold repetition of the words *squeezing* and *brings out*.

[26] On the difficulties of the second line see Kidner, *Proverbs* (Tyndale Old Testament Commentary; Downers Grove, Ill.: InterVarsity, 1964), 161. These difficulties, however, have no bearing on this discussion.

[27] Delitzsch, *Proverbs*, 2:162.

As Kidner puts it, "This proverb is not a plea for slovenliness, physical or moral, but for the readiness to accept upheaval, and a mess to clear up, as the price of growth."[28] What is interesting for our purposes, though, is the role the ox and his "strength" are said to play: I think the ordinary reader would see the ox's strength as a causal condition for plowing a large patch of hard soil in a reasonable time. Perhaps it goes without saying that, as well, oxen have characteristics that make them a better choice for such a task than, say, snakes, cats, or chickens (not to mention stones), and this by virtue of the kind of animal they are (i.e., their natural properties). That is, the ox's causal contribution is an underlying assumption of the proverb.

Proverbs (and other biblical material) sees a straightforward causal relationship between alcoholic drinks and their effects. For an example warning against overindulgence, consider Proverbs 20:1 (NIV):

> Wine is a mocker and beer a brawler;
>   whoever is led astray by them is not wise.

The expression rendered "led astray" can also be translated "intoxicated";[29] and note the presence of the means clause, "Whoever is intoxicated *by means of them* is not wise." Whybray notes that *is not wise* "may mean either that a wise person does not get drunk or that a drunken person behaves stupidly";[30] since in Proverbs "wisdom" refers to that skill which looks ahead and plans behavior morally pleasing to the Lord,[31] it seems that the first of Whybray's options is closer to the truth.[32] In this case, as in 25:16, the wise person will make his plans based on the characteristics of the things he might use.[33]

So as not to lose balance, we should note that the Bible also *commends* wine, again for its causal properties. For example, Psalm 104:15 celebrates as one of the products man gets from the soil (under God's blessing, cf. v. 14), "wine (which) causes a man's heart to be glad." That is, the problem is not with the substance and its causal properties, but with the abuse sinful

---

[28] Kidner, *Proverbs*, 106; cf. also Whybray, *Proverbs*, 212-213.

[29] The verb is *š-g-h*, on which see F. Brown, S. R. Driver, and C. A. Briggs, *A Hebrew and English Lexicon of the Old Testament* (Oxford, England: Oxford University Press, 1951), 993a, sense 2.

[30] Whybray, *Proverbs*, 288.

[31] Cf. D. A. Hubbard, "Wisdom," in J. D. Douglas et al., eds., *The New Bible Dictionary* (Downers Grove, Ill.: InterVarsity, 1982), 1255b-1257a, at 1255a: "Basically, wisdom is the art of being successful, of forming the correct plan to gain the desired results. Its seat is the heart, the centre of moral and intellectual decision."

[32] Actually, since the form is a future, "he will not become wise," it is referring to the preventive influence of drunkenness in the pursuit of wisdom. That is, to *become* wise, one should *act wisely.*

[33] Cf. 23:29-35 for an enlargement on the theme of the dangerous causal properties of wine, and the consequent agency choices the would-be wise are called upon to make. Cf. Gen. 19:30-38 (especially vv. 32-35) for a dreadful agency decision based on the presumed causal properties of wine. In the NT, cf. Eph. 5:18, "don't be getting drunk *by means of* wine."

humans may make of it. For ethics we would recall *abusus usum non tollit* ("abuse does not take away proper use").

Proverbs 11:1 alludes to another way in which people might misuse the properties of God's creation; it refers to a deceiving balance, which the Lord abhors, and a "full stone" (literally; the NIV "accurate weights" is a good interpretation), in which the Lord delights. The background to this is Deuteronomy 25:13-16, which forbids the Israelites to carry around two stones of different sizes or to use different dry measures—a large and a small. The rationale for taking this action is that a larger stone would weigh more than a smaller one, so a crafty man would use one when buying and the other when selling. Similarly the larger dry measure would hold more grain than the smaller one. There is no hint that these properties come from anything other than being the sorts of things they are. This making use of properties in a dishonest way is something the Lord abhors; he wants a full stone and a full dry measure.

The theological context of Proverbs should have led us to expect this picture of a causal web. For example, in 3:19ff. we read that the Lord founded the earth by his *wisdom*, and that he imparts wisdom to those who seek it from him. The effect of this wisdom will be successful moral agency, analogous to successful physical agency, which comes from real insight into the way things are. This gets further development in 8:27-31 (NIV):

> I [Wisdom, personified] was there when he set the heavens in place,
>> when he marked out the horizon on the face of the deep,
> when he established the clouds above
>> and fixed securely the fountains of the deep,
> when he gave the sea its boundary
>> so the waters would not overstep his command,
>> and when he marked out the foundations of the earth.
> Then I was the craftsman at his side.
> I was filled with delight day after day,
>> rejoicing always in his presence,
> rejoicing in his whole world
>> and delighting in mankind.

I think this passage is best understood in conjunction with the creation narrative of Genesis 1. In creating, the Lord imparted actual *being* to things, that is, they are real and they are other than he. And their being and their interactions are imprinted with rationality and purpose (the effect of wisdom). All of this, you will recall, is "very good." For Wisdom to be a "craftsman" suggests that the creation is in some sense like a finely functioning work of skill. The patterns we observe and use for agency decisions—and as analogies for moral decisions—are patterns of real things whose natures come from a rational Creator who calls his people to rational agency. If our ordinary experience of agency and rationality is to have any bearing on our understanding of wisdom ("rational spiritual agency")—which means if spiritual rationality is to have any purchase point in our minds—then it is reasonable to believe that what we take to be rational, including our sense of cause and effect in the natural world, is on the right track.[34]

Moving out of Proverbs, but staying with "wisdom" material, let's consider the parable in Isaiah 5:1-7. In the NIV this reads,

(1) I will sing for the one I love a song about his vineyard:
My loved one had a vineyard on a fertile hillside.
(2) He dug it up and cleared it of stones
and planted it with the choicest vines.
He built a watchtower in it and cut out a winepress as well.
Then he looked for a crop of good grapes,
but it yielded only bad fruit.

(3) Now you dwellers in Jerusalem and men of Judah,
judge between me and my vineyard.
(4) What more could have been done for my vineyard
than I have done for it?
When I looked for good grapes,
why did it yield only bad?
(5) Now I will tell you what I am going to do to my vineyard:
I will take away its hedge, and it will be destroyed;
I will break down its wall, and it will be trampled.
(6) I will make it a wasteland, neither pruned nor cultivated,
and briers and thorns will grow there.
I will command the clouds not to rain on it.
(7) The vineyard of the LORD Almighty is the house of Israel,
and the men of Judah are the garden of his delight.
And he looked for justice, but saw bloodshed;
for righteousness, but heard cries of distress.

---

[34] We might compare also Gen. 1:26-29, where the first humans are told to rule and to bring into subjection the rest of the created order; it seems reasonable to suppose that this implies that the creation is manageable by humans. The only kind of managing we know of is that of making use of natural properties. Similarly, Ps. 104:5 tells us the Lord "established the earth upon its foundations, it will not be moved for ever and ever"; this is best understood as describing the guaranteed stability of the world God made. C. S. Lewis, in chapter 2 of *The Problem of Pain* (London: Geoffrey Bles, 1940), suggested that "not even Omnipotence could create a society of free souls without at the same time creating a relatively independent [independent of our wishes and deserts] and 'inexorable' Nature" as the backcloth against which we make our choices.

Verse 7 explains what the parable is an analogy for, and this warns us not to allegorize the details. Nevertheless, for the analogy to be effective it must have a root in common experience—in this case the common experience of cultivating grapes in the hill country of Judah. The soil of that land is very full of stones but is fertile if well-worked. Hence in verse 2 the "loved one" took the necessary steps to procure a good crop from which he would get plenty of good wine. Verse 4 is the "loved one's" protestation that he did in fact fulfill all the causal conditions. Therefore, the conclusion is, there is something wrong with what we may call the "nature" of the vineyard (if it were a person, this something wrong would be perversity, and this is the point of verse 7).

Note that the perception of causality goes further, in verses 5-6. The hedge and the wall are for keeping (domestic) animals out, to prevent them from eating the cultivated plants. When these are removed, the animals will eat ("destroyed" in v. 5 is better "devoured") and trample.[35] In verse 6, it appears that not pruning and not cultivating (literally "hoeing") are what result in the thorns and briers growing (at least anyone with gardening experience will naturally think of this); and the rain is stopped because it is a necessity for anything desirable to grow (cf. Deut. 11:14, 17). Hence the parable views a number of natural objects and events as causes: the removal of stones and cultivation, the wall and hedge, the animals' teeth and hooves, the rain.

Moving to some parables of Jesus, we see a similar picture. For example, in Matthew 7:24-27, Jesus makes an analogy (NIV):

> (24) "Therefore everyone who hears these words of mine and puts them into practice is like a wise man who built his house on the rock. (25) The rain came down, the streams rose, and the winds blew and beat against that house; yet it did not fall, because it had its foundation on the rock. (26) But everyone who hears these words of mine and does not put them into practice is like a foolish man who built his house on sand. (27) The rain came down, the streams rose, and the winds blew and beat against that house, and it fell with a great crash."

Most people recognize the good sense that lies behind the analogy: Of course you would want to build your house on solid, high ground—especially when one considers the torrential rain in Palestine—rather than

---

[35] For discussion of some of the linguistic issues in this verse, cf. C. John Collins, *Homonymous Verbs in Biblical Hebrew: An Investigation of the Role of Comparative Philology* (Ph.D. dissertation, University of Liverpool, 1988), 52-56.

on sandy soil; and that is because we think the high, rocky ground has a number of properties that make it preferable to the sand.[36] And it seems pretty plain that Jesus endorsed this recognition when he used the little word translated "because" in verse 25; that is, the being founded on the rock, and the causal properties of that rock, are explicitly said to be the *cause* for the house not falling.[37] We are warranted in drawing similar causal conclusions about the sand in verse 27.

Now consider Matthew 13:24-30 (NIV):

> (24) "The kingdom of heaven is like a man who sowed good seed in his field. (25) But while everyone was sleeping, his enemy came and sowed weeds among the wheat, and went away. (26) When the wheat sprouted and formed heads, then the weeds also appeared.
>
> (27) "The owner's servants came to him and said, 'Sir, didn't you sow good seed in your field? Where then did the weeds come from?'
>
> (28) "'An enemy did this,' he replied.
>
> "The servants asked him, 'Do you want us to go and pull them up?'
>
> (29) "'No,' he answered, 'because while you are pulling the weeds, you may root up the wheat with them. (30) Let both grow together until the harvest. At that time I will tell the harvesters: First collect the weeds and tie them in bundles to be burned; then gather the wheat and bring it into my barn.'"

The weeds (Greek ζιζάνια, traditionally translated "tares" or "darnel") are a plant that "in their early stages of growth appear as grass-like as wheat, but can easily be distinguished at harvest-time."[38] The landowner knows what kind of seed he sowed, and what he expects to see grow as a result (cf. Gen. 1:11-12). Based on the appearance of a different kind of plant, he is able correctly to infer the activity of another agent besides himself (v. 28). He also knows that the attempt to pull up the weeds might be the cause of damage to the wheat (v. 29). He also knows that when the harvest comes, he will be able reliably to distinguish between the wheat and the weeds, based on the features of each. Again, such reasoning seems eminently rational in a world in which things have properties by which we may distinguish them.

In Luke 14:31-32, Jesus tells a parable based on warfare (NIV):

---

[36] I recall that in the San Francisco earthquake during the 1989 World Series, a portion of the town that was built on landfill became about as stable as Jello.

[37] Cf. the version of the same parable in Luke 6:47-49; in v. 48 (NIV), "When a flood came, the torrent struck that house but *could not* [Gk. οὐκ ἴσχυσεν] shake it, *because* [Gk. διά + infinitive] it was well built."

[38] F. N. Hepper, "Grain," in J. D. Douglas et al., eds., *The New Bible Dictionary* (Downers Grove, Ill.: InterVarsity, 1982), 444.

"Or suppose a king is about to go to war against another king. Will he not first sit down and consider whether he is able with ten thousand men to oppose the one coming against him with twenty thousand? If he is not able, he will send a delegation while the other is still a long way off and will ask for terms of peace."

This is the second of two parables about reckoning up the cost of being Jesus' disciple (vv. 26-27, 33) before setting out. The parable trades on the common perception that success in battle depends (aside from luck) on the relative strengths of the opposing forces. This king, who has a force half the size of his opponent, must decide whether there are factors compensating for lower numbers, e.g., superior troop equipment, morale, seasoning, etc. If not, he'd better not risk it. This calculation is rational because the king is expected to do the best figuring he can in view of his knowledge of what he thinks is the natural course of things. The parable trades on the rationality of this kind of figuring, and thus endorses it.[39]

Going beyond the wisdom material, we might also consider those passages in the Bible that speak of the begetting of children. Most men that I know who have fathered children—irrespective of ethnic or cultural origin—can identify with Jacob's description of Reuben (Gen. 49:3, cf. RSV): "You are my firstborn, my might [literally, my *kōaḥ*], the first fruits of my strength [Hebrew *rē'šît 'ônî*]." Jacob feels that he has indisputably expressed his causal power, his vitality, by the act of begetting a child.[40] When the biblical writers mention begetting, they do so in terms of the normally perceived causal relationship between sexual relations, pregnancy, and birth. For example, in Genesis 16:1-4, Sarai interprets her childlessness as being due to her own infertility (which she ascribes to God's inexplicable will, v. 2); she therefore suggests that she and her husband (Abram) get children by Abram taking Hagar the handmaid as a second wife. In verse 4, Abram "went in to Hagar" (a euphemism for entering her quarters for sexual relations) and, presumably as a natural consequence, she "became pregnant" and bore Ishmael.[41]

---

[39] To this we may add the passages in the OT about Israel's prospects in war: In Num. 20:20-21, Israel decides not to fight Edom's heavy force, since they have no promise of special divine aid; cf. Judg. 1:19, which ascribes, on the one hand, Judah's success to special help, and on the other, their failure to clear out some other inhabitants to the superior iron chariotry of the natives.

[40] Of course, only a fool would think he was in any sense *the* cause of the child's being. A man with any sense at all is humbled and awe-struck by the whole process at the same time as he delights in his privilege of contributing to it.

[41] This view of the narrative gets support from the fact that in Gal. 4 Paul calls Ishmael the one who "was born/begotten according to flesh" (κατὰ σάρκα γεγέννηται, v. 23, cf. v. 29), in contrast to Isaac who was born/begotten "through promise" (δι' ἐπαγγελίας, v. 23) or "according to the Spirit" (τὸν κατὰ πνεῦμα [γεννηθέντα], v. 29). That is, Ishmael was begotten by Abram and Sarai relying on their "nature" instead of relying on God's promise and expressing that reliance by their conduct. Paul applies that contrast to the Galatians who rely on their own law-keeping (which was an expression of reliance on their own abilities, i.e., "nature," since God was not about to supply any help in the effort!) to procure favor with God instead of the reliance on God's promise of unmerited favor which Paul taught.

Similarly, most readers will suppose that there is a causal connection between David's adulterous relations with Bathsheba and her pregnancy (2 Sam. 11:4-5). This is enhanced by the narrator's addition of the note in verse 4, "and she was purifying herself from her [menstrual][42] uncleanness"; that is, the time was a week after her period began, and this implies both that she was not pregnant by her absent husband Uriah (he was away on campaign), and that she was entering the fertile part of her cycle.[43] The causal connection further becomes clear in David's unsuccessful attempt to get Uriah to spend the night in his own house and sleep with his wife, presumably in hopes that the child would be ascribed to that circumstance (vv. 9-13). When Uriah proved himself too loyal a soldier to do such a thing, that sealed his doom and David arranged for his murder (vv. 14-15). Interestingly enough, Nathan the prophet (God's reliable spokesman) called the child "the son that is (to be) born to you" (12:14), indicating David's causal role in the begetting of that boy. Then in 12:24, the penitent David "went in to Bathsheba and lay with her and she bore a son" (Solomon, their second son); again, we read the temporal sequence as expressive of a causal connection.[44]

It is this acknowledged causal connection that allows people to make the correct inference: When a woman is pregnant it is because she has lain with a man.[45] In Genesis 38:24-25, Judah's twice-widowed and hitherto childless daughter-in-law Tamar is discovered to be pregnant. Since she is not married, the conclusion is that she has fornicated.[46] Tamar explains that she is pregnant by the man to whom certain tokens belong, and this turns out to be Judah himself (cf. vv. 15-18)!

In all of these passages there is no challenge to the "ordinary" perception of causality in the begetting of children. There is no hint that any author would encourage us to read "he went in to her and lay with her and she

---

[42] Cf. Lev. 18:19 for the use of *ṭumʾâ* "uncleanness" to denote the woman's forbiddenness to a man during her monthly period.

[43] Cf. Y. Kiel, *Sēfer Šĕmûʾēl* (Samuel, Daʾat Miqra; Jerusalem: Mossad Harav Kook, 1981), 414, who also notes that this explains the "washing" of v. 2. The NASB renders this clause "and when she had purified herself from her uncleanness," making it subsequent to her relations with David and prior to her return to her house. This is an inexcusable rendering of the clause, which is just a circumstantial clause, cf. Joüon-Muraoka, §159d. NIV and RSV are much more accurate here.

[44] This acknowledged connection explains Onan's strategy in Gen. 38:9: Instead of begetting a child for the name of his deceased brother Er, whenever he "went in to" Er's widow Tamar, Onan "would spoil his semen onto the ground so as not to give a descendant to his brother" (presumably his goal was to get sexual pleasure for himself and avoid the consequences). This only makes sense if Onan saw a causal relationship between where he deposited the semen and whether or not Tamar got pregnant. It also explains why, in Gen. 30:14-16, Leah considered it worthwhile to "hire" Jacob's services for the night from her sister and rival wife Rachel. And as for the sordid strategy of Lot's daughters (Gen. 19:30-36), we may note that they employed their concept of the causal powers both of wine and of sexual intercourse.

[45] All of these considerations will form the background for the discussion of the unique conception of Jesus.

[46] The Hebrew verb is *z-n-h*, which refers to illicit sexual activity in general. The NASB translation "she has played the harlot," though it captures the connection with v. 15 where Judah thought she was a "harlot" (Heb. *zônâ*), nevertheless may give the false impression of sex-for-pay as the inference of v. 24.

became pregnant" as "he went in to her and lay with her and this was the occasion for God's making her pregnant." Of course, we must acknowledge the presence of passages such as 1 Samuel 1:5, which tells us that Hannah had no children because the Lord had "closed her womb" (cf. Gen. 30:2); or v. 19, which says that Elkanah "knew" his wife Hannah, and the Lord "remembered her," and thus she became pregnant (cf. Gen. 30:16-18, 22); or Ruth 4:13, which says that when Boaz went in to Ruth the Lord "gave her conception"—not to mention passages such as Psalm 139:13 and Jeremiah 1:5, which speak of God actually "forming" or "knitting" people in the womb (which does sound like direct divine action of the occasionalist sort).

I shall address texts such as Psalm 139:13 and Jeremiah 1:5 when I look at passages that do at first blush seem to favor the occasionalist (or providentialist) interpretation; for the rest, it is enough to note that the causal condition of sexual intercourse is always present, and we may explain the passages cited in the previous paragraph as referring to God's sovereign, providential disposition of all events without specifying the mechanism—e.g., in supernaturalist terms, either by concurrence to secure or prevent the natural product of sexual activity, or by a direct ("supernatural") action of God, or by God's opaque-to-us governance. (My own preference is for the concurrence type of explanation.) Hence these texts do not undermine the commonsense perception of causality so much as they remind us that more factors are at work than meet the eye.[47]

Consider next the way in which Israel will conquer the promised land under divine direction, as described in Exodus 23:29-30 and Deuteronomy 7:22 (NIV):

> *Exodus 23:29-30:* "But I will not drive them [i.e., the native inhabitants of the promised land] out in a single year, because the land would become desolate and the wild animals too numerous for you. Little by little I will drive them out before you, until you have increased enough to take possession of the land."

> *Deuteronomy 7:22:* "The LORD your God will drive out those nations before you, little by little. You will not be allowed to eliminate them all at once, or the wild animals will multiply around you."

The natural effect of completely eliminating the human inhabitants from the land would be that the land would become overgrown with weeds and wild animals. Hence the Lord intends to displace the Canaanites little

---

[47] Recall the discussion regarding the definition of "cause," where I pointed out that to focus on one cause is not necessarily to exclude the possibility of other factors being involved.

by little. The Lord apparently expects his people to see that he respects the integrity of the natural order he created, even though he will take special interest in seeing that the Israelites win occupancy of the land. Of course, this hardly implies any limitation, or even self-limitation, on God's part: After all, the creation is the way it is because he made it so, and this because he wanted it so.

We may mention briefly a number of passages that make use of the commonsense view that ascribes death to causes. For example, in Judges 4:21 (cf. 5:26-27) the natural implication is that Sisera died because Jael drove a tent peg through his temple; in 9:53-54, it is straightforward to suppose that the casting of an upper millstone from a window is what caused the crushing of Abimelek's skull, and it would have caused his death had not Abimelek had his armor-bearer run him through—and this action caused death. Genesis 6:17 (cf. 7:21-22) tells us that the waters of the flood will destroy all that have the "breath of life" in them. This implies that this will happen because these creatures cannot breathe water (i.e., they do not have the property to do so), and therefore the water will cause them to die. By the same token, the way of escape is to be a box whose property is to float (the ark). In 1 Kings 22:34-35 we read of an Aramean archer who shoots, without aiming, at Ahab, and hits him in an unprotected place. The king watched the rest of the battle and died that evening. There is no difficulty in supposing that the wound caused him to bleed to death (cf. also the wound in 2 Kings 9:24 [with faster effects because of its location], 27). Second Kings 9:33-37 is a gruesome passage about the death of Jezebel. The impression it gives is that the fall from the window and the trampling by the horses caused her death (v. 33), while the activity of the dogs caused the disappearance of most of her body parts (vv. 35-36).

We may finish this section on indirect references to presupposed natural causal powers by considering a number of texts that tell us that people or things were *not* able to do something, and that explain this inability by "natural causes." For example, in Genesis 36:6 Esau moved his family and livestock away from his brother Jacob, *because* (v. 7) their possessions were too numerous for them to dwell together, and the land where they dwelt was not able to bear them on account of their livestock. The implication is that, had their livestock remained fewer, the land would have had the natural capacity to provide adequate grazing.[48] In Exodus 7:21, 24 the Egyptians could not drink the fouled water of the Nile; in 9:11 the Egyptian magicians

---

[48] Cf. Gen. 13:6 for similar wording.

could not stand before Moses because of their severely painful "boils"; and in 15:23 the Israelites could not drink the water at Mara because it was bitter. In Matthew 8:28, the two Gadarene demoniacs were so violent that no one was able (Greek ὥστε μὴ ἰσχύειν τινα, "no one had the strength," i.e., to overcome the demoniacs) to pass by there, while in 26:40-41 the disciples were unable to stay awake because their bodies were tired. In John 21:6 the catch of fish was so large that the disciples did not have the strength to haul the net into the boat. Finally, in Acts 27:16 the weather was so severe that the sea-goers were scarcely able to control the ship's boat.

In each of these cases, the ordinary reader has no difficulty in ascribing the inability to the "nature" of things; e.g., I identify with the disciples' struggle to haul the net, because I have experience of things that are too heavy. And further, if things were otherwise—e.g., if I were stronger or if the item were not so heavy, i.e., if the properties of the things involved were different—the outcome would have been different. Such at least is my "common sense" perception of the way things are in my experience, and the biblical narratives seem entirely at one with this perception.

We are in a position to summarize this chapter: As long as what we mean by "nature" and "cause" corresponds to the definitions set out in chapter 4, and as long as we recognize that they are not the whole story in any event in a world that infallibly serves God's purposes, we can see that the biblical authors endorse the validity of these notions. This comes through both in explicit ascriptions of natural properties and causal powers to created things, and in the structure of presuppositions that must underlie a host of other biblical statements. It is also significant that these texts come from communicative contexts from which we can expect comment on things in a straightforward manner, albeit in "ordinary language" rather than technical terms. For example, this material draws primarily on narrative, wisdom literature, and the sermonic form of Deuteronomy. Interestingly, the passages that we will explore in chapter 7 come from a different set of communicative contexts.

Six

Special Divine Action

In this chapter we examine several biblical passages that seem to describe what I am calling "*qualitatively* special divine action." By this awkward and ugly phrase I want to do several things: 1) recognize that any traditionally theistic worldview sees everything that happens as in some way expressive of God's action and purpose, including what we call "natural" events; 2) avoid any terms such as "intervention" that suggest to some, rightly or wrongly, that somehow God's special action is an intruder in his own world; and 3) emphasize that what seems to be "special" is not the apparent specific attention to individuals and their needs (though that may be there),[1] but the mode by which the event is carried off, i.e., it goes beyond the natural causal powers of the parties involved.[2] Hence the adjective "supernatural," understood in this way, may also be useful.

It has been traditional to refer to this category of events as "miracles," but I prefer not to use that term. One reason is that given in chapter 4, namely that no biblical words properly correspond to that term's etymological element of "wonder." Indeed, I have not governed my selection of material by the presence or absence of the commonly identified "miracle words" in either Hebrew or Greek. Another reason for not using that term is that some restrict the term to events in what we may call "redemptive history" (recall the *OED* definition discussed in chapter 4), and I do not want to prejudge the question of whether supernatural factors may also enter into events in "natural history."

I want it to be clear that to focus on this kind of event in no way implies that a "natural" explanation for some special event in the Bible in some way

---

[1] This becomes necessary because V. White, *The Fall of a Sparrow: A Concept of Special Divine Action* (Exeter, England: Paternoster, 1985), means something like this notion of "subjectively special" when he writes of "special" divine action (e.g., pages 139-142) but without clarifying it.

[2] Hence my term corresponds to Paul Gwynne's "*direct* special divine action," in *Special Divine Action: Key Issues in the Contemporary Debate* (Rome: Gregorian University Press, 1996), 24, which he defines as, "God brings it about that some particular outcome is different from what it would have been had only natural, created factors been operative." Since, however, the doctrines of preservation and concurrence make God's part in everything "direct," I have avoided a potentially misleading term.

reduces the importance or divine origin of the event. As A. R. Millard helpfully pointed out (and this in an essay whose purpose is to defend the propriety of the category "supernatural" in Old Testament historical narratives),[3]

> For the Israelites the perception of a "natural cause" did not diminish the miracle. They believed their God controlled the universe and all in it, therefore he could take any element in it to use its normal forces for his purposes. . . . David's Philistine war had its success because of specific divine aid, his victories over the Jebusites, Moab, Ammon, and Aram are related as straightforward military achievements, the strategy sometimes revealed, accompanied by a plain acknowledgement of God's over-ruling (e.g., 2 Samuel 10:12).

PASSAGES THAT DEPICT NATURAL POWERS BEING EMPLOYED OR SURPASSED BY SPECIAL DIVINE ACTION

Genesis 1:1 presents the origin of the world as something qualitatively special. We may render that verse, "God (had)[4] in the beginning created the heavens and the earth." All things that are not God owe their existence to God's own unconstrained choice to create, to originate their being. Unlike some, I do not find the proof of my interpretation in the presence of the verb translated "created" (Hebrew *bārā'*); instead, it follows from the overall meaning of the sentence. After all, if this took place "in the beginning," what was there before then? Nothing. And if what God created was "the heavens and the earth," which here seems to be an expression for "everything in the material universe," what is left out? Nothing.[5] Hence the Bible opens, as traditionally interpreted, with an affirmation of creation from nothing.[6] No explanation

---

[3] A. R. Millard, "The Old Testament and History: Some Considerations," *Faith and Thought* 110 (1983), 34-53, at 47, 50.

[4] I put in the word *had* to indicate that Moses has made this verse background to his main narrative sequence, Gen. 1:3–2:3. The verb *created* is a "perfect" tense, which at the beginning of a narrative is not part of the main sequence of events an author wants to focus on. It could be used as a summary of the following narrative, e.g., as in Gen. 22:1; it can be used to express discontinuity with the preceding narrative (not an option here!); or it can be used to denote events prior to the main sequence. I favor the third option, first because v. 2 is also providing background ("now as for the earth [whose creation was just mentioned in v. 1], it was formlessness and emptiness . . ."). The second reason is that other biblical writers refer to this passage and get from it a doctrine of creation from nothing (e.g., Isa. 40:26; Heb. 11:3; Rev. 4:11); and if we take Gen. 1:1 as either a summary of the entire account, or as some would have it, "When God began to create . . . ," there is no source of the creation from nothing doctrine. For more discussion, with discourse considerations and theological implications, see A. Niccacci, "Analysis of Biblical Narrative," in R. D. Bergen, ed., *Biblical Hebrew and Discourse Linguistics* (Dallas: SIL, 1994), 175-198, at 183.

[5] Unless we want to mention the angels and their like; but they owe their being to God as well.

[6] For a rebuttal of attempts to argue that the doctrine of creation out of nothing is not a biblical concept but is instead due to pressures on the early church, see Paul Copan, "Is *Creatio ex Nihilo* a Post-biblical Invention? An Examination of Gerhard May's Proposal," *Trinity Journal* 17n.s. (1996), 77-93.

that appeals either to natural properties (since natural properties themselves owe their existence to this event) or to God being under some compulsion (cf. Rev. 4:11, "for you [God] created all things and *by reason of your will* they were and were created") will fly with the biblical authors.

The creation narrative of Genesis 1:1–2:3 has indications of additional special divine action upon the creation, especially the presence of God's Spirit in 1:2 and the places in which God speaks a wish that is then fulfilled (1:3, 6, 9, 11, 14, 20, 24, 26). We will need to come back to this in chapter 11 when we discuss origins. For now it is enough to note that writers of the intertestamental period picked up on the idea of God's "word" being the instrument that carries out his will, following the lead of Psalm 33:6, 9 ("by the word [Hebrew *dābār*] of the Lord the heavens were made . . . for he said [Hebrew *ʾāmar*, the verb used in Gen. 1], and it was, he commanded, and it stood fast"). Most interesting to us is the book of Wisdom, which recounts this in 9:1:

> O God of (the) fathers and Lord of mercy,
> who made all things by means of your word.

It becomes clear that this author thought of the "word" (Greek λόγος) as God's agency for qualitatively special action; as he says in 16:12, referring to the bronze snake, a special cure for snakebite in Numbers 21:6-9 (cf. NRSV):

> For neither herb nor poultice cured them,
> but (it was) your own word [λόγος],
>   Lord, which heals [or, was healing] all.[7]

Then in 18:15 (NRSV) he describes the death of the Egyptian firstborn (Ex. 11:1-8; 12:29-32):

> Your all-powerful word [λόγος] leaped from heaven,
>   from the royal throne,
> into the midst of the land that was doomed . . .[8]

---

[7] Cf. Wisd. 16:7, which explicitly eschews any natural explanation: "For the one who turned toward it [the bronze snake] was saved, not on account of the thing that was looked at, but on account of you, the Savior of all."

[8] Interestingly enough, this is accurate exegesis of how the biblical account describes the event. In Ex. 12:29, which begins "and it came about in the middle of the night, and the Lord *he* smote every first-born. . . ." the word order of the clause "and the Lord, *he* smote" is peculiar, because the subject comes first and is attached to the conjunction, rather than the expected *wayyiqtol* form, "and he smote." This puts special focus on "the Lord"; as the Israeli commentator Hakham notes, the word order stresses that it was the Lord himself and no intermediary who did the smiting (*Sēfer Šēmôt* [*Exodus*, Da'at Miqra; Jerusalem: Mossad Harav Kook, 1991], 201 [ad loc.], 233).

Next, consider the narratives that describe the unique conception of Jesus. Luke 1:26-38 details the visit of the angel Gabriel to Nazareth to inform a young betrothed girl that she will become pregnant with the promised heir of David (i.e., the Messiah).[9] Luke is clear that she is a "virgin" (παρθένος) in v. 27. Curiously, when Gabriel tells her, "You will become pregnant and bear a son" (v. 31), Mary apparently interprets the simple future tenses as referring to the *immediate* future, and before she takes up residence with her fiancé Joseph.[10] Hence she asks (v. 34):

> How will this be, . . . since I do not know [i.e., have sexual relations with] a man [or husband]?

We may compare Mary's question with that of Zacharias, some months earlier, in verse 18. Zacharias, a pious priest and husband of Mary's kinswoman Elizabeth, was childless (presumably not for want of trying but because of infertility, v. 7). This same angel Gabriel visited Zacharias and explained that he and Elizabeth would finally have a son, who would have a special mission to Israel. Zacharias, however, focused on the difficulties, and so he asked,

> By what[11] shall I know this? For *I* am an old man, and *my wife* is advanced in her days.

Gabriel is offended by Zacharias' question, which he takes as expressing unwarranted disbelief (vv. 19-20).[12] On the other hand, Mary's question in verse 34 does not meet with the same reception from Gabriel. Instead he agrees with her, and interprets her simple "how" as a perplexed but reasonable request for a causal explanation.[13] Gabriel therefore explains in verse 35:

> The Holy Spirit will come upon you,
> and the Power of the Most High will overshadow you,
> therefore also the child (to be) born/begotten (is) holy;
> he will be called Son of God.

---

[9] Cf. the commentaries of J. A. Fitzmyer, *Luke I-IX* (Anchor Bible; Garden City, N.Y.: Doubleday, 1981); and I. H. Marshall, *Luke* (New International Greek Text Commentary; Grand Rapids, Mich.: Eerdmans, 1978).

[10] Fitzmyer, 1:350, suggests that the question is there only to advance the dialogue and to give the angel the opening to explain the miraculous conception, and Mary did not necessarily say it "historically." Marshall, 70, is also hesitant. But if, as Fitzmyer himself observes (347), the announcement follows an OT pattern which is addressed to a woman who is already pregnant or who will conceive in the very near future, there is no reason to be so skeptical about its genuineness.

[11] Gk. κατὰ τί, "in accordance with what?" (cf. BAGD, 407a, s.v. κατά ii.5.a.δ), is a different question from Mary's πῶς, "how?" although English versions tend to render both the same.

[12] M. Zerwick, *Grammatical Analysis of the Greek New Testament* (Rome: Editrice Pontificio Istituto Biblico, 1993), interprets Zacharias' question as equivalent to "How can I be sure of this?"

[13] Take our material on begetting (chapter 5) for background on Israelite views of how pregnancies come about.

The parallelism between "Holy Spirit" and "Power of the Most High" shows that these are two mutually illuminating phrases for the same thing. And, as Fitzmyer puts it, "The latter phrase ["Power of the Most High"] indicates that the Spirit is understood in the Old Testament sense of God's creative and active power";[14] that is, in our terms, the Spirit is an energy from outside God's ordinary work in "nature." No explanation based on "natural properties" will satisfy the requirements of this language. That makes this an instance of qualitatively special divine action.[15]

Gabriel then goes on to mention Elizabeth's extraordinary pregnancy, and he concludes with (v. 37), "for nothing is impossible with God."[16]

The parallel passage in Matthew's Gospel, though different (perhaps "complementary" is a better adjective) in many of its details, is entirely in agreement with Luke as to the kind of divine action involved. Matthew 1:18 introduces us to Jesus' mother Mary, betrothed to Joseph; and it makes explicit that,

> Before they came together [i.e., as husband and wife, including sexual relations] she was found to be pregnant from the Holy Spirit.

When Joseph learned of Mary's pregnancy, he resolved to divorce her quietly—and this because he was operating under the assumption that everyone else makes about how women come to be pregnant. He knew he hadn't done it, so there must be someone else. In view of the Old Testament material discussed in chapter 5, this was eminently rational on Joseph's part. Indeed, it looks like the Lord thought so, too, since in verse 20 we read that he sent an angel to appear to Joseph in a revelatory dream, to explain to this poor man just where Mary's pregnancy had come from and what Joseph was to do about it:

> "Joseph son of David, don't be afraid to take Mary your wife; for what is begotten in her is from the Holy Spirit."

[14] Fitzmyer, *Luke,* 1:350.
[15] This renders futile the attempts of R. J. Berry, "The Virgin Birth of Christ," *Science and Christian Belief* 8 (1996), 101-110, at 106-109, to find a natural mechanism for the conception. At 108 he says, "I must emphasize that there is no certain record of parthenogenesis in humans, nor of a male being conceived without fertilisation by a Y-bearing sperm. My point is that the possibility is not completely outside the realms of biological imagination. . . . My purpose in describing them is simply to reduce the assumption of incredibility that seems to dog the doctrine of the Virgin Birth." This indicates that Berry most probably fits into the "providentialist" family in our typology. If we followed the supernaturalist line, we would find the effort of J. Stafford Wright, "Virgin Birth," in J. D. Douglas et al., eds., *The New Bible Dictionary* (Downers Grove, Ill.: InterVarsity, 1982), 1238, more compelling: "If without irreverence we ask how the ultimate mystery of the incarnation can be linked to the physical, it would seem that, in order that the Second Person of the Trinity might become man, the Holy Spirit fashioned the necessary genes and chromosomes that could be the vehicle of Christ's person in uniting with those in the body of the virgin."
[16] In view of the wording, which is a clear adaptation of Gen. 18:14 LXX (which refers to Sarah's pregnancy with Isaac) and the connector "for," it is easiest to see this as explanatory of Elizabeth's pregnancy first; but of course the principle is generally valid and would equally apply to Mary's pregnancy.

These passages express in the clearest possible terms that Jesus' conception was the product of qualitatively special divine action, since they refer it to the special work of the Holy Spirit.[17] At the same time, as we have seen, they also endorse the notion of "natural cause" and the inferences people make from that notion: Mary's question in Luke 1:34, and Joseph's intention in Matthew 1:19, were seen as quite reasonable, to be met with assurance that something qualitatively different was happening.

In describing the resurrection of Jesus, the New Testament authors spend little time on its metaphysics. I think that is because it is an event so obviously impossible if natural created factors and ordinary divine concurrence are the only relevant considerations, that no comment is necessary.[18] In a few places, however, some of this becomes explicit. For example, in his address to the Athenian philosophers (Acts 17:22-31), Paul finishes by declaring the coming day of judgment for all people—as decisive an "intervention" in the "natural course of things" as we could ask for. And, Paul tells them, God has "provided a token of faith to all people by raising him [Jesus] from the dead"; the resurrection is therefore a proof or foretaste of the great eschatological supernatural event, because it is itself a supremely supernatural event.

This qualitatively special aspect of Jesus' resurrection is in focus as well in John 10:18, where Jesus declares, "No one takes it [my life] from me, but I myself lay it down of my own accord; I have authority to lay it down, and I have authority to take it back. This command I received from my Father" (i.e., it is not part of "nature" at all). It also appears in Romans 1:4, where Jesus is described as having been "marked out as Son of God in power according to the Spirit of Holiness by (his) resurrection from the dead"; i.e., the resurrection was a special operation of divine power.

Similarly, when Paul speaks of the resurrection of believers, as he does in Philippians 3:21, he says that at his return the now-glorious Jesus will "transform the body of our humble state to be conformed to the body of his glory, according to the working that enables him even to subject all things to himself."[19] And in 1 Corinthians 15:42-44 (especially verse 44) Paul

---

[17] Cf. BAGD, 234b, s.v. ἐκ 3.a, which explains that this preposition (translated "from" in vv. 18, 20) is used to denote the role of the male parent or of the female parent in contexts dealing with begetting. Since we know Mary to be the mother, this implies that the Holy Spirit in some way supplied the part of the father (although clearly not by carnal means). This enhances the attractiveness of Stafford Wright's speculation, mentioned above.

[18] Similarly the raisings of dead people Jesus performed during his earthly ministry: e.g., the widow's son of Nain, Luke 7:11-17; Jairus' daughter, Luke 8:49-56 (cf. v. 55, "her spirit returned," clearly beyond any created power to achieve); Lazarus, John 11:38-46.

[19] Cf. also Rom. 8:11; 1 John 3:2.

specifically contrasts the "natural" (Greek ψυχικόν) body we now have with
the "spiritual" or "supernatural" body we will then have (πνευματικόν).[20]

Generally, the Gospel writers simply designate the mighty works Jesus
did during his earthly ministry as "signs," "acts of power," "works," and the
like, and leave out questions of their mode. They probably leave us to draw
our own conclusions. However, in a few places they do become more
explicit. In John 3:2, Nicodemus acknowledges that Jesus must be a teacher
who has come from God, "for no one can do these signs which you are doing,
unless God be with him" (referring to the unspecified "signs" of 2:23 that
had led many to believe in him; most likely these were works of healing).
That is, natural powers were not enough to explain Christ's work.[21] In Luke
8:46, when the woman with a flow of blood touched Jesus' garment, Jesus
was aware that "power" (δύναμις) went out of him, which accomplished her
healing. And in Luke 13:11-13, a woman who had a spirit of sickness was
bent over and not able to stand up straight at all, but Jesus freed her from
her sickness and immediately she became erect: That is, Jesus' authority was
greater than that of the spirit, and overcame her "inability" (which was due
to human nature being less powerful than demonic nature).

Jesus' follower Peter, after healing a lame man, asked (Acts 3:12, NIV),
"Men of Israel, why does this surprise you? Why do you stare at us as if by
our own power [δύναμις] or godliness we had made this man walk?" Peter
presupposes that humans have power; his point, however, is that merely
human power is not enough to explain the healing. That is, he considered it
supernatural.

I have mentioned the Holy Spirit, and this leads to the passages in the
Old Testament about the Holy Spirit "coming suddenly upon" someone;
what do these passages add to our discussion? There are a number of expressions to denote this particular activity of the Spirit, but I will select just a few
passages.[22] For example, quite frequently these expressions describe the
Spirit coming upon someone and moving him to inspired speech (e.g., Num.
11:25-26; 24:2; 1 Sam. 10:6, 10; 19:23; 1 Chron. 12:18 [Hebrew v. 19];
2 Chron. 24:20); and this is the likely background for the inspired speeches
resulting from the "filling with the Spirit" in Luke 1:41, 67; 2:27. In other

---

[20] I shall discuss the opposition of these Greek words below in regard to 1 Cor. 2:14-15. In the context
of 1 Cor. 15, the adjective *natural* (ψυχικόν, literally "soulish") probably comes from the base noun *soul*
(ψυχή) in v. 45, which quotes Gen. 2:7. To make the connection clearer, that part of the verse should probably be rendered "the first man, Adam, became a living *natural* being."

[21] That the author of John endorses the view of Nicodemus is clear, not only from his prologue, which
tells us that God was "with" Jesus in an extraordinary way (i.e., by incarnation), but also from the function he gives to the "signs": People are culpable if they see the signs and fail to believe. Cf. also Acts 10:38.

[22] For fuller treatment of linguistic issues, see C. John Collins, *Homonymous Verbs in Biblical Hebrew: An
Investigation of the Role of Comparative Philology* (Ph.D. dissertation, University of Liverpool, 1988),
394-408.

cases, Samson is suddenly enabled to kill a lion or Philistines (Judg. 14:6, 19; 15:14) and Saul and David to perform their kingly duties (1 Sam. 11:6; 16:13). Some of these same expressions are also used for the coming of an evil spirit upon someone, notably upon Saul (1 Sam. 16:14; 18:10; 19:9). These last passages indicate that the expressions do denote the belief that the influence comes from outside the man himself, whatever moderns may think about insanity and whatnot.[23] Thus, at least sometimes (e.g., prophesying, see the next section) the terms denote a special divine action. In general, when the expressions speak of the Spirit of God, they refer to the Spirit equipping and enabling someone to perform a task for the benefit of the people of God.[24]

It is at least possible that not all of the passages should be taken that way. For example, we could view Saul's anger that led to his delivering Jabesh Gilead (1 Sam. 11:6) as simply God's employment of Saul's natural capacities without in any way going beyond them (similarly Gideon in Judg. 6:34). I do not think we have enough information from the text to decide the issue, which suggests that the author did not consider it relevant to his communicative purpose for us to be able to tell.[25]

What shall we make of Samson, however? It certainly seems that his exploits are extraordinary: killing a lion with his bare hands (Judg. 14:6), killing thirty men of Ashkelon apparently single-handedly (14:19), and bursting ropes and killing a thousand Philistine warriors with only the jawbone of a donkey (15:14-15). Perhaps Samson was just exceptionally strong, exceptionally agile, and exceptionally "lucky," all of which God employed providentially for his own purposes. Popular versions of the Samson story make him out to be a muscle-bound dolt, but there are reasons to reject this image even though it is popular (we can leave in the dolt part, as we'll see!).

Let's give a careful reading to the story of Samson's relationship with Delilah, who wheedled out of him the secret of his strength and betrayed him to the Philistines (Judg. 16:4-21). Delilah wants Samson to tell her "by what

---

[23] They also raise a number of vexing problems: e.g., since the evil spirit is twice "an/the evil spirit of God" (16:16; 18:10), once "an/the evil spirit of the Lord" (19:9), and once even "a/the spirit of God" (16:23), it is difficult to know just who or what this spirit is supposed to be. Is it God's own Spirit; or is it like the "spirit of deceit" of 1 Kings 22:19-23, who, though distinct from the Lord, nevertheless is his agent (allowing for the vision form of the 1 Kings text)? And if we decide for the latter, as I am inclined to do, shall we allow the use of the term *supernatural* for such influence? I note that the expression may be rendered "a harmful spirit of God" (cf. NIV margin at 1 Sam. 16:14, "injurious"), which at least gets us out of ascribing moral evil to God. And after all, it was sent upon Saul, who had veered away from obedience to the Lord; and we do not know what kind of torment it gave—it could for all we know be the torment of a guilty conscience, which would have caused a better man to repent.

[24] Thus they have a bearing on how we should interpret the NT terms for the baptism and filling of the Holy Spirit, but I will not pursue that subject here.

[25] Or else the use of terms does signify something special, and we just do not have enough of the language habits to pick up on that.

means his strength is great" (a grammatical rendering of the phrase in v. 5; cf. vv. 6, 15). After the first deception, the text says that Samson's strength was not "known" (v. 9); I have argued elsewhere that the nuance of "known" here is "known as to its source," and this exactly fits the context.[26] Indeed, in verse 19 Samson's "strength" left him (the Hebrew verb is *sûr*, constructed with *mēʿālāyw*, "to depart from being upon someone"), while in verse 20 "the Lord left him" (*sûr mēʿālāyw* again); this strength is not his "natural" strength. This ties in with those expressions in the Samson narratives about the Spirit of the Lord "impelling him" (13:25) and coming upon him mightily (e.g., 14:6, 19; 15:14), which tell us that the Spirit equipped and enabled him for some task. And finally, note Samson's reply to Delilah in 16:7, 11, 13, 17: Under such conditions he would become like "any other man," i.e., without the great strength that is an *addition* to his human powers. Thus we can say that the author of Judges saw Samson's strength as a result of special divine action.

When it comes to Jonathan's exploits, the metaphysical explanation is not quite so easy. In 1 Samuel 14, Jonathan and his armor-bearer crossed a wadi to attack a Philistine outpost and killed about twenty men in the initial hand-to-hand combat. This caused such a fright among the Philistine occupation forces that it attracted the attention of Jonathan's father Saul, who then led the main Israelite force into battle and routed the Philistines. In the course of these events, Saul made a foolish oath that no one was to eat, but Jonathan was unaware of the oath (and thought it silly when he learned of it), and ate some honey (vv. 24-30). For this he was to be punished under the terms of Saul's oath; but in verse 45 the Israelites refused to allow Jonathan to be harmed, even though he was guilty. They explained their refusal with "for with God he has worked today" (*kî-ʿim-ʾelōhîm ʿāśâ hayyôm hazzeh*).

They seem to be saying that Jonathan has done something beyond his "natural" (or at least his *expected*) powers. It is hard for us to know whether this is a reference to spectacular luck (under God's providential guidance, of course) or to some qualitatively special divine assistance. Perhaps in light of verses 6, 10, 12, the author intends to favor the special assistance interpretation (NIV):

(6) Jonathan said to his young armor-bearer, "Come, let's go over to the outpost of those uncircumcised fellows. Perhaps the LORD will act [Hebrew *ʿāśâ*] in our behalf. Nothing can hinder the LORD from saving, whether by many or by few."

---

[26] For discussion see Collins, *Homonymous Verbs*, 707.

(10) "But if they say, 'Come up to us,' we will climb up, because that will be our sign that the LORD has given them into our hands."

(12) The men of the outpost shouted to Jonathan and his armor-bearer, "Come up to us and we'll teach you a lesson."

So Jonathan said to his armor-bearer, "Climb up after me; the LORD has given them into the hand of Israel."

We must admit, however, that we cannot be sure that giving the information to enable us to answer our question was part of the author's communicative intent. (An important part of that intent was to build a case against Saul as one unfit to be king; and here, regardless of the mode of God's action, he just does not get the picture.)[27] A providentialist could perhaps imagine a scenario filled with lucky breaks; and however implausible such a scenario might be, we cannot with certainty refute it from the text.[28]

There are no uncertainties about the communicative intent of Numbers 22:28. This verse occurs in a passage about Balaam, the pagan prophet. The angel of the Lord blocked Balaam's way as he tried to ride his donkey; the donkey saw the angel and Balaam did not. The donkey veered off the path and refused to go where Balaam wanted it to go, and Balaam lost his temper and beat the donkey. Then we read that the Lord "opened the donkey's mouth" so that the beast spoke. We have no idea why Balaam didn't keel over in a faint when his donkey spoke; but in any case, as the commentator Ashley dryly observes,[29]

> Since speaking animals were apparently unusual in Israel, the narrator makes it clear that this is an act of Yahweh himself. To discuss whether donkeys have sufficient vocal cords to speak overlooks the fact that this is an act of Almighty Yahweh. The question of how the donkey could speak does not concern the narrator.

For my money this is a sound reading of the text, against which R. K. Harrison's providentialist-sounding exposition sounds marvelously strained:[30]

---

[27] Cf. the writings of V. Philips Long on this point, especially *The Reign and Rejection of King Saul: A Case for Literary and Theological Coherence* (Atlanta: Scholars Press, 1989).

[28] A similar uncertainty attaches to Prov. 19:14 (NIV): "Houses and wealth are inherited from parents, but a prudent wife is from the LORD." Of course the houses and wealth are under God's providential control; but does that *require* us to interpret the prudent wife as being the result of qualitatively special action? Probably not; as Whybray comments (*Proverbs*, 281), "If a man who has already been blessed by good fortune through the normal law of inheritance has his happiness completed by a happy marriage, this is a mark of exceptional divine favour."

[29] Timothy Ashley, *Numbers* (New International Commentary on the Old Testament; Grand Rapids, Mich.: Eerdmans, 1993), 457.

[30] R. K. Harrison, *Numbers* (Grand Rapids, Mich.: Baker, 1992), 300-301.

As the donkey brayed, she conveyed a message of anger and resent-
ment that the seer understood in his mind in a verbal form and to
which he quite properly responded verbally. Through her opened
mouth the braying animal retaliated against her undeserved treatment by uttering sounds that were unintelligible to the other
onlookers but that Balaam was able to comprehend through processes of mental apperception that are not well understood. . . . In
connection with the Balaam incident, God spoke through the braying of the donkey in a manner that was intended for only one recip-
ient: the animal's owner.

Ashley's reading is more convincing, I think, because the text says the angel
"opened the donkey's mouth" (i.e., not Balaam's ears or mind!). I do not
know how to interpret that except as a special operation.

Finally, consider the case of 1 Samuel 6:9,[31] which comes in the narrative of the captivity of the ark of the covenant (4:1b–7:2). In 6:7-9 the
Philistine clergy (*kōhănîm wĕqōsĕmîm*, "priests and diviners," v. 2, i.e., people with insight into the supernatural) propose a simple test by which they
can infer whether their troubles ("tumors," v. 5) are the product of agent causation (i.e., divine intervention) or not: by seeing whether the cows drawing
the ark act according to their "natural properties." If the cows do not return
to their calves (i.e., if they act contrary to their "natural" action),[32] the
Philistines will know that Israel's God has brought this great trouble (v. 9a);
if the cows do return to their calves, then the Philistines will know that it was
not God's hand (i.e., intervention) that touched them, but that it happened
to them *miqreh* (9b). I have argued elsewhere that this last word should be
translated "as an ordinary event," i.e., things acting according to their ordinary or natural behavior. We the readers know the cause of the Philistines'
troubles, and by their (very sensible) experiment the Philistines find it out,
too: It was special divine causation, connected with the ark of the covenant,
the place where God makes his presence manifest in a special mode.

PASSAGES THAT DESCRIBE SPECIAL DIVINE ACTION IN REVELATION

When it comes to knowledge, biblical passages support two propositions:
First, humans are, by virtue of being human, able to know things, even

---

[31] For full exegetical details on this text, cf. C. John Collins, "*Miqreh* in 1 Sam 6:9: 'Chance' or 'Event'?"
forthcoming in *The Bible Translator* 51:1 (January 2000).

[32] Cf. Robert Gordon's comment on the outcome in v. 12: "Contrary to what might have been expected
of them, the cows moved off toward Beth Shemesh, albeit making a noise about it" (*I and II Samuel: A
Commentary* [Grand Rapids, Mich.: Zondervan, 1986], 102).

important things;[33] and second, there are some things that humans cannot know unless God should reveal them by some special action.

Both sides of this come out clearly in the narratives about Joseph and Daniel as interpreters of revelatory dreams. In Genesis 40:8; 41:8, 15-16, Joseph explains why a special work is necessary for the interpretation of a dream, which is held to be a message from the supernatural realm about the future. He does not say either that the dream did *not* in fact come from beyond, nor that humans cannot know anything about anything. Rather, he accepts the assumption that the dream came from beyond, and this explains why the interpretation must come from beyond "nature." Joseph declares that "Interpretations belong to God" (40:8), and "It is apart from me; it is God who will answer the well-being of Pharaoh" (41:16). After Joseph gives a full interpretation with advice for action, Pharaoh decides that Joseph is "a man in whom is the spirit of gods/God" (v. 38).[34]

We have a very similar situation in the Daniel story. In Daniel 2, King Nebuchadnezzar of Babylon has a dream, which he takes to be revelatory. He asks his court diviners, not simply to interpret the dream but even to narrate it to him first! In verses 10-11, the diviners explain to Nebuchadnezzar that no man on earth could do that, that in fact only the gods who do not dwell with (mere) flesh could do it. Finally a royal official tells the king that Daniel, an exile from Judah, can give the king what he wants. When Nebuchadnezzar asks Daniel, "Are you able to tell me the dream and its interpretation?" (v. 26), Daniel, like Joseph, declares:

> No wise man, enchanter, magician or diviner can explain to the king the mystery he has asked about, but there is a God in heaven who reveals mysteries. He has shown King Nebuchadnezzar what will happen in days to come. (vv. 27-28)

In verse 47 the king acknowledges the greatness of Daniel's God as evidenced by Daniel's ability both to recount and to explain the dream. Daniel 5:8-12, about the diviners' inability to read the writing on the wall and Daniel's reputation as having an "extraordinary spirit," carries on this theme.

Then consider the passages that describe prophetic inspiration. The most important in the Old Testament is Deuteronomy 18:9-22 (NIV):

---

[33] This follows in general from the doctrine of humans as created in God's image (Gen. 1:26-27); cf. the descendants of Cain as pioneers in various crafts (Gen. 4:17-24), in addition to the passages discussed in this section. See the section on "Human Nature and the Possibility of Science" in my forthcoming *Christian Faith in an Age of Science.*

[34] It is hard to ascertain whether *'ĕlōhîm* in the expression *rûaḥ 'ĕlōhîm* is supposed to mean "gods" or God; perhaps the Israelite author wanted to report the kind of words a polytheist would use ("gods") but in such a way that the pious Israelite would recognize that it is really the one true God. In any case the NASB "divine spirit" is disappointing. Cf. also Dan. 4:8 [Aramaic v. 5]; 5:11.

(9) When you enter the land the LORD your God is giving you, do not learn to imitate the detestable ways of the nations there. (10) Let no one be found among you who sacrifices his son or daughter in the fire, who practices divination or sorcery, interprets omens, engages in witchcraft, (11) or casts spells, or who is a medium or spiritist or who consults the dead. (12) Anyone who does these things is detestable to the LORD, and because of these detestable practices the LORD your God will drive out those nations before you. (13) You must be blameless before the LORD your God.

(14) The nations you will dispossess listen to those who practice sorcery or divination. But as for you, the LORD your God has not permitted you to do so. (15) The LORD your God will raise up for you a prophet like me from among your own brothers. You must listen to him. (16) For this is what you asked of the LORD your God at Horeb on the day of the assembly when you said, "Let us not hear the voice of the LORD our God nor see this great fire anymore, or we will die."

(17) The LORD said to me: "What they say is good. (18) I will raise up for them a prophet like you from among their brothers; I will put my words in his mouth, and he will tell them everything I command him. (19) If anyone does not listen to my words that the prophet speaks in my name, I myself will call him to account. (20) But a prophet who presumes to speak in my name anything I have not commanded him to say, or a prophet who speaks in the name of other gods, must be put to death."

(21) You may say to yourselves, "How can we know when a message has not been spoken by the LORD?" (22) If what a prophet proclaims in the name of the LORD does not take place or come true, that is a message the LORD has not spoken. That prophet has spoken presumptuously. Do not be afraid of him.

Verses 9-14 describe the forbidden ways of trying to secure success in the future: The covenant people must rely on the Lord and express that reliance with lives of obedience. Verse 15-20 describe the fundamental feature of the office of a prophet, namely that he has a special message from God. The language about God putting his words in the prophet's mouth and the prophet speaking "in the name of the LORD" (as his authorized representative) informs us that the prophet's words are more than just extra spiritual insight or keen observation of the social and spiritual scene. The very words come from beyond what a human being can know simply by virtue of being human. Verses 21-22 offer a sign by which anyone who claims to be a prophet can prove that his message is from beyond nature: He can prove the divine origin of his message by telling the future—which, as in the Joseph story, is the property of God alone, and can only be known through means from beyond nature.[35]

This forms the background to a text such as Jeremiah 23:16, where the false prophets speak "a vision of their (own) heart" rather than one that is "from the mouth of the Lord." In context this speaks of so-called prophets of Jeremiah's day whose message to the complacent was "there, there" rather than "repent!" They spoke as mere humans, i.e., from within their own natural abilities and with their own sinful agenda (cf. v. 32, "I [the Lord] did not send them," i.e., their action is not the result of God's special intention). The true prophet is the one who has stood in the council of the Lord and announces his words (vv. 18, 22).

Second Peter 1:20-21 is also explicit (NIV):

> Above all, you must understand that no prophecy of Scripture came about by the prophet's own interpretation. For prophecy never had its origin in the will of man, but men spoke from God as they were carried along by the Holy Spirit.

In context, this refers to Old Testament prophecies about the Messiah, which the life and work of Jesus, particularly the Transfiguration, have confirmed. This rejects any possibility of a "natural" explanation—even of the providentialist sort—for the origin of prophecy.

The late R. K. Harrison, an Old Testament scholar of evangelical convictions and painstaking study, provides a good example of providentialist-type explanations for predictive prophecy:[36]

> Permeating [the prophets'] utterances invariably was some distinctly predictive element, which was based in part upon the spiritual awareness that the individual prophet had of the future consequences of past and present iniquity and the consistent rejection of the Covenant ideal. This was reinforced by the fact that the prophets delivered their utterances in the name of the Ruler of History, within whose power lay the destiny of individuals and peoples, and who guided the processes of history according to the immutable principles that characterized His nature. . . .
>
> This type of individual [who could make predictions] shared in the capacity for intuitive grasp of wide fields of perception that, as [William F.] Albright has remarked, has also characterized certain figures of the last two hundred and fifty years (he mentions Jules

---

35 Num. 12:6-8 tells us the "normal" mode of prophetic inspiration, namely, through visions and dreams. Moses had a more direct communication.

36 R. K. Harrison, *Introduction to the Old Testament* (Grand Rapids, Mich.: Eerdmans, 1969), 757-758.

Verne and Heinrich Heine), at least in sporadic moments of exalta-
tion, and which is conspicuously absent in the personalities of those
trained in accordance with the modern scientific method. . . .

The prophets continually predicted the future, on the perfectly
logical basis that, as Augustine and others have expressed it, what
is to happen is already inherent in the present situation.

I do not think Harrison's account of prophetic prediction is adequate for
the biblical material assembled here.

PASSAGES THAT DESCRIBE SPECIAL DIVINE ACTION IN RELIGIOUS RENEWAL AND TRANSFORMATION

When biblical writers reflect on the success of their ministries, they are
emphatic in ascribing these results to God. For example, in 1 Corinthians
3:6 Paul likens the gospel message to seed cast into a field: "I planted,
Apollos watered, but God caused the growth." And in 2 Corinthians 4:3-6
(NIV) he says,

> And even if our gospel is veiled, it is veiled to those who are per-
> ishing. The god of this age has blinded the minds of unbelievers, so
> that they cannot see the light of the gospel of the glory of Christ,
> who is the image of God. For we do not preach ourselves, but Jesus
> Christ as Lord, and ourselves as your servants for Jesus' sake. For
> God, who said, "Let light shine out of darkness," made his light
> shine in our hearts to give us the light of the knowledge of the glory
> of God in the face of Christ.

What is the general biblical picture regarding the metaphysics of regeneration, progress of ministry, and character transformation? This topic is
important in itself, because it has so many implications for the conduct of
ministry; but it is also important because many of the mighty works of Jesus
are used as analogies for moral renewal, and we want to see how the analogy will work. We will consider that in chapter 8.

The classic Old Testament text is Ezekiel 36:25-27, which describes
God's intention to give spiritual genuineness to his people after they return
from the exile (NIV):[37]

> "'I will sprinkle clean water on you, and you will be clean; I will
> cleanse you from all your impurities and from all your idols. I will
> give you a new heart and put a new spirit in you; I will remove from

---

[37] This is the background for John 3:3, 5, the birth of water and Spirit.

you your heart of stone and give you a heart of flesh. And I will put my Spirit in you and move you to follow my decrees and be careful to keep my laws.'"

In Old Testament psychology, the "heart" refers to the center of a person's motives, the system of likes and dislikes by which he or she chooses (Prov. 4:23), and which is in turn affected by those choices (e.g., by becoming "hard"). Ezekiel describes, not a change in this property of the people, but God's giving them a new set of likes and dislikes, new motivations and abilities (the Spirit in them). This is not presented as an outgrowth of their own deliberations or choices, nor as a contravening of human nature, but as a qualitatively special divine act. This is similar to Deuteronomy 29:4 [Hebrew v. 3], "And the Lord has not given to you a heart to know, and eyes to see, and ears to hear, to this day," which apparently traces the "giving" to a special act of God.

We find similar ideas in, e.g., 2 Corinthians 5:17, where someone in Christ is a "new creation";[38] or in Hebrews 6:4-5, which describes participants in the life of the Christian community as "those who have once been enlightened, who have tasted the heavenly gift, who have shared in the Holy Spirit, who have tasted the goodness of the word of God and the powers of the coming age" (NIV); i.e., something from outside "nature" has invaded their lives (which is what makes their rejection of it so serious).

In 1 Corinthians 2:14-15 Paul contrasts the unbeliever, who does not accept or understand the things that come from the Spirit of God, with the believer. The terms he uses are the Greek words ψυχικός and πνευματικός; our English versions render ψυχικός as "a natural man" (NASB) or "the man without the Spirit" (NIV). Based on the usage of this same opposition in 15:44-46,[39] it is possible to say that the ψυχικός is the one in whom only the ψυχή (natural life, that which God has not "interfered with") operates, while the πνευματικός is the one in whom God's Spirit (πνεῦμα) is doing his qualitatively special work of subduing opposition to God and impelling toward Christian faith and obedience.[40]

A providentialist account of moral awakening comes from R. K. Harrison's comment on Deuteronomy 29:4 (text discussed above):[41]

---

[38] The same concepts, but with different imagery, appear in Eph. 2:5, which speaks of believers, who when they were unbelievers were dead in sin, as having been made alive with Christ, i.e., having been made partakers of the benefits of his resurrection.

[39] Cf. above, where I discuss the resurrection of Christ and his followers and this passage.

[40] Cf. also James 3:15. BAGD, s.v. ψυχικός, 894a, makes the same "natural" and "supernatural" contrast between the two terms.

[41] R. K. Harrison, "Deuteronomy," in D. Guthrie et al., *The New Bible Commentary: Revised* (Grand Rapids, Mich.: Eerdmans, 1970), 225.

They did not possess sufficient spiritual insight to appreciate properly the mercies of God. In attributing such incapabilities to God, the Hebrew lawgiver is merely following OT traditions generally in relating everything to Him as the ultimate source or ground of existence.

Paul Helm seems also to speak this way when he writes,[42] "God can so order the events of a person's life as to ensure that he or she becomes a Christian," and does not apparently think we need to look for anything more than special providence in the process.

Nevertheless the biblical material seems pretty well to support the opinion of John Murray,[43]

There is a change that God effects in man, radical and reconstructive in its nature, called new birth, new creation, regeneration, renewal—a change that cannot be accounted for by anything that is in lower terms than the interposition of the almighty power of God. No combination, permutation or accumulation of earth-born forces can explain it or effect it.

Or perhaps more vividly, Blaise Pascal:

To make a man a saint, grace [supernatural action] is certainly needed, and anyone who doubts this does not know what a saint, or what a man, really is.[44]

When Paul describes the effects and integrity of his ministry, as he does in 2 Corinthians 2-6, he is very clear that he takes no credit for it. In fact, in 3:5-6 he says (NIV),

Not that we are *competent* in ourselves to claim anything for ourselves, but our *competence* comes from God. He has made us *competent* as ministers of a new covenant—not of the letter but of the Spirit; for the letter kills, but the Spirit gives life. (italics added)

That there is such a thing in the biblical view as "ordinary" human competency should be clear from the discussion in chapter 5 above; but this kind of competency is not sufficient for the ministry to which Paul was called.[45]

---

[42] Paul Helm, *The Providence of God* (Downers Grove, Ill.: InterVarsity, 1994), 120. This is surprising in view of his earlier affirmation of a more "supernaturalistic" account in *The Beginnings: Word and Spirit in Conversion* (Edinburgh: Banner of Truth, 1986), 14-21.

[43] John Murray, *Collected Writings* (Edinburgh: Banner of Truth, 1984), ii:171; see the whole chapter on regeneration, 167-201.

[44] Blaise Pascal, *Pensées*, no. 508 (Brunschvicg) /no. 869 (Krailsheimer): "Pour faire d'un homme un saint, il faut bien que ce soit la grâce, et qui en doute ne sait ce que c'est que saint et qu'homme."

[45] Cf. his contrast in 2 Cor. 10:3-5 between the "fleshly" weapons of ordinary human warfare and the divinely powerful weapons God has equipped him with for his spiritual war for souls.

It is this conviction that supported Paul's integrity in his refusal to resort to anything manipulative and to keep his courage when results were not externally impressive (4:1-6).[46]

Now of course Paul did not interpret this doctrine as suggesting that the effects were unrelated to the means. Far from it: He himself labored, suffered, worried, fasted, prayed (Acts 20:18-21; 1 Cor. 15:10; 2 Cor. 11:27-28; 1 Thess. 2:1-20; 3:9-10), went without his own rights for the sake of not erecting unnecessary barriers to belief (1 Cor. 9:14-23), set an example of holiness for others (1 Cor. 11:1); and he exhorted his disciple Timothy to a life of study, holiness, and faithful public ministry, that in so doing he might "save" (i.e., bring to eternal glory through perseverance in faith and obedience) both himself and his flock (1 Tim. 4:6-16). Indeed, in the middle of his blatantly "predestinarian" section of Romans, Paul even asked,

> How, then, can they call on the one they have not believed in? And how can they believe in the one of whom they have not heard? And how can they hear without someone preaching to them? And how can they preach unless they are sent? (Rom. 10:14-15a, NIV)

And then in verse 17, "Consequently, faith comes from hearing the message, and the message is heard through the word of Christ." Hence, the diligent use of the means is important, but the results are beyond the natural powers of the means themselves, because of what sinful humans are.[47] This theology gives motivation to diligence and cheerfulness when the results are not what one had hoped for, and humility when there are results.

To compare the natural with the supernatural in character development, consider "nature" at its best,[48] as represented in Aristotle's *Nicomachean Ethics*, II.i.4:

---

[46] It is fascinating to compare Paul's philosophy of ministry with the language in Iain Murray's *Revival and Revivalism: The Making and Marring of American Evangelicalism, 1750–1858* (Edinburgh: Banner of Truth, 1994). Murray notes (82-83), "It cannot be supposed that, in the high excitement attending a work of the Spirit of God, God's saving work can be instantly distinguished from what moves men only temporarily or from what can be accounted for in psychological terms" (recall Paul's "spiritual"—"soulish/psychological" opposition in 1 Cor. 2:14-15). Murray quotes a minister who said, "I never fully understood the apostle's comparison of ministers to 'earthen vessels' [2 Cor. 4:7], till I saw, in a revival, the utter inefficacy of my own preaching to save a single soul, without divine influence" (128 n.3). And he mentions some "wise pastors," in whose view "to lay importance on outward signs of conviction, such as tears, was a sure way to confuse the natural with the spiritual" (209). These sentiments, I think, well represent the spirit of Paul.

[47] Benjamin Warfield, "On Faith in Its Psychological Aspects," in Warfield, *Biblical and Theological Studies* (Philadelphia: Presbyterian and Reformed, 1968), 375-403, points out why this must be so: "But evidence cannot produce belief, faith, except in a mind open to this evidence, and capable of receiving, weighing, and responding to it. . . . The sinful human heart—which is enmity toward God—is incapable of that supreme act of trust in God. . . . The mode of the divine giving of faith is represented rather as involving the creation by God the Holy Spirit of a capacity for faith under the evidence submitted" (397, 398).

[48] Some may doubt that it is theologically proper to speak of "nature" this way; but consider Rom. 2:14, which speaks of unbelieving Gentiles doing good things "by nature" (Gk. φύσει), i.e., apart from the influence of the covenantal revelation of God and his Holy Spirit.

But we receive the virtues, by having first practiced them, just as [we do] with the other skills: for the things we must do once we *have* learned, these we learn *while doing*. . . . Likewise by performing righteous deeds we become righteous people, [by performing] temperate deeds [we become] temperate people, [by performing] courageous deeds [we become] courageous people.[49] (italics added)

This is so striking and attractive, that such Christian teachers as Bishop Joseph Butler, Alexander Whyte, and C. S. Lewis have taken it over, but with a key difference: In Christian sanctification the Holy Spirit, an agent from outside the web of cause and effect, pours his energy into us to make our actions of obedience produce results *beyond* nature, namely the formation of Christ's own character in his people.[50] As Lewis put it,

Now the moment you realize "Here I am, dressing up as Christ," it is extremely likely that you will see at once some way in which at that very moment the pretence could be made less of a pretence and more of a reality. . . .
You see what is happening. The Christ Himself, the Son of God who is man (just like you) and God (just like His Father) is actually at your side and is already at that moment beginning to turn your pretence into a reality. . . .
The real Son of God is at your side. He is beginning to turn you into the same kind of thing as Himself. He is beginning, so to speak, to "inject" His kind of life and thought, His *Zoe*, into you; beginning to turn the tin soldier into a live man. The part of you that doesn't like it is the part that is still tin.

This understanding finds support if we put a number of biblical passages together. For example, 2 Corinthians 3:18 speaks of those who behold the glory (special presence) of the Lord being transformed in stages, from glory to glory, and this is from the Lord, the Spirit. But how does this transformation take place? Romans 8:13 describes the life of persevering in faith to the end, as "by the Spirit you are putting to death the deeds of the body," which verse 14 paraphrases as "being led by the Spirit." In 2 Peter 1:3-4, we read of God's precious and magnificent promises, whose purpose is that by them we might become partakers of the divine nature, having escaped the corruption that is in the world by lust.

---

[49] τὰς δ' ἀρετὰς λαμβάνομεν, ἐνεργήσαντες πρότερον, ὥσπερ καὶ ἐπὶ τῶν ἄλλων τεχνῶν· ἃ γὰρ δεῖ μαθόντας ποιεῖν, ταῦτα ποιοῦντες μανθάνομεν. . . . οὕτω δὲ καὶ τὰ μὲν δίκαια πράττοντες δίκαιοι γινόμεθα, τὰ δὲ σώφρονα σώφρονες, τὰ δὲ ἀνδρεῖα ἀνδρεῖοι.
[50] Alexander Whyte, *Bunyan Characters* (Edinburgh and London: Oliphant, Anderson and Ferrier, 1898), 2-9 (drawing on Butler); C. S. Lewis, *Mere Christianity* (London: Geoffrey Bles, 1952), book iv, chapter 7, "Let's Pretend."

In verses 5-11 Peter goes on to picture the life of such partaking as being diligent to advance one's character. Hebrews 5:14 defines the mature believers as "those who by practice have their faculties trained to discern good and evil."[51] We find out what kind of use trains our faculties from James 1:2-4, which tells believers to count it joy when they encounter various temptations,[52] since such trials provide an opportunity to prove the genuineness of their faith, and that proof goes on to work endurance, which goes on to work maturity. Likewise, Romans 5:3-5 speaks of tribulations working endurance, which works proven faith, which works hope for eschatological glory.

Hence, like the theology of ministry, the outcome is not independent of the means; but it is greater than the means themselves could have produced. The Holy Spirit *adds* something to nature.[53]

---

[51] See Donald Guthrie, *Hebrews* (Tyndale New Testament Commentary; Grand Rapids, Mich.: Eerdmans, 1983), 136: "In fact the words *by practice* . . . could be translated 'by habit', which would bring out perhaps more clearly the building up of experience through a continued process in the past. . . . Spiritual maturity comes neither from isolated events nor from a great spiritual burst. It comes from a steady application of spiritual discipline." 1 Tim. 4:7 uses the same image: "Train yourself towards godliness."

[52] BAGD, 641a, s.v. πειρασμός 2.b, finds this sense here rather than "trials" (RSV, NASB, NIV). That this is right appears from the verbal connections between vv. 2-4 and 12 (e.g., "endure," "proven") which support the linking of πειρασμός as "temptation" here (which it certainly is in v. 12). Cf. 1 Pet. 1:6-7, with similar wording and the same issues.

[53] Development of *Christian* character hence presupposes the prevenient operation of the Holy Spirit in regeneration, as well as his impulsion toward and energizing of obedience ("leading," Rom. 8:14). Our actions are thus *instrumentalities* (i.e., not *meritorious causes*) by means of which the Spirit produces the results. Thus we maintain the reality and even necessity of our cooperation without detracting from the supremacy of grace.

$\mathcal{S}$even

Passages That Seem to Support Occasionalism or Providentialism, Evaluated in Light of Their Communicative Purpose

So far, the biblical passages treated seem to be pointing in a supernaturalist direction: That is, they affirm a real-but-radically-dependent nature, over which God rules and upon which he can work by qualitatively special action. In this chapter we will consider a number of key texts adduced by both providentialists and occasionalists in support of their positions.[1] The providentialists take these texts as showing that, since all "natural" events are God's providential actions, it is therefore invalid (or at least unnecessary) to think of qualitatively special divine action. The occasionalists take these texts as showing that, since every "natural" event is really supernatural, it is therefore invalid to think of any natural causation at all. If these texts can prove what these proponents say they do, we could 1) go back and reinterpret our previous passages to be consistent with them, or 2) throw up our hands in despair of ever getting *one* model out of such a diverse set of books as the Bible. We have to be clear, however, that the providentialists and occasionalists have their work cut out for them: It will not be enough to prove from these texts such things as 1) that God is immediately and causally present in every natural event, or 2) that God is able to rule all events so that they turn out *entirely* the way he wants, or 3) that the creation has no independent existence, since these issues are not in dispute. What the providential-

---

[1] I have culled these texts from a number of places. I have especially focused on the passages put forward in Nicolas Malebranche, *The Search after Truth and Elucidations of the Search after Truth*, T. M. Lennon and P. J. Oscamp, trans. (Columbus: Ohio State University Press, 1980), 672-682; and G. C. Berkouwer, *The Providence of God* (Grand Rapids, Mich.: Eerdmans, 1952), passim.

ist must prove is that, although such a thing as nature exists, there is no such thing as qualitatively special divine action (at least in the sub-arena in which he is a providentialist); and the occasionalist must prove from Scripture that there is no causal nexus to which created things make a contribution. Are these texts up to the challenge?

RADICAL DEPENDENCE ON THE CREATOR

Two very similar New Testament texts affirm the dependency of the creation on its Creator, specifically on Christ: Colossians 1:17 and Hebrews 1:3. Colossians 1:15-18a is printed as poetry in my Greek New Testament and contains a magnificent hymn-like description of Christ. He is the image of the invisible God (v. 15), in whom, through whom, and for whom everything was created (v. 16), who is before all things and in whom all things hold together (v. 17), and he is head of the church (v. 18a). We may see verse 17 as asserting that in Christ all things that exist remain in existence, and in context this means, so that they may serve his purposes of cosmic reconciliation (v. 20).

Hebrews 1:2-4 has some strong points of connection with the Colossians passage. We read that the Son through whom God has spoken has been set as heir of all things, and that through him God made the world (v. 2); this Son is the radiance of God's glory and the representation of God's being, and bears (or supports) all things by the word of his power; and having carried out a cleansing of sins, he sat down at the right hand of divine Majesty (v. 3), having become as much better than the angels as the name he has inherited is more distinguished than they are (v. 4). The excellence of the Son is seen not only in what he is to the creation (vv. 2b-3a) but in what he has done to procure salvation for his people.

There seems to be little room for disagreement that these verses assert that the creation owes to Christ's good pleasure, not just its initiation, but its continuation, including the continuation of any properties, powers, or effects. These verses are compatible with any of the three metaphysical positions I am examining, as long as the position in question acknowledges that created things have real existence. (Occasionalism does not necessarily deny that created things have real existence; it only denies that they have causal powers.)

Discussions on providence often use Paul's statements in Acts 17, especially verses 25-28 (NIV):

(25) "And he [God] is not served by human hands, as if he needed anything, because he himself gives all men life and breath and

everything else. (26) From one man he made every nation of men, that they should inhabit the whole earth; and he determined the times set for them and the exact places where they should live. (27) God did this so that men would seek him and perhaps reach out for him and find him, though he is not far from each one of us. (28) 'For in him we live and move and have our being.' As some of your own poets have said, 'We are his offspring.'"

The supernaturalist William G. T. Shedd says,[2] "The immediate operation of God in his providence is taught in Acts 17:28"; i.e., Shedd uses this passage to support the doctrine of concurrence. The (almost?) occasionalist Francis Pieper cites this text to prove that "it is only by divine power that creatures have their life."[3] Malebranche himself cited verse 25.[4]

Since these verses are not about special divine actions, they are neutral with respect to providentialism and supernaturalism. For this passage to support occasionalism, it would have to be asserting that God's giving life and breath (v. 25), and our living, moving, and having our being in him (v. 28) rules out all creaturely causes. But let's remember the context of this speech: It is addressed to a group of Athenian philosophers, and is intended to lead them to see the relevance of Christ's person and resurrection (v. 31). It would take us too far from our main point to look at all the details of this fascinating speech, but we should be aware that it bristles with references to the Old Testament and to the doctrines believed by some of the philosophers, especially the Stoics.[5] The first part of verse 28, "in him we live and move and have our being," is in quotation marks in the NIV because the translators recognized that here Paul has quoted from a Stoic poem (the same passage from which he gets his quote in Titus 1:12) to illustrate his argument.[6] As Lake and Cadbury point out, "The whole argument of the original pagan writing as quoted is: Zeus cannot be dead, as the Cretans who show his tomb say,

---

[2] W. G. T. Shedd, *Dogmatic Theology* (Nashville: Nelson, 1980 [originally 1888]), i:529.

[3] Francis Pieper, *Christian Dogmatics* (St. Louis: Concordia, 1950), i:487. I am unsure whether to label Pieper a true occasionalist, because he is not clear here. But on balance I would say his heart is with the occasionalists. This conclusion gains some credibility from the fact that it is possible to construe Martin Luther, Pieper's hero, as an occasionalist due to his strongly nominalist tendencies, as does Gary B. Deason, "Reformation Theology and the Mechanistic Conception of Nature," in David Lindberg and Ronald Numbers, *God and Nature: Historical Essays on the Encounter Between Christianity and Science* (Berkeley, Calif.: University of California Press, 1986), 167-191.

[4] Malebranche, 672, among the "infinity of such passages" that "attribute to God the alleged efficacy of secondary causes." According to Edward B. Davis, "Newton's Rejection of the 'Newtonian World View': The Role of Divine Will in Newton's Natural Philosophy," *Science and Christian Belief* 3:1 (1991), 103-117, at 114, Samuel Clarke (1675–1729), a close associate of Isaac Newton (1642–1717), also appealed to this verse in support of a generally occasionalist (or in Davis's terms, "voluntarist") metaphysic.

[5] A good commentary will point these out, e.g., F. F. Bruce, *Acts* (New International Commentary on the New Testament; Grand Rapids, Mich.: Eerdmans, 1988). See also the discussion of this passage in my forthcoming *Christian Faith in an Age of Science*.

[6] As discussed in Bruce, *Acts*, 338-339.

since our living depends on him. The argument is from living men to a living God." Since we live, he must be alive, too. The specific thrust of the address is that the things we know about ourselves positively demand a transcendent Creator to explain them, and this Creator has given a historical manifestation of his purposes in Christ's resurrection, which is a pledge of his power to judge the whole world. For verse 28 to support occasionalism, then, we would have to show 1) that the Stoic source implied some such doctrine, 2) that Paul in quoting the verse meant to affirm everything the original poet meant to affirm, and 3) that such an affirmation is actually relevant to his theme in the speech. Good luck on any of the three.

Verse 25 is likely dependent on Isaiah 42:5. Paul's point is that "the God who created all could not be envisaged as requiring anything from his creatures. . . . Far from their being able to supply any need of his, it is he who supplies every need of theirs: to them all he gives 'life, breath, and everything.'"[7] Nothing in this interpretation precludes the presence of means by which God does this, since the focus is on the ultimate source; nor does it preclude the possibility that the "giving" is God's act in his concurrence.

None of the verses cited in this section can in any sense be said to tip the balance in favor of, much less to *require*, either an occasionalist or a providentialist interpretation.

PERVASIVE DIVINE INVOLVEMENT

A large number of texts assert divine involvement in even the most mundane matters. The occasionalist will take these texts to mean that all such matters are direct acts of God with no causal contribution from the created things; the providentialist will take them as instances of complementary descriptions of processes for which a "scientific" description (i.e., purely in terms of natural cause and effect) is also valid.

For example, consider what Jesus says in two well-known passages from Matthew's Gospel, 6:25-34 and 10:28-31 (NIV):[8]

> *Matthew 6:25-34:* (25) "Therefore I tell you, do not worry about your life, what you will eat or drink; or about your body, what you will wear. Is not life more important than food, and the body more important than clothes? (26) Look at the birds of the air; they do not sow or reap or store away in barns, and yet your heavenly Father feeds them. Are you not much more valuable than they? (27) Who of you by worrying can add a single hour to his life?

---

[7] Bruce, *Acts*, 337.
[8] Malebranche, 673, cites only 6:28-30, but with no discussion.

(28) "And why do you worry about clothes? See how the lilies of the field grow. They do not labor or spin. (29) Yet I tell you that not even Solomon in all his splendor was dressed like one of these. (30) If that is how God clothes the grass of the field, which is here today and tomorrow is thrown into the fire, will he not much more clothe you, O you of little faith? (31) So do not worry, saying, 'What shall we eat?' or 'What shall we drink?' or 'What shall we wear?' (32) For the pagans run after all these things, and your heavenly Father knows that you need them. (33) But seek first his kingdom and his righteousness, and all these things will be given to you as well. (34) Therefore do not worry about tomorrow, for tomorrow will worry about itself. Each day has enough trouble of its own."

Matthew 10:28-31: (28) "Do not be afraid of those who kill the body but cannot kill the soul. Rather, be afraid of the One who can destroy both soul and body in hell. (29) Are not two sparrows sold for a penny? Yet not one of them will fall to the ground apart from the will of your Father. (30) And even the very hairs of your head are all numbered. (31) So don't be afraid; you are worth more than many sparrows."

It would seem that Jesus wanted his followers to see every detail in the world, even down to the feeding and falling of birds, as God's own activity. Surely here is the proof for occasionalism. But in reply one must say, "Not so fast!" The first thing to do is to take note of the communicative purpose of these two passages. They both are about why Jesus' followers should not have to worry.

Matthew 6:25-34 is explanatory of verse 24 ("no one can serve two masters"), and gives reasons why disciples can resist the temptation to compromise their loyalty to Jesus out of concern for their material well-being. The summary of the rationale is verse 32: "For the pagans run after all these things, and your heavenly Father knows that you need them." Hence the believer is free to pursue the kingdom without worry (vv. 33-34). Two things about this passage show that it does not prove occasionalism: 1) there is no denial of means that God might use in feeding the birds and clothing the lilies (vv. 26, 30), and any discussion of that mechanism would be a distraction from the main point. Indeed, if Proverbs is taken as the background, we have no reason to suppose Jesus expected his followers to get their food and clothing except as payment (even the "professional ministers" were paid in return for their work [cf. 1 Cor. 9:13-14] or else had to work in "regular jobs" as Paul did); 2) verse 32 tells us that our Father knows that we *need* these things—what does that mean except that food, drink, and clothing have causal properties that preserve our life in this world? This text has the same philosophy as Deuteronomy 11:13ff., as discussed above in chapter 5.

To understand the meaning of Matthew 10:28-31, we must do two things. First, we note the repetition of "be afraid" in verse 31, which brings us back to verse 28; this means that verses 29-30 are in support of this injunction. And second, we should be careful when we interpret the expression in verse 29 "apart from the will of" (Greek ἄνευ, which simply means "without"). In light of the parallel in Luke 12:6, which has "not one of them is forgotten before God," the translation in Matthew 10:29 would be better, "Yet not one of them will fall to the ground *without the knowledge and consent* of your Father."[9] As a matter of fact, this explains the significance of the hairs being "numbered": There is no limit to God's knowledge of the circumstances and needs of his people. Jesus' disciples need not fear what people can do to them, since nothing can happen to them apart from God's knowledge and consent; and God can at any time foil the plans of an enemy, should it please him to do so.

But wait, there's more! What of those passages from the Psalms, of which 104:10-30 is typical (NIV):[10]

> (10) He makes springs pour water into the ravines;
>   it flows between the mountains.
> (11) They give water to all the beasts of the field;
>   the wild donkeys quench their thirst.
> (12) The birds of the air nest by the waters;
>   they sing among the branches.
> (13) He waters the mountains from his upper chambers;
>   the earth is satisfied by the fruit of his work.
> (14) He makes grass grow for the cattle,
>   and plants for man to cultivate—
>   bringing forth food from the earth:
> (15) wine that gladdens the heart of man,
>   oil to make his face shine,
>   and bread that sustains his heart.
> (16) The trees of the LORD are well watered,
>   the cedars of Lebanon that he planted.
> (17) There the birds make their nests;
>   the stork has its home in the pine trees.
> (18) The high mountains belong to the wild goats;
>   the crags are a refuge for the coneys.

---

[9] Cf. BAGD, 65b, s.v. ἄνευ, sense 1.

[10] Malebranche, 672 cited the Latin "producens foenum jumentis, et herbam servituti hominum, ut educas panem de terra," as coming from "Ps. 103." This is our Ps. 104:14 (Ps. 103:14 in the Vulgate). He also mentioned Ps. 148, but perhaps meant 147:8-9, 16-17; and he probably would have included 135:6-7 and 145:14-16.

(19) The moon marks off the seasons,
   and the sun knows when to go down.
(20) You bring darkness, it becomes night,
   and all the beasts of the forest prowl.
(21) The lions roar for their prey
   and seek their food from God.
(22) The sun rises, and they steal away;
   they return and lie down in their dens.
(23) Then man goes out to his work,
   to his labor until evening.

(24) How many are your works, O LORD!
   In wisdom you made them all;
   the earth is full of your creatures.
(25) There is the sea, vast and spacious,
   teeming with creatures beyond number—
   living things both large and small.
(26) There the ships go to and fro,
   and the leviathan, which you formed to frolic there.

(27) These all look to you
   to give them their food at the proper time.
(28) When you give it to them, they gather it up;
   when you open your hand, they are satisfied with good things.
(29) When you hide your face, they are terrified;
   when you take away their breath,
   they die and return to the dust.
(30) When you send your Spirit, they are created,
   and you renew the face of the earth.

The German commentator H. J. Kraus drew the following "biblical-theology"-oriented conclusion from this psalm:[11]

> In the interpretation of OT hymns that deal with creation, the term "nature" should straightaway be eliminated. "Israel was not familiar with the concept of nature, nor did she speak about the world as a cosmos, i.e., about an ordered structure that is self-contained and subject to definite laws. To her the world was primarily much more an event than a being, and certainly much more a personal experience than a neutral subject for investigation" (G. von Rad, "The reality of God," *God at work in Israel* [1974], 116).

---

[11] H. J. Kraus, *Die Psalmen* (English translation, Continental Commentary; Minneapolis: Augsburg, 1989; originally Biblischer Kommentar Altes Testaments; Neukirchen, Germany: Neukirchener Verlag, 1978), 304.

The first thing we have to recognize about these texts is that they are poetry; and by that I do not intend to dismiss them, but to recognize that poetry has different communicative functions than prose. In general, poetry uses language artistically (i.e., unusually, more elaborately) in order to help us see things differently than we might otherwise see them. Poetry uses imaginative descriptions, enabling us to feel what it was like to be there; the language may be harder to process than that of prose, and it may contain allusion and repetition, because it demands labor to get its point. The author wants us to celebrate something special, or to mourn over something sad (or to get us to mourn over something we didn't see as sad), or to enjoy the retelling of a tale. As a psalm, the poem performs these functions in public worship by putting these words in the mouths of God's people to sing to him. How do passages such as Psalm 104:10-30 perform these functions?

Derek Kidner has argued pretty well that Psalm 104 takes Genesis 1:1–2:3 as its starting point.[12] Its function is to remind us to see the world, not just as something God made and then left to its own devices, but as something in which he continues to involve himself, in which he actually delights. And all its operations are completely at his disposal (recall Deut. 11:13-17), governed by his purposes. As Kidner puts it:[13]

> The psalm speaks the sober truth of God's maintenance of all life. It gives a rounded view of this by pointing to its visible and invisible operation: that is, at one level, the natural order and its bounty . . . and behind all this, the outflowing energy of God which holds all things in being.

Such a concern is no less applicable in our technological society than it was in the ancient agrarian one; but we should notice that this has nothing to do with *overthrowing* our ordinary perception of the world—rather, it intends to *augment* that perception. Natural processes are not autonomous, they are not the whole story, they do not operate independently of God's purposes. The purposiveness of providence, as we shall see in chapter 10, is normally invisible to humans; it is something one must take God's word for, and this is a faith that needs nourishing! As John Rogerson observed,[14]

---

[12] Derek Kidner, *Psalms* (Tyndale Old Testament Commentary; Downers Grove, Ill.: InterVarsity, 1973), 368.

[13] Kidner, *Psalms,* 372.

[14] John Rogerson, "The Old Testament View of Nature: Some Preliminary Questions," in H. A. Brongers et al., eds., *Instruction and Interpretation* (Oudtestamentische Studiën 20; Leiden: Brill, 1977), 67-84, at 79, 84.

These passages [i.e., those that express pervasive divine activity] do not represent what the average Israelite felt; they are religious texts, containing a religious interpretation of the natural world, a religious interpretation that was certainly not "given" along with ordinary perception of the world, and which was by no means self-evident to anyone who reflected on the processes of the natural world. . . . The attempt of the Old Testament writers to claim the sovereignty of God over nature and its workings was not something easily attained with the help of thought processes or an "outlook" that readily saw the divine in everything. It was rather a courageous act of faith, persisted in when there was often much in personal experience and competing religions and outlooks, that suggested that such a conviction was false.

By the way, it is probably worth remembering that Psalm 104 in no way denies the causal properties of water, soil, vegetation, wine, and various kinds of food (grass for cattle, bread for humans, meat for feline predators). And verse 29, which sounds like a direct act of God, need not be any stronger than "the suspension or withdrawing of the various benefits before described" (J. A. Alexander).[15] These causal properties are all at God's disposal.

The second part of Isaiah's prophecy contains a number of passages that use participles, which some may interpret as ongoing activity. For example, Isaiah 44:24 has God saying (NIV),

I am the LORD, who *has made* all things,
who alone *stretched out* the heavens,
who *spread out* the earth by myself.

The verbs which I have italicized are Hebrew participles, a grammatical form that could in some contexts convey ongoing action. Malebranche based his treatment of this verse on a Latin translation which read, "making all things, stretching out the heavens alone, establishing the world and no one is with me," i.e., inferring that God alone does these things and not second causes.[16] This, however, is a misunderstanding by the Latin translator, and the NIV is probably right in its interpretation of the verbs as referring especially to a past event.[17]

Malebranche also uses Isaiah 45:7 as a proof-text, which he quotes to

---

[15] J. A. Alexander, *Psalms* (Grand Rapids, Mich.: Zondervan, n.d. [originally 1864]), 427.

[16] Malebranche, 672: "Ego sum Dominus faciens omnia, extendens coelos solus, stabiliens terram, et nullus mecum."

[17] See P. Joüon and T. Muraoka, *A Grammar of Biblical Hebrew* (Rome: Editrice Pontificio Istituto Biblico, 1993), §138e, cf. §121i.

the effect, "who creates the darkness as well as the light, who makes both good and evil."[18] According to Malebranche, only God can cause us evil; and this verse tells us that no evil occurs that God does not produce (cf. also Amos 3:6). We should first note that versions which render the word as "calamity/disaster/woe" instead of "evil" (e.g., RSV, NASB, NIV, NRSV) are probably on the right track in view of the opposition to "peace" (Hebrew *šālôm*; the word "good" in Malebranche's text is inexplicable).[19] Second, the verse says nothing that a supernaturalist or providentialist would have difficulty with: It asserts God's ultimate sovereignty over all circumstances and leaves out of view the means he might use to exercise that sovereignty. The main thing that is relevant to the context is that such sovereignty is "hidden" (v. 15), and is to be clung to by faith.

I have already mentioned two verses about the origin of children, namely Jeremiah 1:5 and Psalm 139:13, both of which refer to God "forming" the embryo in its mother's womb.[20] To begin with, we note the contexts and communicative purposes of these texts. Jeremiah recounts his call to prophetic ministry in exalted terms in Jeremiah 1:4-10. In particular, God had settled on Jeremiah as a prophet before he was born, before God "formed" him in the womb. It is sufficient for our purposes here to recognize that the text says nothing about the presence or lack of *means* God may have used for the forming; instead, the particular communication needs to focus on God's sovereign role in the whole process in order to convey the weightiness of Jeremiah's mission.

Psalm 139:13-16 presents a similar picture. The psalmist has written a hymn for every member of the covenant people to sing in worship (i.e., it is not just the author's spiritual autobiography). It is common to think of this psalm as a celebration of God's omniscience, but it is not really concerned with omniscience as such. Instead the psalm enables God's people to sing words of delight in the fact that God knows them through and through, and there is no place in the whole universe they could go that would keep God from showering his love and grace on them. Some people think that in verses 7-12 the author has a guilty conscience and *wants* to flee, but that cannot be so. He opened in verses 1-6 with an affirmation of faith and of a clear conscience, and in verse 10 he speaks of God "leading" him, which is a word for God's tender care (cf. Ps. 23:3; 73:24). And in verses 11-13 he argues that not even darkness could hide him from God's care.

---

[18] Malebranche, 682, but the note gives the reference as Isa. 47:7.

[19] The footnote gives the Latin: "faciens pacem [note: this is 'peace', corresponding to the Hebrew; the text has the translation 'good'] et creans malum" (Isa. 45:7 in the Vulgate).

[20] Malebranche, 672, lists Job 10:8; 2 Macc. 7:22-23, to which these comments would also apply.

And what is the proof for the psalmist's argument? Verses 13-18, which describe his life in a "dark place," i.e., his mother's womb (note how v. 13 begins with "for," which means that it explains what comes before). As a believing member of the covenant people, the psalmist recognizes that God's special covenant love had been active in his life even when he was an embryo.[21] And so, in verse 17 he declares how precious he finds God's thoughts; and verses 23-24 are a prayer that God will help him continue to experience that special love all his life long and on into eternity.[22] Hence the stress in these verses is on the intimacy of God's involvement with the psalmist at the earliest stages of his life, and the divine supervision and special care in all these details. That is, the psalmist does not want the users of this psalm to lose sight of this crucial component of the religious worldview. Like the Jeremiah passage, however, this psalm makes no comment on the presence or lack of instrumentalities—and why should it, since such considerations would only cloud the picture with concerns foreign to the communicative purpose?

Finally, consider two passages that describe great military exploits of Israelites. The first summarizes what happened as a result of Deborah's encouraging Barak to fight the Canaanite army of Jabin, whose general was Sisera. There was a hard-fought battle, and Jael killed Sisera in her tent by a ruse; in Judges 4:23 we read, "On that day God subdued Jabin, the Canaanite king, before the Israelites." See? *God* did it.

Second Samuel 23:9-12, a passage about two of David's heroic warriors, is even more pointed (NIV):

> Next to him was Eleazar son of Dodai the Ahohite. As one of the three mighty men, he was with David when they taunted the Philistines gathered [at Pas Dammim] for battle. Then the men of Israel retreated, but he stood his ground and struck down the Philistines till his hand grew tired and froze to the sword. The LORD brought about a great victory that day. The troops returned to Eleazar, but only to strip the dead.
>
> Next to him was Shammah son of Agee the Hararite. When the Philistines banded together at a place where there was a field full of lentils, Israel's troops fled from them. But Shammah took his stand

---

[21] For a discussion of the proper interpretation of the Hebrew phrase of v. 14, frequently rendered "I am fearfully and wonderfully made," but which is more accurately "I have been awesomely distinguished [i.e., marked out as a member of God's people]," cf. my "Psalm 139:14: 'Fearfully and Wonderfully Made'?" *Presbyterion* 25:2 (Fall 1999) 115-120.

[22] According to Franz Delitzsch, *Psalms* (Keil-Delitzsch; English translation, Grand Rapids, Mich.: Eerdmans, 1980 [original German 1867]), the "hurtful/offensive way" in v. 24 should be taken as the "way to torment," while the "everlasting way" is the "way to eternal life."

in the middle of the field. He defended it and struck the Philistines down, and the LORD brought about a great victory.

Eleazar and Shammah took their lives in their hands, fought intense and bloody hand-to-hand combat, and found themselves exhausted at the end—and "*the LORD brought about a great victory that day.*" We can't help wondering what Eleazar and Shammah thought of that! However that may be, these passages say nothing to deny the causal contributions of Deborah, Barak, Jael, Eleazar, and Shammah; they instead invite readers to see beyond these to the purposes of God that are being carried out amid human courage.

In chapter 10 I intend to discuss briefly the limits to the intelligibility of God's providential oversight of the world's events, and limits to the recognizability of his wisdom that makes all those events serve his personally oriented purposes. These passages must be set against that background, and are part of the Bible's inculcation and nourishment of the outlook of faith. Hence I would be far from dismissing them when I try to identify their communicative purpose. That purpose, however, in no way supports occasionalism.

DIVINE SOVEREIGNTY

Many biblical passages assert the completeness of God's sovereignty over his world. For example, Ephesians 1:11 describes God as "the one who works all things according to the counsel of his will." And the prophet Isaiah spoke of God's sovereignty in a practical way; that is, God is so great that the great world power of Assyria cannot prevent him from carrying out his plan (14:24-27):

> The Lord of Hosts has sworn, saying, "Is it not just as I planned, thus it happened, and just as I purposed, so it will stand? (Namely,) to break Assyria in my land, and upon my hills I shall trample him; and his [Assyria's] yoke will leave from being upon them [Judeans], and his burden will leave from being upon his [Judah's] shoulder.
> "This is the purpose that is purposed upon all the earth, and this is the hand that is stretched out over all the nations. For the Lord of Hosts has purposed, and who will frustrate (his purpose); and his hand is stretched out, and who will turn it back?"

Other texts include even the evil actions of people (Gen. 50:20; Acts 2:23; 4:28) under the rubric of God's sovereignty. This is indeed a problem, which I intend to comment on in chapter 10; but it is not a problem that, say, supernaturalism has and occasionalism solves. The problem comes from asserting that human choices are real, not from asserting that there is such a thing as nature. Indeed, if we set the notion of nature in the context of the divine verdict of "very good" (Gen. 1:31), we see that it in no way provides a barrier to the fulfilling of God's plan. After all, "good" means "according to God's wishes"!

I conclude that none of the passages treated in this chapter is in any way incompatible with supernaturalism. They may be construed in a way that suits providentialism, but only at the expense of the biblical idea of special divine action. Occasionalism typically claims these verses for itself; and though some of the texts on their surface tend that way, upon closer examination they do not. Indeed, many of them actually take for granted the causal contribution of created things!

Part Three

THEOLOGICAL
EVALUATION

Eight

Evaluation of Rival Views

In this chapter I want to revisit the cases for occasionalism and providentialism presented in chapter 3, in light of the exegetical work of chapters 4–7. I do this because occasionalism and providentialism are typically seen as alternatives to the more conventional supernaturalism. In chapter 9 we will consider supernaturalism more fully.

Supernaturalism, we recall, affirms the reality of God's action in both the "natural" events (created things upheld by divine preservation and concurrence) and the "supernatural" ones (qualitatively special divine action). Providentialism holds that all events are, in principle, both "natural" and "providential" (i.e., divine preservation and concurrence are sufficient to explain them). Occasionalism denies the category of "natural" altogether, and claims that what we call "causes" are merely the *occasions* for God to produce the effects—without created things making any causal contribution.

ASSESSMENT OF THE "BIBLICAL THEOLOGY" CASE FOR OCCASIONALISM

Recall from chapter 3 that "biblical theology" authors commonly begin with a suspicion of philosophical enterprises as "Greek" in their outlook. I have argued that this is not in any way automatically the case. If a philosopher is dry, or even if he is a hair-splitter in treating biblical material, that may mean he is insensitive to the nature of the texts he is supposedly dealing with. But, *abusus usum non tollit:* "abuse does not nullify proper use."

When it comes to particular exegesis, the common assertions about the "Hebrew mind" being unable to think in terms other than God's direct action in everything do not seem to me to be based on sound interpretation of the texts from which these assertions supposedly derive. For example, put J. P. Ross's statement, "When he is asked *why*, the answer that leaps to the Israelite's mind is in terms of God; the language of physical causation does not occur to him," against Proverbs 30:33, "For squeezing milk *brings out* butter, and squeezing the nose *brings out* blood, and squeezing anger *brings out* strife," or 1 Samuel 28:20, "Moreover there was no strength in him *because* he had not eaten bread all the day and all the night." These texts and many others do in fact use the language of physical causation; and, it would appear, they do so because the authors took it for granted that such causation was operative.

So when Ross says, "Israel did not believe in an autonomous nature, and consequently did not have to ask how God intervened in it—the modern problem of miracles," he is saying nothing worth discussing, since he has employed the word *autonomous* in a skewed fashion.

Eichrodt's claim that the Old Testament asserts that "the bestowal of rain and fertility is the direct gift of Yahweh" is also misleading. The passages discussed certainly present such things as being under God's control to accomplish his purposes; but those passages do not explicate a mechanism by which God exercises this control. In fact, Deuteronomy 11:13-17, which asserts divine control over the rain, assumes that the rain has causal powers that make its giving a blessing and its withholding something to be feared.

ASSESSMENT OF BERKOUWER'S CASE FOR OCCASIONALISM

Berkouwer is much more sophisticated than the "biblical theologians" but no more successful. His contention that "the use of the terms first and second causes implies that God is only the most important cause among equal causes" is probably untrue historically, except as a critique of an abuse. And hence we would repeat, *abusus usum non tollit.* We would say the same to his fear that such talk leads to the "staticizing of the God-concept," since nothing proves that this language *must* lead to such a result. And when he says, "We are unmistakably taught the absolute dependence of all creatures on the work of God. There is no terrain in which man can escape being defined by the activity of God," nothing I have treated in chapter 7 is opposed to that; indeed nothing in supernaturalism at its best is opposed to it.

As I pointed out in chapter 3, when Berkouwer refers to "an incidental intervention into an otherwise hermetically sealed nature," this is a caricature of the supernaturalist position and does not need to be taken seriously.

Because of his importance and influence, I want to consider some of Berkouwer's exegetical specifics more closely. For example, he argues that, "The virgin birth is not presented in Scripture as a formal *contra naturam*. It is presented in the light of redemption and of the revelation of God in the flesh through the assumption of human nature."[1] We should reject this as an argument against supernaturalism, for the following reasons: 1) the actual texts of Matthew 1:18-20; Luke 1:34-35, as treated in chapter 6; 2) *contra naturam* ("against nature") is not necessarily the best term for this supernatural event (cf. chapter 9 below); 3) it is not obvious how a supernatural act of God and an alleged scriptural presentation "in the light of redemption," etc., are actually contrary.

Berkouwer goes on to say that, "In the miracles following this one [i.e., the virgin birth], miracles worked by Christ himself, we observe the powerful signs of the approaching kingdom";[2] and, in discussing the healing of the man born blind (John 9), "Everything in the story circles, not around a logical and natural deduction from a determined fact to God as 'first cause'. . . but around the meaning of the miracle, which culminates in salvation and which summons faith and calls to worship."[3] But Berkouwer seems to have missed a key point, namely that it is precisely *because* the miracles of Jesus are often emblematic of the coming of salvation that a supernaturalist description of them is so suitable (the advance of the kingdom is the work of the Holy Spirit).[4] Note that the passage in John 9 explicitly makes this connection in verses 39-41, where there is a direct parallel between physical and spiritual blindness, and our blindness of heart needs a supernatural cure. Hence if we suppose that the Gospel writers wanted to make a valid analogy between these healings and the transformation of one's inner life, then in light of the material on religious renewal treated in chapter 6, which favors the supernaturalist interpretation, we should suppose that the healing is itself a special operation of divine power on "nature."

ASSESSMENT OF MALEBRANCHE'S EXEGETICAL CASE FOR OCCASIONALISM

Malebranche's exegetical case for occasionalism, as we have seen, appears most fully in his fifteenth elucidation. It depends on a number of interpretive moves, each of which needs to be questioned. In places I have offered what seems to me a stronger argument for his position than he himself did. And his rule for resolving apparent contradictions by only taking literally those affirmations that are contrary to common opinion, which is another version of Berkeley's "think with the learned and speak with the vulgar,"

---

[1] G. C. Berkouwer, *The Providence of God* (Grand Rapids, Mich.: Eerdmans, 1952), 209-210.

[2] Berkouwer, 210.

[3] Berkouwer, 219.

[4] As Pascal, *Pensées*, no. 851 (Brunschvicg) / no. 903 (Krailsheimer) put it, "Miracles prove the power which God has over hearts, by that which he exercises over bodies" ("Les miracles prouvent le pouvoir que Dieu a sur les coeurs, par celui qu'il exerce sur les corps").

seems to wear a bit thin when we examine the actual passages to which he wanted to apply this rule. It also involves an a priori commitment to a hermeneutic that is not based on the principle of conversational cooperation which discourse analysts have shown to be in effect in an act of communication; indeed, it actually flouts that principle.

None of what Malebranche called the "infinity of such passages" to prove his position requires us to overthrow the simple interpretation of a host of other passages. In fact, it is quite natural to interpret these texts in a way that is entirely consistent with supernaturalism; they enrich it by keeping before the believer's eyes certain facets of the theological position that are easy to overlook.

So the exegetical and theological arguments that have been marshaled in favor of occasionalism cannot pass critical scrutiny. What about providentialism?

ASSESSMENT OF PROVIDENTIALISM

Recall from chapter 3 that it is difficult to find a thoroughgoing providentialist. What we find instead are writers who have a marked preference for this kind of explanation, and writers who are providentialists in specific areas of study (e.g., in the origin of life). If we look at some of the explanations that such authors have suggested for biblical events, some of them have plausibility (e.g., the first nine Egyptian plagues, but see chapter 9 below), and some of them do not (e.g., the unique conception of Jesus). So as a general principle, Millard's comments are valid:[5]

> Natural explanations of the events in many of the stories [in the Bible] can be seriously entertained, following the indications of the texts themselves. . . . To disclose the mechanism of a "miracle" is not to deny its nature, for that lay more in its timeliness than its manner.

Nevertheless (as Millard himself insists) the biblical authors present some events as unusual, not simply in the actuarial sense of "rare" but in the very mechanism by which they came about. In chapter 6 we saw that the creation, the tenth plague in Egypt, the virgin conception of Jesus, his mighty works, his resurrection, and his (future) return to call all humanity to judgment clearly fit into this latter class. Providentialism has no capacity for these, and we should therefore reject it.

But what about the story of life's origin? Does providentialism accurately represent the biblical material there? I shall consider that in chapter 11.

---

[5] A. R. Millard, "The Old Testament and History: Some Considerations," *Faith and Thought* 110 (1983), 34-53, at 51.

Nine

Theological Conclusions

In chapter 4 we recognized that the existence of something we could call "nature," and "natural properties" and "causal powers," is a part of the "common sense" apparatus with which every human being deals with the world. Both supernaturalism and providentialism affirm this "common sense," with some important modifications. In particular, neither of these views allows that "nature" is in any way self-existent or independent of God; instead they insist that it is a creation, it is real, and we can know something of it. Supernaturalism in particular has the doctrines of divine concurrence and government built into it. It does not claim that this recognition of radical dependence arises from observation of nature itself. I also have tried to specify what sorts of things we would need to find in the biblical texts if we were to go beyond important *revisions* to "common sense" to a complete *overthrow* of it.

I believe that providentialism has shown itself woefully inadequate as an interpretive scheme for the biblical literature. I am only slightly less confident in rejecting occasionalism. At the very least, the proponent of occasionalism must admit that the biblical texts alleged to require a radical rejection of our ordinary perception of the world do no such thing. This in itself would warrant retention of supernaturalism; but in light of the evident endorsement of causation in the texts examined in chapter 5, there really is no reason to look outside of supernaturalism.

However, that does not fully settle all the questions. Can we articulate more carefully just what we should mean by "nature" and "supernature," so as not to allow for the kinds of abuses and misunderstandings that have provoked sensitive theologians? Can we find a way to describe conditions under which special operations of divine power would be detectable? Can we give criteria on whether a particular biblical event is supernatural, and to what extent? Can we say something about how prayer fits into this scheme?

DEFINING "NATURAL" AND "SUPERNATURAL"

In the light of what we have discussed so far, we can support the following definitions:

> *Natural:* God made the universe from nothing and endowed the things that exist with "natural properties"; he preserves those properties, and he also confirms their interactions in a web of cause-and-effect relations.

> *Supernatural:* God is also free to "inject" special operations of his power into this web at any time, e.g., by adding objects, directly causing events, enabling an agent to do what its own natural properties would never have made it capable of, and by imposing organization, according to his purposes.

For a reference point, compare this with Blaise Pascal's definition of *miracle* as "an effect which exceeds the natural power of the means which are employed for it; and what is not a miracle is an effect which does not exceed the natural power of the means which are employed for it."[1] My definitions are akin to Pascal's.[2]

Note several things about these definitions: To begin with, the distinction between "natural" and "supernatural" events is not the degree of directness or immediacy of God's action, or the presence or absence of means: Concurrence (crucial to natural events) is immediate, and Jesus healed "using" mud made from dirt and spit (John 9:6, a supernatural event; cf. vv. 16, 31-33). These definitions are also free of such language as "violation of the laws of nature" as David Hume used. This will have important consequences when we think about apologetics.

A final feature for us to notice about these definitions is that they make detection of a supernatural event analogous to the detection of "imposed design," for which Stonehenge will provide a good example. This leads us to our next section.

THE DETECTABILITY OF SUPERNATURAL EVENTS

If I define "imposed design" as,[3]

---

[1] Blaise Pascal, *Pensées*, no. 804 (Brunschvicg) / no. 891 (Krailsheimer): "*Miracle.* C'est un effet qui excède la force naturelle des moyens qu'on y emploie; et non-miracle est un effet qui n'excède pas la force naturelle des moyens qu'on y emploie."

[2] This is also similar to Paul Gwynne's definition of "special divine action" in *Special Divine Action* (Rome: Gregorian University Press, 1996), 24: "God brings it about that some particular outcome is different from what it would have been had only natural, created factors been operative."

[3] We could also call this "design-with-respect-to-organization" or "teleological design."

the imposition of structure upon some object or collection of
objects for some purpose, where the structure and the purpose are
not inherent in the properties of the components but make use of
these properties,

then I have an intuitive criterion for identifying such "design," and possibly
for identifying at least some supernatural events.

It is of course a shortcoming of this notion that it is intuitive. There is
research underway to make it more than that,[4] but that may be of limited use
in examining, say, biblical passages that do not have the necessary amount
of information. We may also feel cautious about using our criterion, since
we do not know everything there is to know about the relevant natural properties. On the other hand, we know enough about some things that we can
have confidence when speaking of them (for example, the creation and Jesus'
conception, resurrection, and future return, as mentioned at the end of chapter 8). As C. S. Lewis pointed out in *Miracles*, "No doubt a modern gynae-
cologist knows several things about birth and begetting which St. Joseph did
not know. But those things do not concern the main point—that a virgin
birth is contrary to the course of nature. And St. Joseph obviously knew
that."[5] But I shall return to this point in chapter 10.

At this point someone is likely to complain that this leads to "the God-
of-the-gaps." This label designates the fallacy of ascribing anything we do not
understand to special divine action. This is upsetting to faith since, as we
come to understand more of the world, these "gaps" shrink and the whole
process appears to squeeze God out. From within a supernaturalist perspective there are several parts to the answer to this, and I shall take it up
again in discussing "intelligent design" in chapter 11. I would of course point
out that the "ordinary" or "natural" course of things is in fact God's action,
so he is not being crowded out. I would also mention that some contexts are
more appropriate than others for appealing to such special divine action.

But more to the present point, I would observe that there are "gaps" and
then there are "gaps." That is, the gaps come from different sources. I cannot explain why a volcano erupted when it did; the explanatory gap is due
to my *ignorance* of the processes (which are in principle explicable, other
things being equal). But I also cannot explain what it is about the rocks in

---

[4] William Dembski, *The Design Inference: Eliminating Chance Through Small Probabilities* (Cambridge,
England: Cambridge University Press, 1998; originally Ph.D. dissertation, University of Illinois at Chicago,
1996). Jonathan Edwards's *Treatise Concerning Religious Affections* (*The Works of Jonathan Edwards*
[Edinburgh: Banner of Truth, 1974], i:234-343) is an attempt to provide criteria for identifying supernatural moral transformation.
[5] C. S. Lewis, *Miracles: A Preliminary Study* (New York: Macmillan/Simon and Schuster, 1960), chapter
7, paragraph 5.

Stonehenge that leads to their being in their configuration. I think any reasonable person would recognize that this is not a matter of ignorance of the properties of rocks, but a matter of the *properties* of the rocks themselves. That is, the first kind of gap may be called a *lacuna ignorantiae causâ* (a gap due to ignorance) while the second is a *lacuna naturae causâ* (a gap due to the natures of the components). The identification of "imposed design" amounts to identifying *lacunae naturae causâ*.

This will not solve every problem that we might face in ascertaining whether a given event is the product of imposed design. But it will enable us to look for some clues to the biblical authors' assumptions about the metaphysical status of the events they record.

CAN WE IDENTIFY WHICH BIBLICAL EVENTS ARE "SUPERNATURAL"?

In chapter 6 I discussed a number of biblical passages that are fairly clear about the qualitatively special divine action involved in them. The virgin conception of Jesus is quite explicit, as we saw. We will have to admit, however, that not every biblical event that has been called a "miracle" comes with as much information on the means involved. In many cases the biblical author did not consider such information relevant to his point. In other cases we may make some reasonable assumptions, but we recognize that we end up having to take the author's word for what happened.

In the section at the end of chapter 4 regarding biblical vocabulary, we saw that the Bible does not clearly have special terms for supernatural events, so we cannot go by terminology exclusively. Instead we shall have to examine each case on its own and see how the author describes it.

For example, what shall we make of the Egyptian plagues? I mentioned in chapter 3 that many scholars have been impressed with Greta Hort's studies, which have related the first nine of the ten plagues to natural processes.[6] Even so, the tenth plague (death of the firstborn) must be reckoned as belonging "wholly to the realm of the supernatural."[7] But let's look a little closer: Just what might we legitimately mean by saying that the first nine plagues "bear a direct relation to natural phenomena in the Nile valley," in the light of the definitions and observations given above? We should pay careful attention to the actual text, and in Exodus 7:10-11 we have an indi-

---

[6] E.g., James Hoffmeier, "Egypt, Plagues In," in David Freedman et al., eds., *Anchor Bible Dictionary* (New York, Doubleday, 1992), ii:374a-378a; K. A. Kitchen, "Plagues of Egypt," in J. D. Douglas et al., eds., *The New Bible Dictionary* (Downers Grove, Ill.: InterVarsity, 1982), 943a-944b.

[7] Kitchen, 943a; cf. Hoffmeier, 375b. In chapter 6 I noted that the author of Wisdom also saw the final plague this way, and I gave exegetical reasons for endorsing his view.

cation. There we read that Moses and Aaron did what the Lord told them; then the Egyptian sorcerers did the same thing "by their secret arts" (Hebrew *bĕlahăṭêhem*). This continued until in the third plague (the gnats) the Egyptians could not counter Moses. We could at least suppose that Moses had supernatural knowledge of the coming progress of events in the Nile cycle; but this text actually implies more. The pattern is that Moses and Aaron acted and got a result, and then the sorcerers acted and got their result. This implies that some level of "operation" was taking place, since there is no hint that the "secret arts" of the Egyptians are merely a sham (only that they are not as powerful as Yahweh). Hence it is better to see these plagues as involving a supernatural employment of natural processes. As T. D. Alexander put it,[8]

> Furthermore, the text emphasizes the divine source of the events. This is indicated, for example, by the many references to Moses or Aaron stretching out their hands, or a staff, in order to bring about the sign. Although some of the signs may be associated with natural phenomena, their occurrence is clearly attributed to divine intervention.

By the same token, we can connect the parting of the Red Sea with "natural conditions prevailing in the area," namely the interactions of the water and the sand, the tides, and the winds that Cassuto describes.[9] The mention of a wind (Ex. 14:21) could favor a "special providence" interpretation (namely that the event resulted from a timely confluence of natural factors rather than from a special operation of God's power). Nevertheless, at the very least Moses knew when to raise his staff (v. 21), and he did this with the plagues, too (cf. 10:13). Also, note that the definition of "supernatural event" in no way rules out the use of means. Hence it seems to me that Cassuto's comments are in order, as long as we put them in a supernaturalist framework:[10]

> I have no wish whatsoever to rationalize the biblical story. The narrative clearly intends to relate a miraculous event, and whoever attempts to explain the entire episode rationally [read: naturalisti-

---

[8] T. D. Alexander, "Exodus," in D. A. Carson et al., eds., *The New Bible Commentary: Twenty-first Century Edition* (Downers Grove, Ill.: InterVarsity, 1994), 100a, b. Some authors, such as Kitchen and Hoffmeier, and U. Cassuto, *Exodus* (Jerusalem: Magnes, 1967), 98, use potentially ambiguous language about "making use of the created order." While I do not disagree with this, I am trying to be more specific about what that making use was supposed to be.

[9] Cassuto, *Exodus*, 167-168.

[10] Cassuto, *Exodus*, 168. Cf. also A. Hakham, *Sēfer Šēmôt* (*Exodus*, Da'at Miqra; Jerusalem: Mossad Harav Kook, 1991), 286-287.

cally] does not in fact interpret the text but projects his own ideas in place of those expressed by Scripture. But we should endeavour to understand how our text pictures the wondrous happening of which it tells, and what is the natural basis of the miracle described, for it is clear that *the Torah does not imply that laws of nature were changed but that a wonderful use was made of those laws.* (italics added)

After crossing the Red Sea dry shod, the Israelites came to a place they called Marah ("Bitter") because of the bitter water there (i.e., it contained large amounts of salts).[11] When the people could not drink the water, the Lord showed Moses a tree to throw into the water to sweeten it (Ex. 15:22-26). Recall the discussion in chapter 5 that showed that the Jewish teacher Ben Sira interpreted this as the divine revealing of natural properties of the wood (Ben Sira 38:5). Some commentators have supposed that instead the event is to be taken as supernatural, i.e., unrelated to any features of the wood, which would mean that Ben Sira was misusing the verse.[12] Nevertheless, Cassuto interpreted our text as,[13]

> *and the Lord showed him a* particular *tree*, the nature of which is to absorb the salt in the water and thus sweeten it. This property is found, according to the testimony of travellers, in one of the varieties of local brier.

The supernatural element would thus be the special revelation of this tree, as indicated by the expression "and the Lord showed him." This is significant because of the relationship of that verb with the noun *tôrâ*, the "instruction" God gave his people through Moses. Indeed, the text goes on (Ex. 15:26) to speak of the Israelites' need to attend to the Lord's expressed will, which they will receive from Moses. We may connect this with the theme in Proverbs that submitting to divine wisdom equips us to live in touch with reality.

Let's move out of the Pentateuch and consider just a few more events. In 1 Kings 18:30-38, Elijah wanted to prove to the people of Israel that Yahweh is the true God, and not Baal (whom they were inclined to serve, but whose 450 prophets had just failed to get him to light the fire of their sacrifice, vv. 20-29). Elijah built an altar, dug a trench, arranged the wood and meat on the altar, and soaked everything with water three times, filling the trench. After Elijah had prayed, "Fire of the Lord fell and consumed the

---

[11] So Cassuto, *Exodus*, 183.

[12] This is the position of Oesterley's commentary on Ben Sira, as we saw.

[13] Cassuto, *Exodus*, 184. The italics are in the original, and come from the way in which the commentary interweaves the Bible text (italics) with its comments.

sacrifice and the wood and the stones and the dirt and licked up the water which was in the trench" (v. 38). As we saw in chapter 3, Colin Brown suggested that, "The fire falling on the sacrifice of Elijah on Mount Carmel was probably a thunderbolt."[14] It appears that Brown prefers a natural explanation for the event. Does this satisfy the text? Probably not. Whether or not the means was a lightning strike does not settle whether or not this was a supernatural event. As a number of commentators point out, if this is lightning it fell from a cloudless sky (the clouds did not come until later, v. 45).[15] Further, as the Israeli scholar M. H. Segal noted, the pouring of water ensures that no one can say that the fire resulted from the dryness and heat of the drought.[16] From the perspective of this study we may say that the application of water is specifically to show that natural factors alone are not enough to explain the event.[17]

Consider also the three friends of Daniel, whom the Babylonian king Nebuchadnezzar ordered thrown into a furnace (Dan. 3:19-30). In verse 19 the king became angry with Shadrach, Meshach, and Abednego because they would not bow down before the golden image he had set up; so he ordered the furnace (into which refusers were to be cast, cf. v. 6) heated up to seven times its normal heat. Nebuchadnezzar's warriors tied up the three Jews in their full clothing to throw them into the furnace, and in throwing the men into the furnace the warriors themselves were killed by its heat, while the three Jews fell into the furnace still tied up (vv. 20-23). To the watching Nebuchadnezzar's astonishment, however, he saw the three Jews walking around the inside of the furnace, untied and unharmed, accompanied by a fourth person who looked like "a son of the gods."[18] Nebuchadnezzar bade the men come out, and all his court found that the fire had had no effect at all on the men's bodies, hair, or clothing. Not even the smell of fire remained on them. Nebuchadnezzar concluded that the three Jews' God had sent his angel and that this explained their deliverance. As we saw in chapter 3, Brown suggested that, "A sudden gust of flame or explosion killed the men who brought Shadrach, Meshach and Abednego down to where the kilns

---

[14] Colin Brown's section in W. Mundle, O. Hufius, C. Brown, "Miracle, Wonder, Sign," in C. Brown, ed., *New International Dictionary of New Testament Theology* (Exeter, England: Paternoster, 1976), ii:620-635, at 628.

[15] E.g., William S. LaSor, "Kings," in D. Guthrie et al., eds., *The New Bible Commentary: Revised* (Grand Rapids, Mich.: Eerdmans, 1970), 344b (drawing on work by H. H. Rowley); John J. Bimson, "Kings," in Carson et al., eds., *New Bible Commentary: Twenty-first Century Edition*, 359b.

[16] Quoted by Y. Kiel, *Sēfer Mělākîm* (Kings, Da'at Miqra; Jerusalem: Mossad Harav Kook, 1989), 372b.

[17] Cf. also D. J. Wiseman, *1 and 2 Kings* (Tyndale Old Testament Commentary; Downers Grove, Ill.: InterVarsity, 1993), 170; Iain Provan, *1 and 2 Kings* (New International Biblical Commentary; Peabody, Mass.: Hendrickson, 1995), 138-139.

[18] Verse 25: the Aramaic is *dāmēh lěbar 'ělāhîn*, "like a son of the gods" or perhaps "of God" (though the former is more likely in a Babylonian's mouth).

were, but the latter survived their ordeal possibly protected by their clothing mentioned in the narrative." This natural explanation is quite inadequate
for the text. First, note that the heat killed the warriors who had less expo-
sure to the fire than the three Jews. Second, the mention of clothing is more
likely to communicate the suddenness of the seizure of the men rather than
to imply any properties of the clothing. Third, even if these clothes were supposed to be some sort of asbestos (but what evidence do we have that the
author of Daniel was aware of such a substance?), the men would still have
been cooked inside the furnace; and verse 27 tells us that none of their flesh
or hair was singed, and not even any smell clung to them, which is incompatible with such a theory (since their clothing did not cover them entirely).
Fourth, the heavenly being (vv. 25, 28) is most likely an agent of God's special action. And finally, as we saw in chapter 5, the letter to the Hebrews
interpreted the event as a special action due to the three men's faith (Heb.
11:34).[19] The narrator has given us plenty of clues to see that he thought
more factors than just the natural ones were relevant here.

There are of course many other special events narrated in the Bible, connected with Moses, Elijah and Elisha, Daniel, and Jesus and the apostles: the
manna, the quail, the water from the rock, the sudden leprosy on Miriam,
the floating axe-head, special provisions of food, raising of dead people,
walking on water, stilling storms, healings, and so forth. It would take a large
work to comment on all of them. I believe that what I have covered here will
give some idea of how to read carefully in order to answer these questions.

HOW DOES PRAYER FIT IN?

Nothing can be clearer than that the Bible encourages believing people to
pray, and to pray with requests. A simple example is the Lord's Prayer,
with its "Give us today our daily bread." Indeed, James 4:2-3 and Matthew
7:7-8 are unequivocal: The making of the request (in the right frame of
soul) is connected with the outcome, even in a causal way (cf. also James
5:16b-18, which asserts plainly the causal effect). The Bible certainly war-
rants what C. S. Lewis called "Pascal's magnificent dictum":[20] "Why God
established prayer: 1. To communicate to his creatures the dignity of
causality. . . ."

Now there are a host of questions that arise in this matter that I do not
intend to address here, since I am not writing a manual on petitionary prayer

---

[19] Cf. E. J. Young, "Daniel," in Guthrie et al., eds., *New Bible Commentary: Revised*, 692b-693a.
[20] Pascal, *Pensées*, no. 513 (Brunschvicg) / no. 930 (Krailsheimer): "Pourquoi Dieu a établi la prière: 1°
Pour communiquer à ses créatures la dignité de la causalité." The reference to C. S. Lewis is *Prayer: Letters
to Malcolm* (London: Collins, 1966), letter x.

and its conditions for being answered and how this fits into the wisdom and goodness of God and our evident lack of them both. I am going to take for granted that God is represented as telling his people to pray; that he promises to act on those requests in a way that is related to what his people ask for (i.e., the "answering" is not a purely mechanical reply, apart from relational factors; and God does not promise to forsake his own wisdom and goodness); and that he expects his people to do their asking in a humble, penitent, and moral frame of soul. The pious are not asked to solve all the problems, but to perform certain actions, confident that the God whom they worship deserves to be believed. An instructive example of the practical issue comes from Lewis's *The Magician's Nephew*, where Aslan has sent the two children Polly and Digory on a mission with Fledge the flying horse, and they suddenly realize that they do not have any food with them (except grass for the horse):[21]

> Polly and Digory stared at one another in dismay.
> "Well, I *do* think someone might have arranged about our meals," said Digory.
> "I'm sure Aslan would have, if you'd asked him," said Fledge.
> "Wouldn't he know without being asked?" said Polly.
> "I've no doubt he would," said the Horse (still with his mouth full). "But I've a sort of idea he likes to be asked."

I want to reflect on the metaphysics of answered prayer in the light of the understanding of divine action that arises from the Bible. Are we to believe that the outcome of events will be different depending on whether or not we pray? Why should prayer accompany operations on the natural world? And are the "answers" to be explained as supernatural, special providences,[22] concurrence, or what?

We may start with an example from the life of George Müller, who ran an orphanage at Bristol, as John Houghton summarizes:[23]

---

[21] C. S. Lewis, *The Magician's Nephew* (New York: HarperCollins, 1994 [originally 1955]), chapter 12.

[22] I do not want to deny what C. S. Lewis said in *Miracles: A Preliminary Study* (New York: Macmillan/Simon and Schuster, 1960), appendix B, "On 'Special Providences'": "It seems to me, therefore, that we must abandon the idea that there is any special class of events (apart from miracles) which can be distinguished as 'specially providential.' Unless we are to abandon the conception of Providence altogether, and with it the belief in efficacious prayer, it follows that all events are equally providential. If God directs the course of events at all then he directs the movement of every atom at every moment." This is correct as to the metaphysics; but it is convenient to have a category to designate those events in which God's supervision becomes in some sense visible to the pious. In the section in chapter 10 on the problem of evil, we will see that Scripture teaches us to expect that, in ordinary providence, God's purposiveness is *not* discernible by even the best of believers.

[23] John Houghton, *The Search for God: Can Science Help?* (Oxford: Lion, 1995), 163-164. This chapter in Houghton appeared as "What Happens When We Pray?" *Science and Christian Belief* 7 (1995), 3-20.

On 9 March 1842 the situation at the orphanage was completely
desperate, resources being completely exhausted. Prayers were
made for provision. The morning post came with no relief.
However, at the latest possible moment, a letter at first wrongly
delivered arrived, with a gift for £10 from someone living in Dublin.
The answer to those morning prayers began some days before in
Dublin; it involved the donor, the postal service and various modes
of transport culminating in the arrival of the cheque at the crucial
moment. Thousands of similar instances occur in Müller's story.

Now it is clear that for this to be an answer to Müller's prayer, God must have
in some sense "foreseen" him praying and moved the donor to give several
days before and governed a number of ancillary events. There are issues I do
not propose to solve right now, such as the relationship of God to time, and
the connection between his foreknowledge and his decree.[24] I shall simply
state that the Bible sees God as both being able to act in time and as tran-
scending it, since it along with space and matter is his creation. He is also
able to govern future events according to his will (cf. the section on divine
sovereignty in chapter 7).

For an illustration we may use the image given in C. S. Lewis:[25]

If you picture Time as a straight line along which we have to travel,
then you must picture God as the whole page on which the line is
drawn. We come to the parts of the line one by one: we have to leave
A behind before we get to B, and cannot reach C until we leave B
behind. God, from above or outside or all round, contains the whole
line, and sees it all.

This means that God is not constrained by time any more than he is by
space. Lewis's image allows us to focus our questions about the mechanisms
by which God governs these events. Recall from chapter 3 that supernaturalists say that God can govern events by any combination of concurrence,
influencing human decisions, setting anterior conditions, and special operations of his power. In the discussion of Ben Sira 38:1-15 in chapter 5 we saw
that this underlies the prayers that Ben Sira urged the physicians to offer,
even as they employed the natural powers God had enabled them to discover. We may draw on our discussion of special divine action in the moral

---

[24] My own conviction is basically that of Paul Helm in *The Providence of God* (Downers Grove, Ill.:
InterVarsity, 1994).
[25] C. S. Lewis, *Mere Christianity* (New York: Macmillan, 1952), book iv, chapter 3, "Time and Beyond
Time"; similarly in *Miracles*, appendix B, "On 'Special Providences.'" Similar imagery appears in Houghton,
The Search for God, 163-167; Donald MacKay, *Science, Chance and Providence* (New York: Oxford
University Press, 1978), 52-55.

and spiritual sphere to see that Paul's prayers for effective ministry (e.g., Col. 4:3-4) and spiritual growth of his converts (e.g., Col. 1:9-12; Phil. 1:9-11; etc.) are requests for qualitatively special effects, i.e., events not produced solely from within the web of cause and effect.

Some authors express interest in how this correlates with science. For example, Houghton says:[26]

> Because I am a meteorologist, I am often asked what I think about praying about the weather—for instance, praying for rain. If I believe that forecasts of tomorrow's weather are possible because it is dependent on processes in the atmosphere which can be described scientifically, how can I also believe that prayer can have anything to do with it? My answer is that I believe that it is entirely appropriate to pray about the weather, as it is about anything else that is of concern to us. But I also, as a scientist, believe that the movements of the atmosphere follow scientific laws. In [a previous chapter] I spoke of two stories, the "scientific story" (the one that is appropriate to weather forecasting) and the "faith story" (the one that relates to my prayers). I explained that these two stories are complementary; the existence of the "scientific story" in no way invalidates the "faith story".

Now, Houghton himself is a supernaturalist, at least in theory; but some may take this way of thinking too far.[27] That is, they may suppose that the existence of the "scientific story" excludes the possibility of God's feeding new events into nature. But this would be a confusion resulting from the language about "scientific laws." To the extent that such laws are accurate (and with complex matters like the weather that is an important qualifier), they describe the normal behavior of the things under observation. They cannot in any way exclude the possibility of "interference"; they cannot even prevent humans from doing things today that render yesterday's forecast invalid, and *a fortiori* they cannot rule out the possibility of God doing something special.

Would it be responsible for us to pray for such an alteration? I do not think we can answer that question except by returning to the purpose and manner of prayer for the pious. God has, generally speaking, not invited humans to dictate to him the *mechanism* by which he must grant their requests. He has instead instructed them to lay their concerns before him, all the time seeking to be humbly conformed to the character he delights in.

---

[26] Houghton, *The Search for God*, 154.
[27] Donald MacKay almost seems to do so in *Science, Chance and Providence*, 54-55, 65.

In such a frame of soul they can leave it to God to see to the propriety of the request and the suitable mechanism for granting it. As C. S. Lewis put it,[28]

> Your other question is one which, I think, really gets in pious people's way. It was, you remember, "How important must a need or desire be before we can properly make it the subject of petition?" . . .
>
> It may well be that the desire can be laid before God only as a sin to be repented; but one of the best ways of learning this is to lay it before God. . . .
>
> If we lay all the cards on the table, God will help us to moderate the excesses.

But can we tell whether a specific event *is* in fact an answer to our prayers? Again let me draw on Lewis:[29] "It is never possible to prove empirically that a given, non-miraculous event was or was not an answer to prayer."[30] In another place he shows that the demand for experimental testing of the efficacy of prayer is not only blasphemous but actually contrary to the nature of prayer as interpersonal request.[31] He points out that we have the same problem when we ask about the causal efficacy of requests we make of our fellow humans. We must rely, not on "scientific testing,"[32] but on what I call "the calculus of interpersonal relations." Or as Lewis put it,

> Those who best know a man best know whether, when he did what they asked, he did it because they asked. I think those who best know God will best know whether he sent me to the barber's shop because the barber prayed.

This reliance on the believer's judgment is not a defect, but arises from the very nature of the situation. Petitionary prayer does not have as its primary function the convincing of skeptics.

---

[28] Lewis, *Prayer: Letters to Malcolm*, letter iv.

[29] Lewis, *Miracles*, appendix B.

[30] We might add that our ignorance often reduces our ability to say whether some given event was itself supernatural in its origin.

[31] Lewis, "The Efficacy of Prayer," in Lewis, *The World's Last Night* (New York: Harcourt, Brace, Jovanovich, 1973), 3-11 (originally in *Atlantic Monthly*, January, 1959).

[32] I do not agree with the label. I prefer instead to say that we have applied the tools of the *wrong science* to this matter.

Part Four

———

APOLOGETICS
AND SCIENCE

———

Ten

Is the Biblical Picture
Viable Today?

If the biblical view is something along the lines of the supernaturalism outlined in chapter 9, is it intellectually responsible for us modern people to embrace that view? Recall that we began chapter 1 with New Testament scholar Rudolph Bultmann's claim that it is not responsible to do so. Bultmann spoke from the perspective which in chapter 2 I called "theistic naturalism," which takes its cue from the "modern scientific outlook," which makes nature out to be impervious to divine "interference."

There are four kinds of objections to the biblical picture of God's involvement in the world he made, and they need not be atheistic in the strictest sense. The first objection I shall consider is the sort that comes from "rationalism," which tends to equate "laws of nature" with laws of God; for God to "violate" one of these would be for him to be inconsistent with himself. The second objection comes from empiricism, which may on the one hand argue that science has shown the physical world to be regular, and therefore we would not be scientific if we were to look for interferences with it, or may on the other hand argue that there are so many problems connected with believing the claims that such events have occurred that we are better off disbelieving every one of them. The third category of objections comes from postmodernism, which denies that we can really know the world in a way necessary for identifying a supernatural event—or, at least, no one outside the supernaturalist paradigm can be expected to agree to the claim that a supernatural event has occurred. Finally, there are the objections that collect around the traditional problem of evil: If God *can* perform supernatural actions, why doesn't he do so a lot more frequently?

Most discussions in the English-speaking world focus on the objections from the second category (empiricism), with a little notice of the fourth category (problem of evil), very little on the first (rationalism), and virtually none on the third (postmodernism).

THE PLACE OF WORLDVIEW COMMITMENTS IN IDENTIFYING DIVINE ACTION

Can someone who is not a believer be expected to agree that a supernatural event has taken place? Can "miracles" serve a reasonable role in promoting one's faith? Supernaturalists have a range of views on the matter, all the way from the strongly evidentialist approach associated with traditional apologetics (proof that something is a miracle is possible, which then counts as a proof of God's existence) to the more paradigm-relativistic approach of the modern era (since we believe the miracle accounts of Scripture only because we already believe the Bible, we cannot expect a nonbeliever to reason from credible miracles to divine agent).

Samuel Clarke represents a good summary of the evidentialist approach:[1]

> The Christian Revelation is positively and directly proved, to be actually and immediately sent to us from God, by the many infallible *Signs and Miracles*, which the Author of it worked publicly as the evidence of his Divine Commission.

The objection to this approach is that it involves us in a circular argument: After all, it is from the "Christian Revelation" itself that we get the *accounts* of "Signs and Miracles," so how do we know whether to believe them?

Both sides can appeal to biblical references: For example, Jesus in John 10:37-38 offers his "works" (which in John means his supernatural works such as healings; NIV renders the term interpretively as "miracles") as evidence for his person:[2]

> If I am not doing the works of my Father, don't believe me. But if I am doing them, even if you don't believe *me*, believe the *works*, that you might come to know and keep knowing that the Father is in me and I am in the Father.

---

[1] Samuel Clarke (1675–1729) was a philosophical theologian who is best remembered for his Boyle Lectures of 1704 (*Being and Attributes of God*) and of 1705 (*Discourse on Natural and Revealed Religion*). This quote is from the 1705 lectures, cited in Paul Helm, "The Miraculous," *Science and Christian Belief* 3 (1991), 83-95, at 84. Helm inclines toward the paradigm-relative side of the spectrum, as does Stephen T. Davis, "The Miracle at Cana: A Philosopher's Perspective," in D. Wenham and C. Blomberg, eds., *Gospel Perspectives, VI: The Miracles of Jesus* (Sheffield: JSOT Press, 1986), 419-442.
[2] Cf. also 2:23; 5:36; 10:25; 14:11; 15:24; Matt. 11:1-6.

On the other hand, Jesus refused to give "signs" on demand (e.g., Matt. 12:38-39), and even in places seemed to play down the role of signs in producing faith, e.g., Luke 16:31 where in a parable Abraham says to the rich man who asks to have Lazarus come back from the dead to warn his brothers (NIV):

> If they do not listen to Moses and the Prophets, they will not be convinced even if someone rises from the dead.

Philosophically, this ties in to the question about how people come to know things, and how their structure of commitments (worldview) relates to their experiences (empirical data). Under the influence of philosophers such as Thomas Kuhn (*The Structure of Scientific Revolutions*), it is appealing to say that we never know anything apart from the way our "paradigm" mediates it. Hence an adherent of a naturalistic paradigm will only interpret events in the light of his naturalism, which means he will only accept naturalistic explanations for data. Since, by this way of thinking, data do not of themselves produce paradigms, no amount of data can force the naturalist to reevaluate the paradigm.

I shall not here enter into a full evaluation of Kuhn and his line of thinking, but shall have to content myself with a few remarks before getting back to the theology.[3] In his monumental *Religion in an Age of Science*, the prominent writer on science and religion Ian Barbour describes the four criteria that theories must satisfy: agreement with data, internal coherence and simplicity, comprehensiveness, and the way they open up possibilities for explaining other things.[4] That is, there are standards that a paradigm must meet in order to be worth considering (which means that paradigms are subject to evaluation by criteria higher than themselves). I think further that there is such a thing as knowledge of the external world that transcends paradigms: Consider the common response to skunks among American Indians, European Americans, African Americans, and Asian Americans, all of whom may have very different worldviews but know to run like mad when the skunk takes up its position (and they have learned this either from experience or from testimony). Besides, even in a Kuhnian system, one can accumulate empirical "anomalies" that can lead to paradigm overthrow. Therefore paradigms do not have a protected status.

When it comes to apologetics, I think we can see how this plays out.

---

[3] There are discussions of this subject in, e.g., J. P. Moreland, *Christianity and the Nature of Science* (Grand Rapids, Mich.: Baker, 1989); Del Ratzsch, *Philosophy of Science* (Downers Grove, Ill.: InterVarsity, 1986). Cf. also John Taylor, "Science, Christianity and the Postmodern Agenda," *Science and Christian Belief* 10:2 (1998), 163-178; and my review essay, "Thomas Kuhn: An Assessment," forthcoming in *Presbyterion*.
[4] Ian Barbour, *Religion in an Age of Science* (New York: HarperSanFrancisco, 1990), 34-35.

As already indicated, the speech in Acts 17:22-31 paves a pathway for commending the faith to those outside its influence. Paul's strategy assumes 1) that there are things we all know by virtue of being human, which we take for granted in all we do and which we have to account for (for Paul here it is the universal religious impulse), and 2) that our worldview commitments affect the way we respond to these points, as well as to new inputs (such as Christian evidences)—and we must evaluate those commitments for their presuppositions and for their adequacy in accounting for those things we all know. This, as a matter of fact, is the thrust of the opening chapter in C. S. Lewis's *Miracles*.

All this means that certain kinds of supernatural events can provide such "anomalies" for naturalism that the theist is right to insist on a reevaluation. In the case of Acts 17, the resurrection of Jesus is one of those anomalies. In Acts 13:12 the Roman proconsul Sergius Paulus believed under the combined influence of Paul's message and the display of power over a magician (and note that in v. 7 Luke called him "intelligent"). Further, the biblical authors present God's supernatural effect on the moral life of believers as a testimony to those outside the covenant (e.g., 1 Kings 8:57-61; 1 Pet. 3:1-2).[5]

But of course such accounts do not invariably result in faith. For example, in Acts 17:32, some (Epicureans?) sneered at the mention of the resurrection. This can mean that the argument is not valid, or it can mean that people believe things for more than just the logical validity of the argument. The biblical material supports the latter explanation. For example, in John 9:35-41, those Pharisees who understood the special nature of the healing of the man born blind and yet did not commit themselves to Jesus are held guilty for their stubbornness (cf. also John 11:47-48; Acts 4:16-17). Further, Jesus' refusal to provide signs is in the context of such stubbornness, and the apparently negative evaluation in Luke 16:31 is in the context of moral indifference.[6]

Hence the basic thesis of Douglas Geivett's essay "The Evidential Value of Miracles" (namely that there is a propriety in appealing to certain supernatural events, especially the resurrection of Jesus) finds support in the

---

[5] Cf. also Deut. 4:6-8; Ezek. 36:22-23; Matt. 5:14-16; 1 Pet. 2:12, 15; 3:15-16 (in an "apologetics" setting); Rom. 1:8; 1 Thess. 1:8-9; 1 Tim. 6:1; Titus 2:5, 10. Of course this should be properly nuanced, as C. S. Lewis did in his chapter "Nice People or New Men?" book iv, chapter 10, of *Mere Christianity* (London: Bles, 1952), since a) not all professing Christians are the genuine article; and b) the evidence is the transformation from what these people were before their conversion.

[6] We might here compare Pascal, *Pensées*, no. 834 (Brunschvicg) / no. 855 (Krailsheimer): "Those who follow Jesus Christ because of his miracles honor his power in all the miracles that it produces; but those who, in making profession to follow him for his miracles, only follow him in effect because he consoles them and satisfies them with the goods of the world, dishonor his miracles, when they are contrary to their conveniences" ("Ceux qui suivent Jésus-Christ à cause de ses miracles honorent sa puissance dans tous les miracles qu'elle produit; mais ceux qui, en faisant profession de le suivre pour ses miracles, ne le suivent en effet que parce qu'il les console et les rassasie des biens du monde, ils déshonorent ses miracles, quand ils sont contraires à leurs commodités").

Bible.[7] Nevertheless, as Geivett also recognizes, this appeal does not take place in a vacuum; that is, it is part of an overall presentation that commends the biblical message about God, creation, sin, the need for forgiveness, etc.— all of which give a theological context for God taking an interest in human affairs.[8] I think this is really because Christian belief is not simply an acceptance of certain things as factual: It goes beyond that to personal commitment.[9]

One Class of Objections: From Baruch Spinoza and Rationalism

Baruch (or Benedict de) Spinoza (1632–1677) was a rationalistic Jew who objected to the possibility of supernatural events (which he took to be contrary to the law of nature) because of his definition of nature, which in turn connects to his epistemology. To him, all that God wills is eternal necessity; hence the laws of nature, which follow from God's will, are themselves the operations of logical necessity. So, should some event occur that is contrary to these laws, this would mean that God has done something contrary to necessity, i.e., contrary to his own nature; and this is absurd. Hence what we call "miracle" is really nothing but an event that exceeds the limits of human knowledge of natural law. Spinoza's argument shows up in the influential Christian theologian Friedrich Schleiermacher (1768–1834).

A very helpful analysis of this approach comes from William Dembski.[10] Dembski shows that Schleiermacher made "the standard rationalist move of subsuming causality under logical entailment," and this is the key difficulty in the argument.[11] As Dembski puts it, "Spinoza and Schleiermacher were not atheists, nor were they process theologians. They were hard-core theological determinists whose theology demanded that everything in nature be

---

[7] Douglas Geivett, "The Evidential Value of Miracles," in D. Geivett and G. Habermas, *In Defense of Miracles* (Downers Grove, Ill.: InterVarsity, 1997), 178-195.

[8] We see in this light that Phillip Johnson's question is theological and philosophically meaningful: "What should we do if empirical evidence and materialist philosophy are going in different directions?" (*Defeating Darwinism by Opening Minds* [Downers Grove, Ill.: InterVarsity, 1997], 114.) That is, it is possible that the evidence (in Johnson's case, regarding biological history) is incompatible with the worldview.

[9] My forthcoming *Christian Faith in an Age of Science* has a chapter on "natural revelation" that includes detailed discussion of the Mars Hill speech and its implications for Christian apologetics.

[10] William A. Dembski, "Schleiermacher's Metaphysical Critique of Miracles," *Scottish Journal of Theology* 49:4 (1996), 443-465. Also useful is William Lane Craig, "The Problem of Miracles: A Historical and Philosophical Perspective," in D. Wenham and C. Blomberg, eds., *Gospel Perspectives, VI: The Miracles of Jesus* (Sheffield: JSOT Press, 1986), 9-48, especially at 16-17, 19-22, 32-37.

[11] Rationalism, as stated above, equates "laws of nature" with "laws of God." Hence, to rationalists, everything that we think involves physical causation actually is a matter of logical necessity. Linguistically, this amounts to an equivocation on the word *reason* in the following sentences: 1) The *reason* (= physical cause) that the mouse disappeared is that the cat ate it. 2) The *reason* (= logical cause) that $4 - 2 = 2$ is that $2 + 2 = 4$.

ordained by God." To respond to this, we have to show that divine sovereignty and omnipotence does not collapse into such a picture.

Schleiermacher's determinism becomes plain when he treats the matter of answered prayer:

> Prayer seems really to be heard only when because of it an event happens which would not otherwise have happened: thus there seems to be the suspension of an effect which, according to the interrelatedness of nature should have followed.
>
> Prayer and its fulfilment or refusal are only part of the original divine plan, and consequently the idea that otherwise something else might have happened is wholly meaningless.

Dembski contends that Schleiermacher has failed to recognize what determinists have generally had to recognize, namely that if I am decreed to get well when I am ill, I am decreed to get well (ordinarily) as a result of calling the physician.[12] (This recognition, recall, is a crucial part of the problem of answered prayer, which we discussed in chapter 9.)

But the fundamental question is the matter of contingency: By what right do we suppose that the creation could not have been otherwise? Indeed, the Christian doctrine is that the creation is *contingent*—that is, it *could* have been otherwise. G. K. Chesterton put the relationship between contingency and necessity this way:[13]

> I observed an extraordinary thing. I observed that learned men in spectacles were talking of the actual things that happened—dawn and death and so on—as if *they* were rational and inevitable. They talked as if the fact that trees bear fruit was just as *necessary* as the fact that two and one trees make three. But it is not. There is an enormous difference by the test of fairyland; which is the test of the imagination. You cannot *imagine* two and one not making three. But you can easily imagine trees not growing fruit; you can imagine them growing golden candlesticks or tigers hanging on by the tail.

Or as Dembski put it,[14]

> It seems that there are all sorts of things that God could, at least in principle, ordain. God could ordain that prayers offered in faith get answered and make a difference. God could ordain that nature

---

[12] Cf. *Westminster Confession of Faith*, 3:6, "As God hath appointed the elect unto glory, so hath he, by the eternal and most free purpose of his will, foreordained *all the means thereunto.*"
[13] G. K. Chesterton, *Orthodoxy* (Garden City, N.Y.: Doubleday, 1959 [originally 1908]), 50-51.
[14] Dembski, "Schleiermacher's Critique," 463.

exhibit a certain regularity for a time and thereafter cease to exhibit it. God could ordain a certain event unconditionally (cf. God's promise to Abraham to make him a great nation). God could ordain another event conditionally (cf. God's promise to bless Israel if Israel keeps the law).

We may also add Craig's observation:[15]

> If God is personal and ontologically distinct from the world, there seems to be no reason why even a total alteration of the laws of nature should in any way affect God's being.

Since traditional Christian theology holds that God is distinct from the world, and that the world is a contingent creation, then it simply rejects this kind of critique as question-begging, of winning by controlling the definitions.

ANOTHER CLASS OF OBJECTIONS: FROM DAVID HUME AND EMPIRICISM

The empiricist objections to the possibility of supernatural events are especially associated with David Hume (1711–1776), the Scottish philosopher and skeptic. Hume's *Enquiry Concerning the Human Understanding* (first edition 1748; revised edition published posthumously in 1777) contains a section whose purpose is to deny the a priori possibility of miracles and the a posteriori possibility of recognizing a miracle.[16]

In section x.1 of his *Enquiry,* Hume defines a "miracle" as "a violation of the laws of nature" and he goes on to assert,[17]

> and as a firm and unalterable experience has established these laws, the proof against a miracle . . . is as entire as any argument from experience can possibly be imagined. . . . Nothing is esteemed a miracle, if it ever happen in the common course of nature. It is no miracle that a man, seemingly in good health, should die on a sudden: because such a kind of death, though more unusual than any other, has yet been frequently observed to happen. But it is a miracle, that a dead man should come to life; because that has never been observed in any age or country. There must, therefore, be a uniform experience against every miraculous event, otherwise that event

---

15 Craig, "The Problem of Miracles," 32.

16 Text found in David Hume, *Enquiries Concerning the Human Understanding and Concerning the Principles of Morals,* L. A. Selby-Bigge, ed. (Oxford, England: Oxford University Press, 1902). Section x also appears as the first chapter of Geivett and Habermas, *In Defense of Miracles.*

17 Hume, *Enquiries,* 114-115; Hume, in Geivett and Habermas, 33.

would not merit that appellation. And as a uniform experience amounts to a proof, there is here a direct and full proof, from the nature of the fact, against the existence of any miracle; nor can such a proof be destroyed, or the miracle rendered credible, but by an opposite proof, which is superior.

This is considered the definitive attack, at least in the English-speaking world, on the respectability of believing in miracles. The American intellectual historian John Herman Randall, Jr., said that, "The great philosopher Hume so demolished [miracles'] value that to this day apologists have had their greatest difficulties, not in proving Christianity by miracles, but in explaining how such impossible ideas ever crept into the record."[18]

But should we accept this powerful critique? To begin with, notice the definition, "violation of the laws of nature." Although it is possible to find Christian apologists who employed this definition, many did not; it does not appear, for instance, in Aquinas or Calvin; and we have seen that Pascal's definition is much closer to what we inferred from the Bible's own material.[19] So straightaway we have a problem: Hume is attacking one conception of miracles, and it is not the biblical one.[20]

But let's go further: Recall that Hume appealed to experience for his proof against supernatural events. But according to my definitions, to the extent that experience establishes anything, it enables us to perceive what I have called the "natural properties" of an item: Iron sinks, animals do not talk, and babies come about by the union of a man and a woman.[21] This cannot be used to rule out the possibility of a supernatural action, since this depends on whether or not God exists and would take an interest in human affairs. Besides, as C. S. Lewis and many others pointed out, when we articulate "laws of nature," we usually leave unstated the obvious qualification "provided nothing intervenes" (often called *ceteris paribus*, "other things being equal" qualifications). For example, a full statement of the behavior of billiard balls would be, "When billiard balls are moving on a billiard table, the angle of incidence equals the angle of reflection (always provided no one interferes)." Observation of billiard balls will never tell you how likely it is

[18] John Herman Randall, Jr., *The Making of the Modern Mind* (Boston: Houghton Mifflin, 1940), 292.

[19] Craig, "The Problem of Miracles," 19-22, shows that in the replies to Spinoza efforts were made to define "miracle" that bear a resemblance to the ideas discussed in chapter 9 above. All this means that Hume had available to him a wider range of possibilities to address and did not do so.

[20] This is not surprising, in view of the fact that Hume's contemporary, Dr. Johnson, noted that "Hume owned to a clergyman in the bishoprick of Durham, that he had never read the New Testament with attention." James Boswell, *The Life of Samuel Johnson, LL.D.* (Everyman's Library; London: Dent, 1906 [originally 1791]), i:315 (spoken in 1766).

[21] Perhaps more carefully we would say that empirical investigation allows us to perceive *the interaction of* the natural properties of the things studied: e.g., iron and water have such properties that, if the iron is formed in the shape of an axe-head and placed in water at liquid temperature, the iron object will sink.

that someone might intervene. Observation of natural properties (e.g., in how babies come about) will never tell us how likely it is that God will employ a natural object in a way that exceeds its natural capacities (e.g., in the virgin conception of Jesus).

Hume goes further: We should never *believe* a claim for a supernatural event, because "uniform experience" weighs against the probability of its being true, because the events are so rare. This part of Hume's argument amounts, in other words, to a probability argument. In statistics, if we want to estimate the probability of a particular event A, we take the total number of times A occurred in our experiment and divide it by the total number of events; as long as our sample is big enough, the estimate is taken to be pretty good. Thus, by Hume's argument we can estimate p(miracle), the probability that a given event was a miracle, by the following equation:

$$p(\text{miracle}) = \frac{\text{number of miracles known to have occurred}}{\text{number of events in the history of the world}}$$

Whatever the value of the numerator, the value of the denominator is obviously so big that the whole fraction is effectively zero. Hence, I should not believe a miracle has occurred.

The trouble with this argument is that it does not answer the question we are asking. We are not asking what is the probability of a supernatural event; we are instead asking what is the probability that a *particular* event is supernatural, *given* such factors as the testimony for it, the theological context in which it occurred, and the existence of a deity with an interest in humans; that is, we're looking at a *conditional* probability. The formula for conditional probability is:

$$p(A \textit{ given } B) = \frac{p(A \textit{ and } B)}{p(B)}$$

In our case this would yield,

p(miracle *given* testimony, theological context, deity) =

$$\frac{p(\text{miracle } \textit{and} \text{ testimony } \textit{and} \text{ context } \textit{and} \text{ deity})}{p(\text{testimony } \textit{and} \text{ context } \textit{and} \text{ deity})}$$

There is no way I know of to assign any values to these elements. However, *if* there is a God who cares about us, and who wants to reveal himself to us, and to use supernatural events as a pointer to his revelation (which is the most common purpose of these events in the Bible), it makes plenty of sense to suppose that he did so in such a way that there would be testimony, and there is no need to suppose that he would do it afresh in each generation.[22]

Additionally, many philosophers point out that Hume actually begs the question here. For example, Craig says, "To say that uniform experience is against miracles is implicitly to assume that the miracle in question did not occur. Otherwise the experience could not be said to be truly uniform."[23]

From a literary point of view, Hume's reasoning overlooks one very important fact, namely, the normal reason for telling a story is to report "interesting" or "tellable" events, and not the *usual* ones. This means that a narrative will not be about what we all know about already. This leads to another flaw in Hume's case: A consistent application of Hume's ideas would have us doubting *all* historical accounts of unusual things.[24]

Part 2 of Hume's section x lists a number of reasons why testimony is not good enough to establish *any* miracle claims. These are: 1) the lack of witnesses of the right kind ("of such unquestioned good sense, education, and learning; of such undoubted integrity . . . ; of such credit and reputation"); 2) human gullibility and love for stories of the fabulous; 3) the origin of such tales "among ignorant and barbarous nations"; 4) other religions claim miracles, hence they cancel one another out. A full discussion of these reasons would itself take a book,[25] but there are a few things on which comment is necessary. One must wonder what the criterion is for calling into question the sense, learning, integrity, and reputation of such people as wrote the Bible, and likewise for the assertion that the Bible authors are from ignorant and barbarous peoples. Is it perhaps because they report supernatural events? This becomes a circular argument (as well as being offensively eli-

---

[22] Indeed, in view of these conditioning factors, we may well agree with Pascal, *Pensées*, no. 815 (Brunschvicg) / no. 568 (Krailsheimer), "It is not possible to have a reasonable belief against miracles" ("Il n'est pas possible de croire raisonnablement contre les miracles"). That is, Pascal rejects the empiricist's position on who bears the burden of proof.

[23] Craig, "The Problem of Miracles," 37.

[24] E.g., Richard Whately's 1819 *Historical Doubts Concerning the Existence of Napoleon Bonaparte* is a *reductio ad absurdum* of Hume's doubts about the reliability of testimony to unusual things. Colin Brown, *Miracles and the Critical Mind* (Grand Rapids, Mich.: Eerdmans, 1984), 146-147, argues that Whately has actually confused two different kinds of uniqueness: "On the one hand, there are reports of events that are without strict parallels, but that nevertheless fall within the range of the normal, since they do not violate patterns of recurrent types of behavior. On the other hand, reports of certain miracles testify to events without any parallel within recurrent experience." It is not clear to me that Hume is quite this nuanced, however; indeed, his point is that the accounts are unbelievable precisely because they are unusual.

[25] Cf. Geivett and Habermas, *In Defense of Miracles*, for the book!

tist). I think that close attention to the Bible will show that its authors display the requisite subtlety of thought to be discriminating in this area; and when we add to that the stakes of being wrong (e.g., Deut. 13 and 18 tie the careful assessment of possibly supernatural events to authentic prophecy, i.e., the mediation of God's own voice), we can see that they were highly motivated to apply that discrimination.[26]

Hume's objections are therefore far from being unanswerable. Indeed, they are based on misunderstandings that call his own credibility into question.

This, by the way, also answers the objection from Bultmann with which we started. Bultmann confuses the *practice of scientific investigation* with what is called the *scientific worldview* (i.e., that nature is a closed system, and everything is in principle naturally explicable). The biblical worldview endorses empirical study of the creation, and even holds out some prospect of genuine (but not exhaustive) understanding of it. Bultmann's reference to modern medical discoveries is particularly odd in view of our discussion of Ben Sira 38:1-15 in chapter 5 (where we saw that Ben Sira endorses the medical employment of natural healing powers as an act of faith). And Bultmann strangely overstates the situation of "the New Testament world of spirits and miracles" in the light of the literary observations about "tellability" above. Of course the New Testament focuses on Christ's supernatural works, including his power over demons, because the significance of these works is so stupendous for people who need to be rescued from "the prince of the power of the air" (Eph. 2:2), whose minds "the god of this age" has blinded (2 Cor. 4:4). Rather than assume the validity of the worldview of "the modern world," surely it is far more sensible to query that worldview for its adequacy in accounting for things we all know to be true (such as human choice, rationality, morality). By such a test it will fail.[27]

OBJECTIONS FROM POSTMODERNISM

"Postmodernism" is an amorphous mass of reactions to "modernism" in a variety of endeavors. A one-size-fits-all definition is impossible, so I will have to specify the kind of postmodernism I am addressing. The easiest way to do that will be to make sure we understand what we mean by "modernism." A particularly lucid exposition of modernism comes from Karl Pearson:[28]

---

[26] That the early Christians *did* in fact exercise that discrimination (in defiance of Hume's second factor, by the way) can be seen in the way they rejected the so-called apocryphal accounts of Jesus' and the apostles' miracles. That is, the theological context of the proposed supernatural event mattered.

[27] C. S. Lewis's essay "Modern Theology and Biblical Criticism," in *Christian Reflections*, W. Hooper, ed. (Grand Rapids, Mich.: Eerdmans, 1967), 152-166, has some telling critique of Bultmann as a literary scholar.

[28] Karl Pearson, *The Grammar of Science* (London: Macmillan, 1896), 77. Note that when he refers to metaphysics as "fantasy," he is also excluding all reference to God and to the supernatural. This is similar to what Del Ratzsch calls the Baconian view of science in *Philosophy of Science*, 22.

The scientific method is the sole path by which we can attain to knowledge. The very word "knowledge" indeed only applies to the products of the scientific method in the field. Other methods may lead to fantasy as that of the poet or metaphysician, to belief or superstition, but never to knowledge. As to the scientific method, it consists in the careful and often laborious classification of facts, the comparison of their relationships and sequences, and finally in the discovery by aid of the disciplined imagination of a brief statement or formula, which in a few words resumes a wide range of facts. Such a formula is called a scientific law.

There are lots of possible objections to this view of science and knowledge, such as its loaded definition of "knowledge," which has no connection with how people actually use the word; its problem of self-refutation—it is itself a metaphysical statement that is not a product of what he calls the "scientific method," so why should we believe it?; and its inaccurate description of what scientists actually *do*.

But I want to focus on what is called the postmodern critique of this approach to knowing and science, associated with such names as Michael Polanyi and Thomas Kuhn. This line of critique has very helpfully discussed science in terms of what scientists actually *do*, and how their metaphysical precommitments come into play, and so on; and this has helped to break down philosophers' confidence in the claims of modernism. Does this open up the possibility for supernatural events to make a comeback into respectable conversation? Well, not necessarily, since the influence of this critique on scientists (and probably on the general public) is limited, and also because some have taken the critique too far and gone on to deny either that there *is* an external world that exists independently of the way you and I observe it, or at least to say that, even *if* such a world exists, it is not knowable by us. This is where we get full-blown postmodernism.[29]

In particular, Thomas Kuhn's work is famous because of its term

---

[29] The literature on this subject is quite large, diverse, and uneven, and I can only provide a small sample. A proponent of postmodernism is Richard Rorty, and he speaks for himself in Stephen Louthan, "On Religion—A Discussion with Richard Rorty, Alvin Plantinga and Nicholas Wolterstorff," *Christian Scholar's Review* 26:2 (Winter 1996), 177-183. In the same issue Nancey Murphy has "Philosophical Resources for Postmodern Evangelical Theology," 184-220. Craig Bartholomew gives an overview in "Post/late? Modernity as the Context of Christian Scholarship Today," *Themelios* 22:2 (January 1997), 25-38; cf. Stan Wallace, "Discerning and Defining the Essentials of Postmodernism," *The Real Issue* 16:3 (March 1998), 5-8. Mikael Stenmark examines and critiques postmodern models of rationality in his chapter on "Contextualism and Human Practices" in *Rationality in Science, Religion, and Everyday Life* (Notre Dame, Ind.: University of Notre Dame Press, 1995), 301-353. Insightful critique of certain aspects of postmodernism appear in William Dembski, "The Fallacy of Contextualism," *Themelios* 20:3 (1995), 8-11; and Jay Wesley Richards, "The Logic of Tolerance," *Princeton Theological Review* 4:2 (May 1997), 2-12. Dennis McCallum considers apologetics in such a setting in "The Postmodern Puzzle: When There Are No Absolute Truths and No Rules of Logic, How Do We Defend the Gospel?" *The Real Issue* 16:3 (March 1998), 1, 9-14.

"paradigm," and his argument that "science" does not function independently of *scientists;* their worldviews are intertwined with their theories.[30] Postmodernism tends to take this even further: Since all our knowing is done by humans with worldview commitments, our knowing is relative only; it is common to say, "All data are theory-laden." So we never know anything in itself, but only as our paradigm interprets it—whether that thing be a rock, a text, an ethical maxim, or God.

This leads us to consider some possible ways that a postmodernist might reply to my reply to Hume. One may deny that such a thing as "natural properties" exists; after all, what proof can I give other than "the Bible implies it"? (And what makes me even think that I can know *what* the Bible implies?) And even if there are such properties, what proof can anyone give that when we experience things, we have any way to know their "natural properties"? After all, one problem with experience is that we can make mistakes. And how do I know that someone won't come along later and give a plausible *natural* explanation for something I thought was *supernatural*? And then there is the role of paradigms: If when we experience the world we do so by way of our precommitments and theories, what right do we have to believe these theories are *true*? After all, we no longer believe that the earth is the center of the universe.

Interestingly enough, our contemporary skeptics can find support in the same essay of Hume to which the modernists turn for arguments against believing reports of supernatural events. In an earlier section than the one we have already considered, Hume contended:[31]

> It is impossible, therefore, that any arguments from experience can prove this resemblance of the past to the future, since all these arguments are founded on the supposition of that resemblance. Let the course of things be allowed hitherto ever so regular, that alone, without some new argument or inference, proves not that for the future it will continue so. . . . My practice, you say, refutes my doubts. But you mistake the purport of my question. As an agent, I am quite satisfied in the point; but as a philosopher who has some share of curiosity, I will not say skepticism, I want to learn the foundation of this inference.

My evaluation of these skeptical replies appeals to a fact about each one of us that is so familiar we may overlook it: the fact that we are *agents,*

---

[30] Thomas Kuhn, *The Structure of Scientific Revolutions* (University of Chicago, 1970). Note that I have already indicated some bibliography for critical discussion of Kuhn's ideas.
[31] Hume, *Enquiry Concerning Human Understanding,* iv.2, in Hume, *Enquiries,* 38.

and, within some limits, successful ones. By that I mean, we get around in the world, we learn how to avoid pain and pursue pleasantness. When you walk out your door, you will probably not step in front of a moving car (unless you either want or don't care about the consequences). We have the intuition that when we make our choices, we are doing so in light of our knowledge of the nature of things; e.g., why else would we choose steel over cotton for a knife blade. Further, we are able to infer the activity of other agents based on our sense of the "natural properties" of the objects; e.g., we suppose that Stonehenge is the product of agency, not of the rocks that compose it.

This is a basic, "common sense" intuition, which we should discard only for good reason; and neither the doubts of David Hume nor the theories of Thomas Kuhn are a good reason to do so.

Hume's doubts offer no compelling reason, and his own reference to himself as an agent is the key. He has started from the wrong end of the stick. He should have begun, not with, "By what right do I assume the reliability of the world and of inductive inference?" but with, "What is it about us and about the world that explains why we are such successful agents?" His section iv offers an impoverished epistemology, because he suggests that the only way we "know" is either through logical deduction or through experience; he makes no allowance for the possibility that as agents created by the God who made the world we are endowed with the capacities to function in that world and even to understand it to some extent. I think we do so by way of what we can call "interactive pattern proposal and correction": We try to infer patterns from our experiences and correct our inferences by experience. Linguists agree that this is how children learn language; I suggest that this is how we learn most if not all of our life skills. This is what successful agency consists of.

The fact that we make mistakes does not mean that our faculties are unreliable; it means rather that we have to be careful, humble, and teachable. After all, even to cast doubt on induction requires that you practice inductive inference; typically such doubt comes from drawing conclusions from your experience of making mistakes.

These difficulties arise because people want (rightly) to believe only those things they have good grounds for believing. But, as Hume noted, we cannot prove the validity of inductive inference from our experience, since we have to presuppose that validity to prove it. Does that mean we have no good grounds for believing that inductive inference can be valid? Philosophers have taken different steps to deal with this problem. One is to give up on claims to "knowledge" and content oneself with description ("anti-realism"). A sounder approach is to take the validity of induction as what J. P. Moreland calls a "synthetic a priori": We take it as a necessary truth that we simply know directly; it is an unsupported, and unnecessary to support, basic belief.[32]

This approach can find strong support in what Mikael Stenmark has expounded as "presumptionism." Presumptionism starts from the principle that,[33]

> It makes no sense to define the standards of rationality in such a way that it is not possible for real people to be rational in their believing. . . . We are finite beings with limited cognitive resources. . . . This means that if we want to proceed rationally no time should be spent on valueless or unimportant justifications, inferences, eliminations of inconsistencies, and the like.

He moves on to contend,[34]

> The presumptionist claims instead that the only rational or proper attitude towards our beliefs must be one of (at least, initial) *trust*— not of distrust. This means that our beliefs should be taken to be intellectually innocent until proven guilty, not guilty until proven innocent.

Indeed, as Stenmark notes, no one would ever do anything, not even get out of bed in the morning, without taking this as a given. And if we do so on the basis of what some philosophers might call inadequate evidence, what choice do we have? We might turn the tables on them: What special qualities of prophetic inspiration do those who cast doubts on this enterprise have, that they should lead us to question such a basic intuition? Really, they might as well ask us to *prove* that we exist (we can't, really; we take it as a given and we get on with our living).

Much as I am drawn to Stenmark's way of thinking, I think we must finally realize that this is one of those features of common human existence that cries out for a theistic explanation, and anything less than that is going to leave us dissatisfied.

Back to the skeptic: I am appealing to our common notion of agency, and I note that successful agency *presupposes* the existence and knowability

[32] J. P. Moreland, *Christianity and the Nature of Science: A Philosophical Investigation* (Grand Rapids, Mich.: Baker, 1989), 116-117.
[33] Mikael Stenmark, *Rationality in Science, Religion, and Everyday Life* (Notre Dame, Ind.: University of Notre Dame Press, 1995), 196. Kelly James Clark has a short but perceptive review of this book in *Christian Scholar's Review* 27:1 (Fall, 1997), 123-124.
[34] Stenmark, 212.

of natural properties. But here we need to be clear on what we mean by "know." The modernist said that "to know something objectively" means "to know without personal involvement, and exhaustively." The postmodern critique has shown that we cannot exclude our precommitments from the knowing process, and of course we all know that we will not live long enough to be sure that we know *completely*. Full-blown postmodernism then concludes that we never really "know" objectively. Now this usage is contrary to what the word *know* means in ordinary language, where it means "know well enough for successful agency." I think we should stay close to the ordinary usage of words if we can, and keep our meaning transparent. There is no reason why we have to think that we do not know something unless we know it exhaustively. We know "well enough" for successful agency. Otherwise, it would not be rational to conclude that Stonehenge is the product of agency: After all, we don't know *everything* there is to know about the rocks that make it up! It seems to me that both modernists and postmodernists are using the word *know* for something that no human being is actually able to accomplish, and this leaves us unable to warrant as rational something we know to be rational. Being unwilling to jettison the rationality of the inference to design for Stonehenge, we should instead jettison the philosophy that called it into question.

And see what the biblical picture gets for us: It endorses that rationality, because it endorses the notion of natural properties of the created realm. It explains that those properties are at least to some extent knowable, because the rational God who made it all also made humans in his image to govern his creation. A supernatural event in such a setting will never be arbitrary or willy-nilly; instead it will express the relational interest of the Creator toward his creatures. For this reason one would expect it also to be, at least at times, detectable.

DIVINE ACTION AND THE PROBLEM OF EVIL

Another problem for the biblical picture is "the problem of evil": By what right do we claim a good and all-powerful God made the world, when it is so chock-full of bad things, such as bad people doing bad things to others, or decent people suffering "the slings and arrows of outrageous fortune"? In the context of discussing special operations of divine power (which is the only context in which I shall treat it here), the problem is particularly acute: If God *can* and *does* exert special actions, why does he not do so more often, to relieve suffering and vindicate his own character? And if he does so for some and not for others, those some must be dreadfully few; how can we possibly call this just on God's part? Would it not be more tolerable to suppose that no special divine operations can take place, than to allow this reproach on God to stand? This was the burden of a 1995 essay by James A. Keller.[35]

Any treatment of the problem of evil, if it is to deserve serious attention, must come to grips with a number of facts about ourselves and about how the Bible presents God's dealings with humans; and as a matter of fact, Keller does not even show an awareness of those facts. First, we must face the fact that humans are sinful. This is something that the Bible explains but, as Chesterton pointed out, "is the only part of Christian theology which can really be proved."[36] That is, we are all aware that something is wrong, both with ourselves and with others; the Bible explains this by reference to the first members of the human race and their disobedience that brought evil into human experience.

Second, in view of this basic human problem, any discussion of God's dealings with humans must be in terms of God's intention to *rescue* them from their sinfulness or to punish them for their rebellion. Most of the special divine actions in the Bible (apart from those of creation) fall in this sphere. Now, if humans are in fact rebels who need rescue, that must mean that if we are to receive the rescue we must surrender our opposition to God, on his terms, and submit to whatever program of cleansing he has in mind for us. Since all people are in this same moral condition, God is under no moral obligation to show favor to *any*, let alone to show it to all indiscriminately. And regardless of how we may feel about it, the Bible indicates that it pleased God to focus his favor on one particular group, Abraham's descendants, with a view towards bringing blessing to all kinds of people.

This relationship is in the Bible called a "covenant," and God is free to make a covenant with whomever he chooses. "Redemptive history" is the development of this relationship over time towards the ends that God himself has in view. What we call "special revelation" is perhaps better described as God's covenantal redemptive self-revelation; and the biblical claim is that this self-revelation came to specific people at specific times. Paul Gwynne observes, "For minds committed to egalitarianism, the idea that God acts at certain times and places rather than at others evokes a certain indignation."[37] If on the other hand we question that commitment to egalitarianism, we can see the scene more clearly. Indeed, this limits the problem of evil only to

---

[35] James A. Keller, "A Moral Argument Against Miracles," *Faith and Philosophy* 12:1 (January, 1995), 54-78. Treatment of authors with similar objections appears in Paul Gwynne, *Special Divine Action* (Rome: Gregorian University Press, 1996), 269-292.

[36] G. K. Chesterton, *Orthodoxy*, 15. I do not intend here to substantiate the claim, but Pascal has, I think, shown the way (cf. section ii of Peter Kreeft's edition of the *Pensées*, *Christianity for Modern Pagans* [San Francisco: Ignatius, 1993]).

[37] Gwynne, *Special Divine Action*, 270.

those who are members of God's covenant people.[38] Still, this leaves us with a big problem: How can we, by looking about us, ever be justified in inferring that everything, especially for the believer, goes according to a purpose that is perfect, holy, loving, and wise? How dare we draw such a conclusion in light of human wickedness, on the grand scale of Pol Pot and Stalin (who oppressed believers), to the small scale of everyday human perversity? Or from babies dying in infancy, or from promising lives cut short by cancer (all of which believers suffer from)?

The Bible taken as a whole does not imply that believers' lives will be free from the effects of their own or others' evil, only that in some way this evil has no autonomous existence that God cannot control for his own purposes. The Bible also rejects the idea that those believers (or anyone else) who are suffering must necessarily be getting punished for their unfaithfulness. Consider a few texts:

> *Proverbs 16:8* (NIV): Better a little with righteousness than much gain with injustice.

This implies that the righteous may well be poorly off, while it is quite possible to get wealthy by injustice. However, the righteous are still better off (for why this is so, see 11:4).

> *Luke 13:1-5* (NIV): Now there were some present at that time who told Jesus about the Galileans whose blood Pilate had mixed with their sacrifices. Jesus answered, "Do you think that these Galileans were worse sinners than all the other Galileans because they suffered this way? I tell you, no! But unless you repent, you too will all perish. Or those eighteen who died when the tower in Siloam fell on them—do you think they were more guilty than all the others living in Jerusalem? I tell you, no! But unless you repent, you too will all perish."

> *John 9:1-3* (NIV): As he went along, he saw a man blind from birth. His disciples asked him, "Rabbi, who sinned, this man or his parents, that he was born blind?"
> "Neither this man nor his parents sinned," said Jesus, "but this happened so that the work of God might be displayed in his life."

The special operations of divine power in the Bible are not primarily

---

[38] I am not in any way suggesting that this means that the covenant people may legitimately be complacent about the sufferings of others or write it off as "they're only getting what they deserve." Such conclusions are entirely out of step with the Bible. Nevertheless I do want to focus on the ways in which the existence of evil may legitimately be said to count against *biblical* belief.

concerned with providing material benefits to people; they are instead 1) to attest a messenger as being a spokesman for God (e.g., Ex. 4:1-9; Acts 2:22), and 2) to reassure God's people that only one being's will really has the final word, namely God's.

This last point is worth our attention. The Christian doctrine of providence, namely that all events are the expression of God's perfect and personal purposes for his people, is not an inference from observation. Paul Helm puts things very well:[39]

> Often there is a sharp disjunction between the view that God is in control, and the seeming chaos and meaninglessness of human lives, and human affairs in general. Is not this chaos a *disproof* of the Christian claim that God rules the universe providentially? It *would* be a disproof if the idea of divine providence were an empirical hypothesis, if it were built up only out of a person's direct experience and based wholly upon it. . . . Rather, for Christians, reliance upon the providence of God, and an understanding of the character of that providence, is based upon what God has revealed in Scripture, and is confirmed in their own and others' experience.

Or, as C. S. Lewis put it,[40]

> There is, to be sure, one glaringly obvious ground for denying that any moral purpose at all is operative in the universe: namely, the actual course of events in all its wasteful cruelty and apparent indifference, or hostility, to life.
>
> At all times, then, an inference from the course of events in this world to the goodness and wisdom of the Creator would have been equally preposterous; and it was never made.

In fact, the Bible indicates that to have it otherwise is not actually possible for humans. This comes out well in the book of Ecclesiastes, whose key word is *find* (Hebrew *māṣā'*), which there has the nuance "to find out, fathom by research." For example, consider these verses which use that verb (cited from RSV, with *māṣā'* highlighted):

> *3:11:* He [God] has made everything beautiful in its time; also he has put eternity into man's mind, yet so that he cannot *find out* what God has done from the beginning to the end.

---

[39] Paul Helm, *The Providence of God* (Downers Grove, Ill.: InterVarsity, 1994), 223.

[40] The first paragraph is from *"De Futilitate,"* in *Christian Reflections*, 57-71, at 69; the second is from *The Problem of Pain* (New York: Macmillan, 1962), chapter 1. See also his essay on "Historicism" in *Christian Reflections* on the futility of inferring the divine purpose from our limited knowledge of the actual course of events.

7:14: In the day of prosperity be joyful, and in the day of adversity consider; God has made the one as well as the other, so that man may not *find out* anything that will be after him. [prediction is futile]

8:17: Then I saw all the work of God, that man cannot *find out* the work that is done under the sun. However much man may toil in seeking, he will not *find it out*; even though a wise man claims to know, he cannot *find it out*.

Though one often encounters the interpretation that takes Ecclesiastes as apologetic to the unbeliever, showing that unbelief leads only to despair, this interpretive scheme cannot be sustained. In these examples "man" is the *pious believer;* in this book (as well as in Job) it is believers who will find themselves baffled in their attempts to make sense out of God's providential ordering of things (and they must not make understanding it all a pre-condition for obedience). In a seminal study J. Stafford Wright put it this way:[41]

We go through the world with [the author of Ecclesiastes], looking for the solution to life, and at every turn he forces us to admit that here is only vanity, frustration, bewilderment. *Life does not hold the key to itself.* . . . Even the finest Christian philosophy must own itself baffled.

That is, the intelligibility of the world is tantalizingly partial (and experience should bear this out).

Does this mean that Ecclesiastes would leave us with only a fideistic leap of confidence in God? Let's make sure we know what would have to be true for us to call it "fideistic": It would have God telling us, "Look, you just have to believe me, and I'm not going to give you any reason for believing." Is that how God addresses us? No, it is not. Think instead of trust in a relationship: Trust is built on some experience, but trust always outruns the evidence, and finds confirmation in further experience. That is how God builds our trust in him (which is what "faith" is supposed to be).

Since Ecclesiastes comes in a canonical context, we should not suppose its author wanted it taken apart from the canonical theology. Indeed, when we find the admonition to "fear God and keep his commandments" and the

---

[41] J. Stafford Wright, "The Interpretation of Ecclesiastes," first published in *EvQ* 18 (1946), 18-34; reprinted in W. Kaiser, ed., *Classical Evangelical Essays in Old Testament Interpretation* (Grand Rapids, Mich.: Baker, 1972), 133-150, and in R. B. Zuck, ed., *Reflecting with Solomon* (Grand Rapids, Mich.: Baker, 1994), 17-30. The interpretation appears in popular form in J. I. Packer's *Knowing God* (Downers Grove, Ill.: InterVarsity, 1973), chapter 10, §§2, 4. The unpublished M.A. thesis of Betsy Thomas, *Coherence in Ecclesiastes: A Consideration of Plot Development* (Covenant Theological Seminary, 1997), which employs the tools of discourse analysis, puts this interpretation on a very solid footing.

reference to certain judgment (12:13-14), we should see these as evocations of this theology. That theology is built (among other things) on redemptive historical events, such as the theophanies and deliverance in Exodus, the authentication of prophets, and the works of Jesus and the apostles. The best way to see these events in this connection is to realize that they make God's interest in his people especially visible to eyes that are unable to see his hand in everything. Supposing we hear in church a testimony from a soundly pious believer, who tells us how she has seen God's faithfulness this past week; ought we correct her by saying, "God is always faithful and you lack the faith to see it"? Certainly not: Of course God is always faithful, and we usually do not see it (and in view of the above, we *cannot* see it); nevertheless he is faithfully merciful, too, and sometimes he helps his people to see it. Indeed, this desire for a visible token of God's love and lordship finds expression in a canonical hymn (Ps. 119:126):

> It is time for the Lord to do something,
> for they have violated your laws.

Is this approach rational? If the situation between humans and God is as the Bible says it is—namely, that he is infinitely wiser and holier than we are, and our resources are severely limited—then this approach is indeed rational. If I may make an analogy, consider my relationship to my children. In particular, I have expected them to trust me, to suppose that I know what I am talking about even though they do not, and to suppose also that I care for them; and I expect them to express that trust by obeying me. For example, I tell my young children not to walk across the street without an adult holding their hand. Now, the characteristics of cars and the mistakes that drivers can make are beyond the experience of a young toddler—and what's worse, many children think they can handle any situation that arises, and I know they cannot. Even if I explain some of these things to them, they will not really *understand*—the most they can do is trust and obey. Or again: My children have never experienced mistreatment at the hands of an adult; and yet in this perverted age I have to teach them to be careful of strangers. While they are below a certain age, I cannot even explain to them what some of the dangers are; they just have to take my word for it. And of course, *they're at their most rational when they trust me and obey*.

The key then to dealing with what the philosophers call the "existential problem of evil" (why is there pain *in my life?*) is to realize that we actually have two separate questions: The first question is, "Why has God brought about these events?" and this is something that God does not expect us to answer—either for ourselves or for anyone else; the second question is, "How can I submit to God's sovereign hand?" and I can usually find the answer to that (in Ecclesiastes, cf. 3:12-13, 17; 9:7-10; 12:13-14). The question for me in my pain is, "Has God given me reason to trust him?" and Ecclesiastes (and the Bible in general) reminds me that the answer is a resounding yes!

In view of this, the problem of evil, though still a difficulty for believers to bear, does not constitute a counterargument for the validity of the biblical position on God's action in the world.

Eleven

Origins, Intelligent Design, and God-of-the-Gaps

INTRODUCTION TO INTELLIGENT DESIGN AND OBJECTIONS TO IT

The preceding chapters support the conclusion that a properly nuanced supernaturalism has the best claim to being the biblically supported metaphysic. That is, we should both affirm the existence of "nature" and recognize that natural processes are not sufficient to explain every event in the world's history. This position is robust in the face of intellectual challenges from unbelief.

Now we come to an issue that may divide Christian believers, even if they are supernaturalists. The questions here turn on the time-frame and context of supernatural events: Are they limited to "redemptive history," or may they also have occurred in the "natural history" of the universe (e.g., in the origin of the universe, of life, and of humanity)?

In this chapter I want to discuss the theological and philosophical propriety of "intelligent design" as a scientific program. Put very briefly, the "intelligent design" program contends that it is scientifically legitimate to have the conclusion that something results from "imposed design" as part of our tool kit of explanatory options for things we meet in the natural world. In chapter 9 I defined "imposed design" as:

> the imposition of structure upon some object or collection of objects for some purpose, where the structure and the purpose are not inherent in the properties of the components but make use of these properties.

As a scientific endeavor, the identification of such design does not require us to say *who* the designer is; theists will of course be thinking of God.

One major area for identifying intelligent design in the natural world would be the cosmological anthropic principle: Why are the constants of the universe so finely tuned to support life on this planet?[1] Is it reasonable to suppose that this is the result either of chance or of some as yet unknown natural law? One finds plenty of statements from the cosmologists expressing their awe at the situation, even in religious terms.[2]

A second major area for such identification of design would be in the biological world. This is the burden of Michael Behe's concept of "irreducible complexity," articulated in his *Darwin's Black Box.*[3] According to Behe, we find complex systems in the biological world that cannot be explained by gradualistic development because they need a minimum number of components to be specifically functional before the whole system works (such as blood clotting and bacterial flagella). Hence, the theory goes, a better explanation for why these systems are there is that a designer imposed the structure on the components. Biological design can also be invoked, say, in the origin of life itself: What we know of biochemistry does not favor the idea that a "natural process only" explanation is true.[4] Also, DNA as a message-bearing medium can be called the product of design. Indeed, if DNA *does* carry a message, then its message cannot be the product of the component chemicals or it is not a message at all.

Other possible areas for identifying intelligent design would be the origins of various levels of differentiation among living groups (e.g., phyla) and the origin of human beings themselves.[5] These ideas are opposed to "evolution," if by evolution one means what Howard Van Till called a "historical scenario that proceeds from molecules to mankind along a continuous pathway of natural phenomena." The intelligent design program is neutral, however, on the question of whether all living things share a common ancestor, although many of its proponents doubt that they do.

It is plain that the identification of "intelligent design" proceeds by the finding of insoluble gaps between what we see and the processes we know about that might have produced what we see. That is, there is a "gap" between the information in DNA and the properties of its component chemicals. There is a gap between human capacities (e.g., in the intellectual,

---

[1] See, for example, the presentation of Hugh Ross, "Astronomical Evidences for a Personal, Transcendent God" in J. P. Moreland, ed., *The Creation Hypothesis* (Downers Grove, Ill.: InterVarsity, 1994), 141-172.
[2] For examples cf. Alan Hayward, *Creation and Evolution* (Minneapolis: Bethany, 1995), 58-64; Ian Barbour, *Religion in an Age of Science* (New York: HarperSanFrancisco, 1990), 135-136.
[3] Michael Behe, *Darwin's Black Box* (New York: Free Press, 1996).
[4] Cf. Walter Bradley and Charles Thaxton, "Information and the Origin of Life" in Moreland, ed., *Creation Hypothesis*, 173-210.
[5] On an important facet of the last point, cf. John W. Oller, Jr., and John L. Ohmdahl, "Origin of the Human Language Capacity: In Whose Image?" in Moreland, ed., *Creation Hypothesis*, 235-269.

moral, linguistic, aesthetic, and spiritual spheres) and what we find in every other animal. From these gaps comes the assertion that it took special agent activity to bridge the gaps. And that leads to the chief theological critique of the intelligent design program: It is just an appeal to ignorance and a species of "the God-of-the-gaps." Related to this critique is the argument that scientific and faith-based descriptions of objects and events must be complementary, and that intelligent design involves an improper mixing of categories. Similarly, we have the "functional integrity" type of doctrines, which insists that to look for "gaps" implies a less-than-fully-intelligent Designer who could not come up with a world with all its physical capacities built in.

The philosophical objections to intelligent design generally fall along the following lines:[6] First, there is the argument that whatever the likelihood of the existence of intelligent design, identifying it is not a part of science, which is committed to supplying natural-process-based explanations for everything. Another objection is that to identify intelligent design is incompatible with the scientific enterprise and could encourage laziness; after all, once you declare that something is designed, you no longer look for natural pathways to produce it, and this can inhibit research. A final objection is that intelligent design is not there to be found, so the search is futile anyhow (this typically from those committed to philosophical naturalism).

We shall proceed by first asking whether the biblical materials do in fact support the intelligent design program and if so under what conditions may we expect to find design, then by assessing these conclusions against the common philosophical objections.

DOES THE BIBLE SUPPORT THE SEARCH FOR INTELLIGENT DESIGN?

As I pointed out in chapter 1, the intelligent design program is most credible theologically if the following claims are viable: 1) that the supernaturalist model of divine action is correct; 2) that at least some supernatural events are detectable; and 3) that some specific events in the natural history of our planet have a (detectable) supernatural factor.

The conclusions of chapters 4–9 are that the Bible supports the first two

---

[6] I attended the conference "Naturalism, Theism, and the Scientific Enterprise" (NTSE) put on by the Department of Philosophy at the University of Texas at Austin, held in February, 1997. The goal of this conference was to air the question: Must science be (at least methodologically) naturalistic if it is to be true to itself? Does the nature of science as such exclude all references to intelligent design? This conference was then continued by an E-mail reflector, and a number of people eventually joined this list who had not attended the conference. The objections to intelligent design given here pretty well summarize the objections from these venues.

of these propositions. Hence in this section we must address the third: that some specific events in the natural history of our planet have a (detectable) supernatural factor. Perhaps the best place to begin is with the creation narrative of Genesis.

We have already seen in chapter 6 that Genesis 1:1 presents us with a major discontinuity, namely the origin of the universe itself. We can see further that the communicative purpose of Genesis 1:1–2:3 is to describe the preparation of the earth as a place for humans to live, love, be happy, and worship the Creator of the universe.[7] Hence, it should not surprise us to find evidence of a universe finely tuned to support life; and even if the only biological life the universe can support is ours, that is not a problem. However, the anthropic principle, as this fine-tuning is called, is not clearly a strong argument for *imposed* design, which is what we are after here. Indeed, it has a rejoinder, as John North has noted:[8]

> A. "Only by God's good grace do we inhabit a Universe perfectly suited to our needs, that is, satisfying the conditions necessary for our existence."
> B. "God may well be responsible, but at all events we should not be surprised that we encounter conditions suited to our existence. If they did not exist, we should not exist."

However, as William Lane Craig has pointed out, the reply of B also has a rejoinder:[9]

> Suppose you are to be executed by a firing squad of 100 trained marksmen, all of them aiming rifles at your heart. You are blindfolded; the command is given; you hear the deafening roar of the rifles. And you observe that you are still alive. The 100 marksmen missed!
>
> Taking off the blindfold, you do not observe that you are dead. No surprise there: you *could not* observe that you are dead. Nonetheless, you should be astonished that you are alive. The entire firing squad missed you altogether! Surprise at that extremely improbable fact is wholly justified—and that fact calls for an explanation. You would immediately suspect that they missed you on purpose, by design.

At the very least, then, the emotion of surprise is justified and points to the possibility of purposive agent causation as the explanation. We are not

---

[7] For development of this idea, see my "Reading Genesis 1:1–2:3 as an Act of Communication: Discourse Analysis and Literal Interpretation," in Joseph Pipa, Jr., and David Hall, eds., *Did God Create in Six Days?* (Taylor, S.C.: Southern Presbyterian Press, 1999), 131-151.

[8] John North, *The Norton History of Astronomy and Cosmology* (New York: Norton, 1995), 619.

[9] William Lane Craig, "Cosmos and Creator," *Origins and Design* 17:2 (1996), 18-28, at 23.

dealing with a knock-down argument with compelling logical force here, but with something that, when taken with other factors (especially what we know to be true of ourselves), adds an aesthetic element to the whole discussion and equips us to respond to our Creator warmly, with our whole person.

Let's look more specifically at how the creation narrative describes the history of the preparation of our planet for human life. Genesis 1:1–2:3 very much represents creation as a "project" that was completed over some time, that includes a series of supernatural actions.[10] We can see this most clearly in the presence of the Spirit of God (1:2), who is a supernatural agent,[11] and in the places where God expressed a wish that was then fulfilled (1:3, 6, 9, 11, 14, 20, 24, 26).[12]

We saw in chapter 3 that Howard Van Till and others who are providentialists (at least in the arena of natural history) would find in this reading of Genesis an implied critique of the Creator, as if he had somehow called an incomplete world into existence if it did not have within itself the capacities to fulfill all his purposes (including the development of life and of humans). Those who make this objection want to magnify the competence and artistry of the artisan who made the world, but the objection is theologically valid only if that is indeed the picture of God's creative work that Genesis portrays. If we say, as I did above, that the work of creation being spread over six "days" makes it sound more like a *project* than an *artifact*, then we see that the objection falls to the ground.

Further, we should note that, as God's "work," nature is presented, not as all-sufficient, but as *sufficient for its assigned purposes*. It seems clear that one of nature's purposes is to be "interfered with": After all, God's image-bearers will "rule" (i.e., manage, direct, and interfere with) nature as a result of their being in his image. In doing so they are following the example of the pattern God himself set (e.g., Gen. 2:15, where the human is to "work" the garden's soil and "keep" it, i.e., direct its activity and interfere with it).[13]

---

[10] For comments on many of the particular verses and exegetical issues in this account, see my "Reading Genesis 1:1–2:3 as an Act of Communication," which will supply extensive notes and discussion.

[11] As B. B. Warfield, "The Spirit of God in the Old Testament," *Biblical and Theological Studies* (Philadelphia: Presbyterian and Reformed, 1968), 127-156, remarked (131): "In both Testaments the Spirit of God appears distinctly as *the executive of the Godhead*" (italics mine; cf. also 133-134). Similarly Michael Green, *I Believe in the Holy Spirit* (Grand Rapids, Mich.: Eerdmans, 1975), commented (19): "In speaking of the 'Spirit of the Lord' the Old Testament writers significantly retain this emphasis on God's violent invasion from outside our experience. . . . It is their way of stressing that the Beyond has come into our midst." (I do not agree with Green's reticence, 28-29, in finding the Holy Spirit referred to in Gen. 1:2.)

[12] Grammatically these are instances of the verb *'āmar* ("he said") followed by a volitional verb. As we saw in chapter 6, the intertestamental book of Wisdom also takes this view, where the divine "word" (*logos*) is the agent both of creation and of interventions (9:1; 16:12; 18:15).

[13] The Genesis creation account sees God's creation "week" as the pattern for the ordinary human work-week. This comes out from, among other things, the refrain "there was evening and there was morning," i.e., this designates the worker's daily rest; the divine work and Sabbath in 2:1-3 are the pattern for the human week in Ex. 20:8-11.

Nature, as it were, absorbs these interferences, cooperates with them, and supports their results; for this she was designed and in this she performs admirably. She is a willing and capable subject.

We might ask, however, whether all this has any bearing on what we should expect to find in the natural world. We may be pressing Genesis into service for which it was not intended (the account is, after all, very broad-stroke); and further, the supernatural events may not all be detectable. As to the first issue, it seems fair to conclude from Genesis *that* there are "gaps," but not necessarily *what* those gaps are. As to the second, it seems pretty obvious that at least some of those gaps will be detectable. For example, though humans are like the animals in many ways in these chapters, the bestowal of the "image of God" (Gen. 1:26-27) is a clear point of discontinuity between humans and the other animals. One would expect that the principle of life itself (which is, at the very least, *organization* of the component parts of living things) is also a detectable discontinuity. In fact, as G. K. Chesterton once wrote,[14]

> No philosopher denies that a mystery still attaches to the two great transitions: the origin of the universe itself and the origin of the principle of life itself. Most philosophers have the enlightenment to add that a third mystery attaches to the origin of man himself. In other words, a third bridge was built across a third abyss of the unthinkable when there came into the world what we call reason and what we call will.

Chesterton's three "mysteries" or "abysses of the unthinkable" correspond to what I have called *lacunae naturae causâ* (chapter 9). Should we expect other *lacunae naturae causâ*? Well, quite possibly; but the best thing to do is to go and look, and this, as it turns out, is a research project.

If such *lacunae* exist, can we say under what circumstances we may legitimately identify imposed design in the natural world? We can, by making use of a distinction from the philosophy of science. There are two contexts of scientific description, the *nomothetic* and the *historical*.[15] The nomothetic context is the one that describes the normal behavior of the things described: Like charges repel, opposite charges attract; apples fall at such-and-such an acceleration; bullfrogs eat dragonflies. This is the realm of scientific "laws" (hence the name, *nomo*thetic), and many popular definitions of science restrict themselves to this domain. The historical context is

---

[14] G. K. Chesterton, *The Everlasting Man* (Garden City, N.Y.: Doubleday, 1955 [originally 1925]), 27.

[15] Cf. Stephen Meyer, "The Methodological Equivalence of Design and Descent: Can There Be a Scientific 'Theory of Creation'?" in Moreland, ed., *Creation Hypothesis*, 67-112, at 78-82.

the one in which we try to explain the particular sequence of causes that led to some state of affairs: Why is there a mountain here; why did this species go extinct; how did the victim die? The popular restriction of science to the nomothetic domain is clearly wrong; are not cosmology, geology, and linguistics sciences, even though each has major historical components? Of course the two contexts are related; I will draw on nomothetic conclusions in my historical descriptions.

The Bible would lead us to believe that appeal to special divine action is never appropriate in a nomothetic context. Of course we will assert God's preservation of properties and concurrence in causal effects; but since preservation and concurrence are not physically detectable, they will not enter into scientific descriptions. I have heard believers explain that the "law" that *opposite charges attract* should require that the electrons and protons of an atom would crash into each other and electrons would no longer orbit the nucleus; that they do not can only be explained, the argument goes, by Colossians 1:17, "In him all things hold together." This is an invalid argument and readily liable to the "God-of-the-gaps" complaint: Once the natural mechanism that explains this is discovered, where then is God? A biblical doctrine of creation as "very good" should have prevented this kind of argument.[16]

And what of historical contexts? For a great number, perhaps a majority, of such historical descriptions, we would not invoke supernatural causation. This is not because of any rule, however, but because we do not have beforehand any reason to expect it. For example, when my son was about three I saw a scab on his leg and asked him how he got it. He told me, "God put it there." Now this is an admirable doctrine of providence, but it was not what I was asking! I assumed the scab was fully (physically) explicable in terms of his and other humans' behavior, and the natural properties of his environment (stairs, chairs, etc.) and of his skin; hence I considered his theological explanation *complementary* to the "natural process" one. But what if I am asking about the origin of the universe, or the origin of life, or the origin of humans? I can at least say that the natural properties of their components are pretty poor candidates for explaining them. And this, I think, illustrates the rule of rationality: We may rationally exclude appeals to supernatural activity in this context only if we already have good grounds for believing it not to be relevant. But if some objects or events give evidence of being the products of agency, it is certainly legitimate to ask "*whose* agency?"

---

[16] This was apparently a failure on Newton's part, when he "gave God the responsibility of preventing the stars from collapsing together under the very attraction which he caused" (Edward Davis, "Newton's Rejection of the 'Newtonian World View': The Role of Divine Will in Newton's Natural Philosophy," *Science and Christian Belief* 3:1 [1991], 103-117, at 110).

CONSIDERATION OF THE OBJECTIONS TO INTELLIGENT DESIGN

Now let's revisit and evaluate the most common theological and philosophical criticisms leveled against intelligent design. Some of these criticisms we have already dealt with in articulating just what intelligent design is and is not. For instance, there is no theological requirement that *all* scientific and faith-based explanations must be complementary, since that depends on a providentialist model of God's action as well as a failure to distinguish between nomothetic and historical contexts. Additionally, the doctrine of "functional integrity" is not a sound reading of Genesis; indeed, it is probably driven more by a favored metaphor (the creation as artifact or machine) than by exegesis.[17] Suppose we change the metaphor: Picture the creation as a musical instrument and its history as the tune. There is no problem with the instrument if it does not have the tune within itself.[18] Genesis portrays a creation that is adequate for its assigned purposes, which include being "played" or interacted with.

I have, however, heard someone contend that it is certainly within God's power to design an evolutionary process that will produce information (a reference to the function of DNA). But, as Stephen Meyer observed, this betrays a serious confusion.[19] To say that a *natural process* produced *an information sequence* is actually a contradiction in terms. And even God cannot make that happen! As C. S. Lewis put it,[20]

> Omnipotence means power to do all that is intrinsically possible, not to do the intrinsically impossible. . . . Meaningless combinations of words do not suddenly acquire meaning simply because we prefix to them the two other words 'God can.' It remains true that all *things* are possible with God: the intrinsic impossibilities are not things but nonentities.

The God-of-the-gaps criticism is more serious. One commonly encounters statements to the effect that "gaps in our knowledge of the *physical* world need filling with *physical* explanations, not talk-about-God."[21] But

---

[17] It is possible to charge that the functional integrity approach is based on aesthetic and theological factors that are themselves open to serious question (as I offer here). Besides, as Paul Helm put it, it is not appropriate to argue a priori what God will and will not do with the physical creation, since that is a contingent matter of fact which must be investigated (*The Providence of God* [Downers Grove, Ill.: InterVarsity, 1994], 76).

[18] Of course this is just an image, with limitations, since the creation depends on God for its very being.

[19] Stephen Meyer, "The Origin of Life and the Death of Materialism," *Intercollegiate Review* 31:2 (Spring 1996), 24-43, at 39.

[20] C. S. Lewis, *The Problem of Pain* (New York: Macmillan, 1962), chapter 2.

[21] Michael Poole in Michael Poole and Gordon Wenham, *Creation or Evolution: A False Antithesis?* (Oxford: Latimer House, 1987), 56.

really, this is begging the question. Are physical explanations *always* adequate? By what right may we assume a priori that all "gaps" are *lacunae ignorantiae causâ* and that none are *naturae causâ*? We have to bring in other considerations: Have we good reason to expect that special interferences are not relevant here? I would suggest that, even apart from the Bible, the radical disjunction between, say, humans and other animals is obvious, and the more we know the plainer that becomes. That is, I do not think that alleviation of ignorance is going to change that picture, only accentuate it.[22] This is equivalent to discerning design in the origin of Stonehenge: No one expects that knowing more about rocks will change that inference.

On the other hand, one must be cautious. It is possible that, for example, some cases of "irreducible complexity" *can* eventually be plausibly accounted for by natural processes. It is theoretically possible that some gaps in the fossil record will someday succumb to plausible transitional explanations. It is possible that the Big Bang theory will not survive, and hence will not be available in support of creation *ex nihilo*. This is why we need sound criteria for inferring design, such as those that Dembski offers.[23] Even though there will be some uncertainty *in some cases* (I do not think in all), that in itself is helpful, since it promotes honesty and critical thinking. Does anyone speaking in the name of "science" have the right to tell us that all the alleged discontinuities are in principle explicable naturally and even that we are on the verge of explaining them? Would not honesty about the problems be more becoming?[24]

Let's now turn to the philosophical objection that finding design is not a part of science, since science is committed to natural-process-based expla-

---

[22] I know that many in the cognitive sciences are saying otherwise, e.g., Stephen Pinker (professor of linguistics and cognitive sciences at MIT), *The Language Instinct* (New York: HarperCollins, 1995). In his chapter 11 he shows that language is uniquely human and offers an evolutionary explanation of how this came about (342-369). But his explanation consists of unwarranted modality shifts (including an appeal to what we might call "extinct-missing-links-of-the-gaps"). It is hard to avoid the impression that he finds these things persuasive because of the explanatory appeal of naturalism; e.g., he says "Darwin is history's most important biologist because he showed how such 'organs of extreme perfection and complication' could arise from the purely physical process of natural selection. . . . Natural selection is not just a scientifically respectable alternative to divine creation. It is the *only* alternative that can explain the evolution of a complex organ like the eye" (360). Indeed, I heard the renowned philosopher of mind and language Jerry Fodor say that we know virtually nothing of the pathway to get from an ape to a human brain. As he colorfully put it, "For all we know, all you have to do is spit in the right place on a chimp's brain to get ours" (rough quote from a public lecture at the University of Missouri, March 25, 1998).

[23] William Dembski, *The Design Inference: Eliminating Chance Through Small Probabilities* (Cambridge, England: Cambridge University Press, 1998; originally Ph.D. dissertation, University of Illinois at Chicago, 1996).

[24] William Dembski mentions some of the problem areas for which reserve would be appropriate: "The origin of life, the origin of the genetic code, the origin of multicellular life, the origin of sexuality, the gaps in the fossil record, the biological big bang that occurred in the Cambrian era, the development of complex organ systems, and the development of irreducibly complex molecular machines are just a few of the more serious difficulties that confront every account of the origin and development of life that posits only purposeless, material processes" (Dembski, "Teaching Intelligent Design as Religion or Science?" *Princeton Theological Review* 3:2 [May 1996], 14-18, at 17b).

nations for everything. The problem here is the definition of science, which is in fact controversial among philosophers: Can we reasonably define science in such a way to demarcate it from non-science? I do not intend to enter into the discussion here,[25] except to note that, at the end of the day, I would hope that what we want in a historical description is an account of *what happened*. In our culture the natural sciences hold a position of prominence, serving as a sort of paradigm for all true objective knowledge, to which other claims must submit for evaluation. But as C. S. Lewis observed, rational people should not give in to this:[26]

> The distinction thus made between scientific and non-scientific thoughts will not easily bear the weight we are attempting to put on it. . . . If popular thought feels "science" to be different from all other kinds of knowledge because science is experimentally verifiable, popular thought is mistaken. . . . We should therefore abandon the distinction between scientific and non-scientific thought. The proper distinction is between logical and non-logical thought.

Thus the conclusions of specific scientific disciplines only compel our assent to the extent that they satisfy the criteria of good critical thought, and this includes being properly *self*-critical in regard to precommitments. And this view that science must only provide natural-process-based explanations reflects an a priori conviction that *only* such explanations are there to be found. This is a philosophical position just as much as the theistic interpretation of intelligent design is.

Interestingly, we have an exactly analogous situation in the field of historiography.[27] That is, we often hear that a truly "scientific" history is entirely in terms of natural causes, or even that any account in which "God" or "a god" is a character is *by definition* not "historical." Behind such claims lie at least two assumptions that we ought to evaluate: 1) a loaded definition of the word *scientific* as "committed to naturalistic explanations come what

---

[25] See chapter 1 of my forthcoming *Christian Faith in an Age of Science* for a survey; for more detail cf. J. P. Moreland, *Christianity and the Nature of Science* (Grand Rapids, Mich.: Baker, 1989), 17-58.

[26] C. S. Lewis, *"De Futilitate,"* in *Christian Reflections* (Grand Rapids, Mich.: Eerdmans, 1967), 57-71, at 61-62.

[27] Some sample bibliography: William J. Abraham, *Divine Revelation and the Limits of Historical Criticism* (Oxford, England: Oxford University Press, 1982); V. Philips Long, *The Art of Biblical History* (Grand Rapids, Mich.: Zondervan, 1994); A. R. Millard, "The Old Testament and History: Some Considerations," *Faith and Thought* 110:1-2 (1983), 34-53, and "Sennacherib's Attack on Hezekiah," *Tyndale Bulletin* 36 (1985), 61-77; Iain W. Provan, "Ideologies, Literary and Critical: Reflections on Recent Writing on the History of Israel," *Journal of Biblical Literature* 114:4 (1995), 585-606 (with naturalistic responses from T. L. Thompson and P. R. Davies, 683-705). Millard's work is based on thorough familiarity with ancient Near Eastern literature; Abraham is a philosopher. Long's book is the work of a Bible scholar who has grasped the pertinent philosophical issues and is a trenchant critique of the insistence upon naturalistic accounts as alone qualifying as "history."

may"; and 2) a commitment to the metaphysical position that such explanations are in principle adequate. The first of these assumptions I have already criticized, and the second is the very question at issue! Alan Millard put it quite well,[28]

> Penetrating beyond the words of the text to seek for an explanation in terms of the natural world is unprofitable. Some texts do reveal the mechanics of divine intervention, e.g., "The Lord rained down great hailstones" (Jos. 10:11), or "Mighty Adad . . . uttered his loud cry over them and with heavy clouds and hailstones finished off the remainder" [from Sargon of Assyria's eighth campaign]. In other passages, where the action is simply reported, as in the [Assyrian] Ashurbanipal report, and in the one under discussion [2 Kings 18:13–19:37], *the historian has no alternative but to admit that something happened which is beyond his resources to comprehend.* Nevertheless, he should be prepared to admit that there was an unusual event. Whatever uncertainties remain, there are adequate grounds for deducing that something deflected Sennacherib from pressing his attack on Jerusalem and caused him to return to Nineveh before he received Hezekiah's tribute. To the Hebrew historian, and to all who share his faith today, that was an act of God.

There are criteria for detecting design, as Dembski has shown. What shall we do about it? Here is where we must realize that scientific theorizing does not take place in a vacuum; we integrate our empirical discoveries with the rest of what we believe. But, as we have already noted, there is no reason why people speaking in the name of "science" should instead promulgate naturalism. If we insist on adopting a demarcationist definition of science, then we can at least demand that people own up to the gaps and leave the explanation of those gaps as "outside the bounds of science"—or at least of the particular science. That is, a biologist is not qualified, as a biologist, to tell me that in principle only naturalistic histories exist. As a biologist, however, he is qualified to tell me that DNA carries information and that the capacity to do so is not explicable by anything we now believe.

This, by the way, indicates the reply to the claim that intelligent design is religion, not science. The identification of design need not be a part of an apologetic program. Indeed, given some of the uncertainties in identifying every instance of design, one should be very careful about that anyhow. Nor is it necessary to require anyone to name the Designer. After all, those who believe in "directed panspermia" (life here arose from seeding

---

[28] Millard, "Sennacherib's Attack," 77 (italics added).

by aliens) posit a cause whom they do not name. As we saw in the section in chapter 10 on the problem of evil, this is not the arena from which we get our best apologetic anyhow. On the other hand, if natural objects give evidence of being the products of agency, it is certainly legitimate to ask, "*Whose* agency?"

The objection that to identify intelligent design is a "science-stopper" (i.e., it cuts off the search for natural explanations) presupposes a number of things. First, it is liable to the charge of smuggling in the assumption that only natural processes are relevant, when that is precisely what needs to be shown. Second, it assumes that "scientific research" is an unqualified good. But what if the identification of design closes off an *unfruitful* line of research? Who would listen to someone who proposed to explain Stonehenge by means of the properties of the rocks that make it up? I hope *my* tax dollars would never be used to fund the project! Granted, once we decide that Stonehenge is designed, we leave off that line of questioning; but we do not thereby stop "science." Instead, we may ask what it is about the rocks that supports the design, where those rocks came from and how they got there, who were the people who made it, and so on. All of these are interesting lines of scientific research. On the other hand, it is certainly possible that someone will use intelligent design too soon—but that would be an abuse, not a proper use, and is no counterargument. The answer to that possibility is the same as the answer to all problems of jumping to conclusions: peer review, attempts to falsify, etc. Actually, we can turn the tables: The natural-process-only restriction *limits* the kinds of explanations available. Intelligent design does not reject such explanations from the scientists' toolbox, nor deem them improper in many cases; instead it augments that toolbox and gives a set of criteria for using the extra tools.

A final objection is that intelligent design is not there to be found, so the search is futile anyhow. Richard Dawkins is most famous for his assertion that, "Biology is the study of complicated things that give the appearance of having been designed for a purpose."[29] Now this belief is of course not an empirical result but a metaphysical precommitment. Indeed, to prove that it is true indirectly acknowledges that "design" is an appropriate subject for science—namely, to disprove it. The only answer to objection is, "Put up or shut up!" Let's look at the biological world and be honest about what we see, and explain where we are describing the evidence and where we are trying to integrate that evidence with our worldview. A Christian holds that it is a basic principle of rationality that we cannot know

---

[29] Richard Dawkins, *The Blind Watchmaker* (New York: Norton, 1986).

a contingent matter of fact a priori; instead we have to investigate it. Let the chips fall where they may.

In sum, the conclusions that supernaturalism has biblical support and that when carefully articulated it can hold its own against its most serious objections can be seen to apply in the realm of intelligent design as well as in the realm of redemptive historical miracles. Promotion of these ideas should encourage glad, critical, and constructive participation by Christians in the sciences and in the culture in which the sciences flourish.

Bibliography

BOOKS

Abraham, William J. *Divine Revelation and the Limits of Historical Criticism*. Oxford, England: Oxford University Press, 1982.

Alexander, J. A. *Psalms*. Grand Rapids, Mich.: Zondervan, n.d. (originally 1864).

Aquinas, Thomas. *Summa contra Gentiles*. English translation, Notre Dame, Ind.: University of Notre Dame Press, 1975.

———. *Summa Theologiae*. Rome: Marietti, 1950 (of the various English editions available, the most useful here is Peter Kreeft's annotated *Summa of the Summa*. San Francisco: Ignatius, 1990).

Ashley, Timothy. *Numbers* (New International Commentary on the Old Testament). Grand Rapids, Mich.: Eerdmans, 1993.

Barbour, Ian. *Religion in an Age of Science*. New York: HarperSanFrancisco, 1990.

Barr, James. *The Semantics of Biblical Language*. Oxford, England: Oxford University Press, 1961.

———. *Biblical Words for Time*. London: SCM, 1969.

Bauer, Walter (W. F. Arndt, F. W. Gingrich, F. W. Danker, trans. and eds.). *A Greek-English Lexicon of the New Testament and Other Early Christian Literature*. Chicago: University of Chicago Press, 1979. (Cited in the text as BAGD.)

Behe, Michael. *Darwin's Black Box*. New York: Free Press, 1996.

Berkeley, George. *The Principles of Human Knowledge with Other Writings* (G. J. Warnock, ed.). Glasgow: Collins, 1969 (first published in 1710).

Berkouwer, G. C. *The Providence of God*. Grand Rapids, Mich.: Eerdmans, 1952.

Bilynskyj, Stephen S. *God, Nature, and the Concept of Miracle*. Ph.D. dissertation, University of Notre Dame, 1982.

Boswell, James. *The Life of Samuel Johnson, LL.D.* (Everyman's Library). London: Dent, 1906 (originally 1791).

Brown, Colin. *Miracles and the Critical Mind*. Grand Rapids, Mich.: Eerdmans, 1984.

———. *That You May Believe: Miracles and Faith Then and Now*. Grand Rapids, Mich.: Eerdmans, 1985.

Brown, F., S. R. Driver, and C. A. Briggs. *A Hebrew and English Lexicon of the Old Testament*. Oxford, England: Oxford University Press, 1951.

Bruce, F. F. *Acts* (New International Commentary on the New Testament). Grand Rapids, Mich.: Eerdmans, 1988.

Buell, Jon, and Virginia Hearn, eds. *Darwinism: Science or Philosophy?* Richardson, Tex.: Foundation for Thought and Ethics, 1994.

Bultmann, Rudolph. *Kerygma and Myth*. New York: Harper and Row, 1961.

Burns, R. M. *The Great Debate on Miracles: From Joseph Glanvill to David Hume*. Lewisburg: Bucknell University Press, 1981.

Burrell, David B. *Aquinas: God and Action*. Notre Dame, Ind.: University of Notre Dame Press, 1979.

Cassuto, U. *Exodus*. Jerusalem: Magnes, 1967.

Chesterton, G. K. *Orthodoxy*. Garden City, N.Y.: Doubleday, 1959 (originally 1908).

———. *The Everlasting Man*. Garden City, N.Y.: Doubleday, 1955 (originally 1925).

————. *As I Was Saying: A Chesterton Reader* (Robert Knille, ed.). Grand Rapids, Mich.: Eerdmans, 1985.

Collins, C. John. *Homonymous Verbs in Biblical Hebrew: An Investigation of the Role of Comparative Philology*. Ph.D. dissertation, University of Liverpool, 1988.

————. *Christian Faith in an Age of Science* (forthcoming).

Cotterell, Peter, and Max Turner. *Linguistics and Biblical Interpretation*. Downers Grove, Ill.: InterVarsity, 1989.

Courtenay, William J. *Covenant and Causality in Medieval Thought*. London: Variorum Reprints, 1984.

Craigie, Peter. *Deuteronomy* (New International Commentary on the Old Testament). Grand Rapids, Mich.: Eerdmans, 1976.

Davids, Peter. *James* (New International Greek Testament Commentary). Grand Rapids, Mich.: Eerdmans, 1982.

Dawkins, Richard. *The Blind Watchmaker*. New York: Norton, 1986.

Delitzsch, Franz. *Commentary on the Epistle to the Hebrews*. English translation, Edinburgh: T and T Clark, 1868.

————. *Psalms* (Keil-Delitzsch). English translation, Grand Rapids, Mich.: Eerdmans, 1980 (German original 1867).

————. *Proverbs* (Keil-Delitzsch). English translation, Grand Rapids, Mich.: Eerdmans, 1980 (German original 1872).

Dembski, William. *The Design Inference: Eliminating Chance Through Small Probabilities*. Cambridge, England: Cambridge University Press, 1998.

Edwards, Jonathan. *The Works of Jonathan Edwards* (Sereno Dwight, ed.). Edinburgh: Banner of Truth, 1974.

Eichrodt, Walther. *Theology of the Old Testament* (J. A. Baker, trans.). English translation, London: SCM, 1967.

Fairbairn, Patrick. *The Interpretation of Prophecy*. Edinburgh: Banner of Truth, 1993 (originally 1865).

Farrer, Austin. *Faith and Speculation*. New York: New York University Press, 1967.

Fitzmyer, J. A. *Luke I-IX* (Anchor Bible). Garden City, N.Y.: Doubleday, 1981.

Fuller, R. H. *Interpreting the Miracles*. Philadelphia: Westminster, 1963.

Geivett, Douglas, and Gary Habermas, eds. *In Defense of Miracles*. Downers Grove, Ill.: InterVarsity, 1997.

Gordon, Robert. *I and II Samuel: A Commentary*. Grand Rapids, Mich.: Zondervan, 1986.

Grant, R. M. *Miracle and Natural Law in Graeco-Roman and Early Christian Thought*. Amsterdam: North Holland, 1952.

Green, Michael. *I Believe in the Holy Spirit*. Grand Rapids, Mich.: Eerdmans, 1975.

Guthrie, Donald. *Hebrews* (Tyndale New Testament Commentary). Grand Rapids, Mich.: Eerdmans, 1983.

Gwynne, Paul. *Special Divine Action: Key Issues in the Contemporary Debate*. Rome: Gregorian University Press, 1996.

Hakham, Amos. *Sēfer Šĕmôt* (Exodus, Da'at Miqra). Jerusalem: Mossad Harav Kook, 1991.

Harrison, R. K. *Introduction to the Old Testament*. Grand Rapids, Mich.: Eerdmans, 1969.

————. *Numbers*. Grand Rapids, Mich.: Baker, 1992.

Hebblethwaite, Brian, and Edward Henderson, eds. *Divine Action: Studies Inspired by the Philosophical Theology of Austin Farrer*. Edinburgh: T and T Clark, 1990.

Helm, Paul. *The Beginnings: Word and Spirit in Conversion*. Edinburgh: Banner of Truth, 1986.

————. *Eternal God: A Study of God Without Time*. Oxford: Clarendon Press, 1988.

———. *The Providence of God* (Contours of Christian Theology). Downers Grove, Ill.: InterVarsity, 1994.

Heppe, Heinrich. *Reformed Dogmatics* (G. T. Thomson, trans.). Grand Rapids, Mich.: Baker, 1978 (originally 1950).

Hooykas, Reijer. *Philosophia Libera: Christian Faith and the Freedom of Science.* London: Tyndale, 1957.

———. *The Principle of Uniformity in Geology, Biology, and Theology.* Leiden: E. J. Brill, 1963.

———. *Religion and the Rise of Modern Science.* Grand Rapids, Mich.: Eerdmans, 1972.

Houghton, John. *The Search for God: Can Science Help?* Oxford: Lion, 1995.

Huff, Darrell. *How to Lie with Statistics.* New York: Norton, 1954.

Hume, David. *Enquiries Concerning the Human Understanding and Concerning the Principles of Morals* (L. A. Selby-Bigge, ed.). Oxford: Clarendon Press, 1902.

Johnson, Phillip E. *Defeating Darwinism by Opening Minds.* Downers Grove, Ill.: InterVarsity, 1997.

Joüon, P., and T. Muraoka. *A Grammar of Biblical Hebrew.* Rome: Editrice Pontificio Istituto Biblico, 1993.

Kee, Howard Clark. *Miracle in the Early Christian World.* New Haven: Yale University Press, 1983.

Keller, Ernst, and Marie-Luise Keller. *Miracles in Dispute.* Philadelphia: Fortress, 1969.

Kidner, Derek. *Proverbs* (Tyndale Old Testament Commentary). Downers Grove, Ill.: InterVarsity, 1964.

———. *Genesis* (Tyndale Old Testament Commentary). Downers Grove, Ill.: InterVarsity, 1967.

———. *Psalms* (Tyndale Old Testament Commentary). Downers Grove, Ill.: InterVarsity, 1973.

———. *The Wisdom of Proverbs, Job, and Ecclesiastes.* Downers Grove, Ill.: InterVarsity, 1985.

Kiel, Y. *Sēfer Šěmûʾēl* (*Samuel*, Da'at Miqra). Jerusalem: Mossad Harav Kook, 1981.

———. *Sēfer Mělākîm* (*Kings*, Da'at Miqra). Jerusalem: Mossad Harav Kook, 1989.

Kraus, H. J. *Die Psalmen* (English translation, Continental Commentary). Minneapolis: Augsburg, 1989; originally Biblischer Kommentar Altes Testaments; Neukirchener Verlag, 1978.

Kreeft, Peter, and Ronald K. Tacelli. *Handbook of Christian Apologetics.* Downers Grove, Ill.: InterVarsity, 1994.

Kuhn, Thomas. *The Structure of Scientific Revolutions.* Chicago: University of Chicago Press, 1970.

Lewis, C. S. *The Problem of Pain.* London: Geoffrey Bles, 1940.

———. *Mere Christianity.* London: Geoffrey Bles, 1952.

———. *The Magician's Nephew.* New York: HarperCollins, 1994 (originally 1955).

———. *Miracles: A Preliminary Study.* New York: Macmillan, 1960.

———. *Prayer: Letters to Malcolm.* London: Collins, 1966.

———. *Studies in Words.* Cambridge, England: Cambridge University Press, 1967.

Liddell, H. G., and R. Scott (revised by H. S. Jones and R. McKenzie). *A Greek-English Lexicon.* New York: Oxford University Press, 1996.

Lindberg, David C. *The Beginnings of Western Science.* Chicago: University of Chicago Press, 1992.

Lindberg, David C., ed. *Science in the Middle Ages.* Chicago: University of Chicago Press, 1978.

Lindberg, David C., and Ronald Numbers, eds. *God and Nature: Historical Essays on the*

Encounter Between Christianity and Science. Berkeley, Calif.: University of California Press, 1986.

Long, V. Philips. *The Reign and Rejection of King Saul: A Case for Literary and Theological Coherence.* Atlanta: Scholars Press, 1989.

———. *The Art of Biblical History.* Grand Rapids, Mich.: Zondervan, 1994.

MacKay, Donald M. *The Clockwork Image.* Downers Grove, Ill.: InterVarsity, 1977.

———. *Science, Chance and Providence.* New York: Oxford University Press, 1978.

———. *Science and the Quest for Meaning.* Grand Rapids, Mich.: Eerdmans, 1982.

Malebranche, Nicolas. *The Search after Truth and Elucidations of the Search after Truth* (T. M. Lennon and P. J. Oscamp, trans.). Columbus: Ohio State University Press, 1980.

Marshall, I. H. *Luke* (New International Greek Text Commentary). Grand Rapids, Mich.: Eerdmans, 1978.

Mascall, Eric L. *Christian Theology and Natural Science: Some Questions in Their Relations.* London: Longmans, Green and Co., 1956.

McMullin, Ernan, ed. *Evolution and Creation.* Notre Dame, Ind.: University of Notre Dame Press, 1985.

Meyer, Stephen C. *Of Clues and Causes: A Methodological Interpretation of Origin of Life Studies.* Ph.D. dissertation, University of Cambridge, 1990.

Moreland, J. P. *Christianity and the Nature of Science: A Philosophical Investigation.* Grand Rapids, Mich.: Baker, 1989.

Moreland, J. P., ed. *The Creation Hypothesis.* Downers Grove, Ill.: InterVarsity, 1994.

Morris, T. V., ed. *Divine and Human Action: Essays in the Metaphysics of Theism.* Ithaca, N.Y.: Cornell University Press, 1988.

Moule, C. F. D., ed. *Miracles: Cambridge Studies in Their Philosophy and History.* London: Mowbray, 1965.

Murray, Iain. *Revival and Revivalism: The Making and Marring of American Evangelicalism, 1750–1858.* Edinburgh: Banner of Truth, 1994.

Murray, John. *Collected Writings.* Edinburgh: Banner of Truth, 1984.

North, John. *The Norton History of Astronomy and Cosmology.* New York: Norton, 1995.

Oesterley, W. O. E. *The Wisdom of Jesus Son of Sirach* (Cambridge Bible for Schools and Colleges). Cambridge, England: Cambridge University Press, 1912.

Pascal, Blaise. *Pensées* (introduction and notes by Ch. M. des Granges). Paris: Garnier Frères, 1964 (this uses the Brunschvicg numbers; the common English edition is by A. J. Krailsheimer [London: Penguin, 1995], and uses a different numbering scheme. Peter Kreeft's *Christianity for Modern Pagans* [San Francisco: Ignatius, 1993] is an abridged and annotated edition based on Krailsheimer.)

Peacocke, Arthur R. *Theology for a Scientific Age.* Minneapolis: Fortress, 1993.

Pearson, Karl. *The Grammar of Science.* London: Macmillan, 1896.

Pieper, Francis. *Christian Dogmatics.* St. Louis: Concordia, 1950.

Pinker, Stephen. *The Language Instinct.* New York: HarperCollins, 1995.

Pinnock, Clark, Richard Rice, John Sanders, William Hasker, and David Basinger. *The Openness of God.* Downers Grove, Ill.: InterVarsity, 1994.

Polkinghorne, John. *Science and Providence: God's Interaction with the World.* Boston: Shambhala, 1989.

———. *The Faith of a Physicist: Reflections of a Bottom-up Thinker.* Princeton, N.J.: Princeton University Press, 1994.

———. *Quarks, Chaos, and Christianity.* New York: Crossroad, 1996.

Poole, M. W., and G. J. Wenham. *Creation or Evolution: A False Antithesis?* (Latimer Studies 23/24). Oxford, England: Latimer House, 1987.

Provan, Iain. *1 and 2 Kings* (New International Biblical Commentary). Peabody, Mass.: Hendrickson, 1995.

Randall, John Herman, Jr. *The Making of the Modern Mind.* Boston: Houghton Mifflin, 1940.

Ratzsch, Del. *Philosophy of Science.* Downers Grove, Ill.: InterVarsity, 1986.

Remus, Harold. *Pagan-Christian Conflict over Miracle in the Second Century.* Cambridge: The Philadelphia Patristic Foundation, 1983.

Robinson, H. Wheeler. *Inspiration and Revelation in the Old Testament.* Oxford, England: Oxford University Press, 1946.

Russell, Colin. *Cross-currents: Interactions Between Science and Faith.* London: Christian Impact, 1995.

Russell, Robert John, Nancey Murphy, and Arthur R. Peacocke, eds. *Chaos and Complexity: Scientific Perspectives on Divine Action.* Vatican City State: Vatican Observatory, 1995.

Schmid, Heinrich. *Doctrinal Theology of the Evangelical Lutheran Church* (Charles Hay and Henry Jacobs, trans.). Minneapolis: Augsburg, 1961 (originally 1875).

Shedd, William G. T. *Dogmatic Theology.* Nashville: Nelson, 1980 (originally 1888–1894).

Stenmark, Mikael. *Rationality in Science, Religion, and Everyday Life.* Notre Dame, Ind.: University of Notre Dame Press, 1995.

Thomas, Owen C., ed. *God's Activity in the World: The Contemporary Problem* (AAR Studies in Religion 31). Chico, Calif.: Scholars Press, 1983.

Thompson, J. M. *Miracles in the New Testament.* London: Edward Arnold, 1911.

Van der Meer, Jitse M., ed. *Facets of Faith and Science, Volume 4: Interpreting God's Action in the World.* Lanham, Md.: University Press of America, 1996.

Van Till, Howard J. *The Fourth Day.* Grand Rapids, Mich.: Eerdmans, 1986.

Van Till, Howard J., Robert E. Snow, John H. Stek, and Davis A. Young. *Portraits of Creation.* Grand Rapids, Mich.: Eerdmans, 1990.

White, V. *The Fall of a Sparrow: A Concept of Special Divine Action.* Exeter, England: Paternoster, 1985.

Whybray, R. N. *Proverbs* (New Century Bible Commentary). Grand Rapids, Mich.: Eerdmans, 1994.

Wiseman, D. J. *1 and 2 Kings* (Tyndale Old Testament Commentary). Downers Grove, Ill.: InterVarsity, 1993.

Wolterstorff, Nicholas. *Divine Discourse: Philosophical Reflections on the Claim That God Speaks.* Cambridge, England: Cambridge University Press, 1995.

Zerwick, M. *Grammatical Analysis of the Greek New Testament.* Rome: Editrice Pontificio Istituto Biblico, 1993.

ARTICLES

Addinall, Peter. "A Response to R. J. Berry on 'The Virgin Birth of Christ.'" *Science and Christian Belief* 9:1 (1997), 65-72 (followed by response from R. J. Berry, 73-78).

Alexander, T. D. "Exodus." In D. A. Carson et al., eds. *The New Bible Commentary: Twenty-first Century Edition.* Downers Grove, Ill.: InterVarsity, 1994.

Barr, James. "Biblical Theology." In K. R. Crim et al., eds. *Interpreter's Dictionary of the Bible, Supplement.* Nashville: Abingdon, 1976, 104a-111b.

Berry, R. J. "The Virgin Birth of Christ." *Science and Christian Belief* 8:2 (1996), 101-110.

Bimson, John J. "Kings." In D. A. Carson et al., eds. *The New Bible Commentary: Twenty-first Century Edition.* Downers Grove, Ill.: InterVarsity, 1994.

Bishop, Steve. "Science and Faith: Boa Constrictors and Warthogs?" *Themelios* 19:1 (1994), 4-9.

Bussey, Peter J. "Indeterminacy, Time and the Future." *Science and Christian Belief* 9:1 (1997), 79-84.

Collins, C. John. "How Old Is the Earth? Anthropomorphic Days in Genesis 1:1–2:3." *Presbyterion* 20:2 (1994), 109-130.

———. "Reading Genesis 1:1–2:3 as an Act of Communication: Discourse Analysis and Literal Interpretation." In Joseph Pipa, Jr., and David Hall, eds. *Did God Create in Six Days?* Taylor, S.C.: Southern Presbyterian Press, 1999.

———. "Science, Supernaturalism, and Postmodernism." Presented at "Christianity in a Postmodern World." L'Abri Conference at Clemson University, October 24, 1997.

———. "*Miqreh* in 1 Samuel 6:9: 'Chance' or 'Event'?" forthcoming in *The Bible Translator* 51:1 (2000).

Collins, John J. "Natural Theology and Biblical Tradition: The Case of Hellenistic Judaism." *Catholic Biblical Quarterly* 60:1 (1998), 1-15.

Copan, Paul. "Is *Creatio ex Nihilo* a Post-Biblical Invention? An Examination of Gerhard May's Proposal." *Trinity Journal* 17n.s. (1996), 77-93.

Courtenay, William J. "The Dialectic of Omnipotence in the High and Late Middle Ages." In T. Rudavsky, ed. *Divine Omniscience and Omnipotence in Medieval Philosophy*. Dordrecht: D. Reidel, 1985, 243-269.

Cowan, Steven B. "On the Epistemological Justification of Miracle Claims." *Philosophia Christi* 18 (1995), 25-41.

———. "A *Reductio ad Absurdum* of Divine Temporality." *Religious Studies* 32 (1996), 371-378.

Craig, William Lane. "The Problem of Miracles: A Historical and Philosophical Perspective." In D. Wenham and C. Blomberg, eds. *Gospel Perspectives 6: The Miracles of Jesus*. Sheffield: JSOT Press, 1986, 9-48.

———. "Cosmos and Creator." *Origins and Design* 17:2 (1996), 18-28.

Crain, Steven D. "Divine Action in a World Chaos: An Evaluation of John Polkinghorne's Model of Special Divine Action." *Faith and Philosophy* 14:1 (1997), 41-61.

Cressey, M. H. "Miracles." In J. D. Douglas, ed. *The New Bible Dictionary*. Wheaton, Ill.: Tyndale, 1982, 782a-784a.

Davidson, A. B. "God (in O.T.)." In James Hastings, ed. *A Dictionary of the Bible*. Peabody, Mass.: Hendrickson, 1988 (originally 1898), ii:196a-205b.

Davis, Edward B. "Newton's Rejection of the 'Newtonian World View': The Role of Divine Will in Newton's Natural Philosophy." *Science and Christian Belief* 3:1 (1991), 103-117.

Davis, Stephen T. "The Miracle at Cana: A Philosopher's Perspective." In D. Wenham and C. Blomberg, eds. *Gospel Perspectives 6: The Miracles of Jesus*. Sheffield: JSOT Press, 1986, 419-442.

Deason, Gary B. "Reformation Theology and the Mechanistic Conception of Nature." In David Lindberg and Ronald Numbers. *God and Nature: Historical Essays on the Encounter Between Christianity and Science*. Berkeley, Calif.: University of California Press, 1986, 167-191.

Dembski, William A. "Schleiermacher's Metaphysical Critique of Miracles." *Scottish Journal of Theology* 49:4 (1996), 443-465.

———. "Teaching Intelligent Design as Religion or Science?" *Princeton Theological Review* 3:2 (May 1996), 14-18.

Dowe, Phil. "Chance and Providence." *Science and Christian Belief* 9:1 (1997), 3-20.

Doye, Jonathan, Ian Goldby, Christina Line, Stephen Lloyd, Paul Shellard, and David Tricker.

"Contemporary Perspectives on Chance, Providence and Free Will." *Science and Christian Belief* 7:2 (1995), 117-139.

Duce, Philip P. "Complementarity in Perspective." *Science and Christian Belief* 8:2 (1996), 145-155 (followed with response by Howard Van Till, 157-161).

Fales, Evan. "Divine Intervention." *Faith and Philosophy* 14:2 (1997), 170-194.

Freddoso, Alfred. "Medieval Aristotelianism and the Case Against Secondary Causation in Nature." In T. V. Morris, ed. *Divine and Human Action: Essays in the Metaphysics of Theism.* Ithaca, N.Y.: Cornell University Press, 1988, 74-118.

———. "God's General Concurrence with Secondary Causes: Why Conservation Is Not Enough." *Philosophical Perspectives* 5 (1991), 553-585.

———. "The 'Openness' of God: A Reply to Hasker." *Christian Scholar's Review* 28:1 (Fall, 1998), 124-133 (also available at www.nd.edu/~afreddos/papers/openness.htm).

Giberson, Karl. "Intelligent Design on Trial—a Review Essay." *Christian Scholar's Review* 24 (1995), 459-471.

Gingerich, Owen. "Where in the World Is God?" in Michael Bauman, ed. *Man and Creation: Perspectives on Science and Theology.* Hillsdale, Mich.: Hillsdale College Press, 1993, 209-229.

Gousmett, Chris. "Creation Order and Miracle According to Augustine." *Evangelical Quarterly* 60 (1988), 217-240.

Grizzle, Raymond E. "A Few Suggestions for the Proponents of Intelligent Design." *Perspectives on Science and Christian Faith* 47:3 (September 1995), 186-189.

Harder, G. "Nature." In C. Brown, ed. *New International Dictionary of New Testament Theology.* Exeter, England: Paternoster, 1976, ii:656-662.

Hardon, John. "The Concept of Miracle from St. Augustine to Modern Apologetics." *Theological Studies* 15 (1954), 229-257.

Helm, Paul. "The Miraculous." *Science and Christian Belief* 3:1 (1991), 83-95.

———. "Eternal Creation." *Tyndale Bulletin* 45:2 (1994), 321-338.

Hepper, F. N. "Grain." In J. D. Douglas et al., eds. *The New Bible Dictionary.* Downers Grove, Ill.: InterVarsity, 1982, 444.

Hess, Richard S. "Genesis 1–2 and Recent Studies of Ancient Texts." *Science and Christian Belief* 7:2 (1995), 141-149.

Hoffmeier, James. "Egypt, Plagues In." In David Freedman et al., eds. *Anchor Bible Dictionary.* New York: Doubleday, 1992, ii:374a-378a.

Holland, R. F. "The Miraculous." *American Philosophical Quarterly* 2:1 (January 1965), 43-51.

Hort, G. "The Plagues of Egypt." *Zeitschrift für die Alttestamentliche Wissenschaft* 69 (1957), 84-103.

———. "The Plagues of Egypt (part ii)." *Zeitschrift für die Alttestamentliche Wissenschaft* 70 (1958), 48-59.

———. "The Death of Qorah." *Australian Biblical Review* 7 (1959), 2-26.

Houghton, John. "What Happens When We Pray." *Science and Christian Belief* 7:1 (1995), 3-20.

Hubbard, D. A. "Wisdom." In J. D. Douglas et al., eds. *The New Bible Dictionary.* Downers Grove, Ill.: InterVarsity, 1982, 1255b-1257a.

Judge, Stuart. "How Not to Think about Miracles." *Science and Christian Belief* 3:1 (1991), 97-102.

Keller, James A. "A Moral Argument Against Miracles." *Faith and Philosophy* 12:1 (1995), 54-78.

Kitchen, K. A. "Plagues of Egypt." In J. D. Douglas et al., eds. *The New Bible Dictionary*. Downers Grove, Ill.: InterVarsity, 1982, 943a-944b.

LaSor, William S. "Kings." In D. Guthrie et al., eds. *The New Bible Commentary: Revised*. Grand Rapids, Mich.: Eerdmans, 1970.

Lewis, C. S. "The Efficacy of Prayer." In Lewis. *The World's Last Night*. New York: Harcourt, Brace, Jovanovitch, 1960.

———. *"De Futilitate."* In Lewis. *Christian Reflections* (W. Hooper, ed.). Grand Rapids, Mich.: Eerdmans, 1967, 57-71.

———. "Modern Theology and Biblical Criticism." In Lewis. *Christian Reflections* (W. Hooper, ed.). Grand Rapids, Mich.: Eerdmans, 1967, 152-166.

———. "Petitionary Prayer: A Problem Without an Answer." In Lewis. *Christian Reflections* (W. Hooper, ed.). Grand Rapids, Mich.: Eerdmans, 1967, 142-151.

Meyer, Stephen. "The Origin of Life and the Death of Materialism." *Intercollegiate Review* 31:2 (Spring 1996), 24-43.

Millard, A. R. "The Old Testament and History: Some Considerations." *Faith and Thought* 110:1-2 (1983), 34-53.

———. "Sennacherib's Attack on Hezekiah." *Tyndale Bulletin* 36 (1985), 61-77.

Moreland, J. P. "Complementarity, Agency Theory, and the God-of-the-Gaps." *Perspectives on Science and Christian Faith* 49:1 (March 1997), 2-14.

Mundle, W., O. Hufius, and C. Brown. "Miracle, Wonder, Sign." In C. Brown, ed. *New International Dictionary of New Testament Theology*. Exeter, England: Paternoster, 1976, ii:620-635.

Murray, John. "Calvin's Doctrine of Creation." *Westminster Theological Journal* 17 (1954), 21-43.

O'Connor, Robert C. "Science on Trial: Exploring the Rationality of Methodological Naturalism." *Perspectives on Science and Christian Faith* 49:1 (March 1997), 15-30.

Oswalt, J. N. "The Myth of the Dragon and Old Testament Faith." *Evangelical Quarterly* 49:3 (1977), 163-172.

Padgett, Alan G. "The Mutuality of Theology and Science: An Example from Time and Thermodynamics." *Christian Scholar's Review* 26:1 (Fall 1996), 12-35.

Peacocke, Arthur. "A Response to Polkinghorne." *Science and Christian Belief* 7:2 (1995), 109-115.

Peters, Ted. "Theology and Science: Where Are We?" *Dialog* 34:4 (Fall 1995), 281-296.

Plantinga, Alvin. "Science: Augustinian or Duhemian?" *Faith and Philosophy* 13:3 (1996), 368-394.

Polkinghorne, John. *"Creatio Continua* and Divine Action." *Science and Christian Belief* 7:2 (1995), 101-108.

Provan, Iain W. "Ideologies, Literary and Critical: Reflections on Recent Writing on the History of Israel." *Journal of Biblical Literature* 114:4 (1995), 585-606 (with responses from T. L. Thompson and P. R. Davies, 683-705).

Remus, H. "Does Terminology Distinguish Early Christian from Pagan Miracles?" *Journal of Biblical Literature* 101:4 (1982), 531-551.

———. "Miracle (New Testament)." In D. N. Freedman et al., eds. *Anchor Bible Dictionary*. New York: Doubleday, 1992, iv:856b-869b.

Reppert, Victor. "The Lewis-Anscombe Controversy: A Discussion of the Issues." *Christian Scholar's Review*, 32-48.

Reventlow, H. Graf. "Theology (Biblical, History of)" in D. N. Freedman et al., eds. *Anchor Bible Dictionary*. New York: Doubleday, 1992, vi:483b-505a.

Rogerson, J. W. "The Old Testament View of Nature: Some Preliminary Questions." In H. A.

Brongers et al., eds. *Instruction and Interpretation* (Oudtestamentische Studiën 20). Leiden: E. J. Brill, 1977, 67-84.

Ross, J. P. "Some Notes on Miracle in the Old Testament." In C. F. D. Moule, ed. *Miracles: Cambridge Studies in Their Philosophy and History*. London: Mowbray, 1965, 43-60.

Russell, Robert John. "Theistic Evolution: Does God Really Act in Nature?" ms. (published in *CTNS Bulletin* 15:1 [Winter, 1995], 19-32).

Sharp, John C. "Miracles and the 'Laws of Nature.'" *Scottish Bulletin of Evangelical Theology* 6:1 (Spring 1988), 1-19.

Siertsema, B. "Language and World View (Semantics for Theologians)." *The Bible Translator* 20 (1969), 3-21.

Taylor, John. "Science, Christianity and the Postmodern Agenda." *Science and Christian Belief* 10:2 (1998), 163-178.

Torrance, Thomas F. "The Doctrine of the Virgin Birth." *Scottish Bulletin of Evangelical Theology* 12:1 (Spring 1994), 8-25.

Van Till, Howard J. "Categorial Complementarity and the Creationomic Perspective." *Journal of the ASA* 37:3 (1985), 149-157.

———. "Special Creationism in Designer Clothing: A Response to *The Creation Hypothesis*." *Perspectives on Science and Christian Faith* 47:2 (June 1995), 123-131.

———. "Basil, Augustine, and the Doctrine of Creation's Functional Integrity." *Science and Christian Belief* 8:1 (1996), 21-38.

Waltke, Bruce K. "The Literary Genre of Genesis, Chapter One." *Crux* 27:4 (December 1991), 2-10.

Warfield, Benjamin B. "Calvin's Doctrine of the Creation." In Warfield. *Calvin and Calvinism*. New York: Oxford University Press, 1931, 287-349 (originally published in *Princeton Theological Review* 13 [1915], 190-255).

———. "Christian Supernaturalism." In Warfield. *Biblical and Theological Studies*. Philadelphia: Presbyterian and Reformed, 1963, 1-21.

———. "On Faith in Its Psychological Aspects." In Warfield. *Biblical and Theological Studies*. Philadelphia: Presbyterian and Reformed, 1968, 375-403.

———. "The Question of Miracles." In J. E. Meeter, ed. *Selected Shorter Writings of Benjamin B. Warfield (II)*. Nutley, N.J.: Presbyterian and Reformed, 1973, 167-204.

———. "The Spirit of God in the Old Testament." *Biblical and Theological Studies* Philadelphia: Presbyterian and Reformed, 1968, 127-156.

———. "The Supernatural Birth of Jesus." In Warfield. *Biblical and Theological Studies*. Philadelphia: Presbyterian and Reformed, 1963, 157-168.

Wright, J. Stafford. "The Interpretation of Ecclesiastes." *Evangelical Quarterly* 18 (1946), 18-34.

———. "Virgin Birth." In J. D. Douglas et al., eds. *The New Bible Dictionary*. Downers Grove, Ill.: InterVarsity, 1982, 1238.

Young, E. J. "Daniel." In D. Guthrie et al., eds. *The New Bible Commentary: Revised*. Grand Rapids, Mich.: Eerdmans, 1970.

Zakovitch, Yair. "Miracle (Old Testament)." In D. N. Freedman et al., eds. *Anchor Bible Dictionary*. New York: Doubleday, 1992, iv:845-856.

General Index

Scripture Index